To Tim: From the beginning.
What a good man you've become! I'm so proud of you.

Acknowledgments

IN A BOOK SUCH AS THIS ONE, it's hard to know where to start. There are so many people working behind the scenes, each one as valuable as the next. First, I'd like to thank Megan Belanger and Stacy Hiquet for believing in me enough to let me write this book. To Kim Benbow, whose patience, support, and sense of humor (not to mention her wonderful grammatical skills) kept me going through the process. To Kyann Ward, who kept me on the right technical track. To Jill Flores for exercising all her layout talents in making this a beautiful book. To Larry Sweazy, Sue Boshers, Mike Tanamachi, and all the others working madly behind the scenes to get this book into print: thank you from the bottom of my heart.

And finally, a huge note of appreciation goes to my husband of 41 years. Vern, thank you for your patience and understanding of the many late-night hours, for fending for yourself or both of us at supper time, and for keeping me encouraged and supplied with Diet Coke and working chocolate. I love you. Maybe it's Wheel of Fortune time!

About the Author

DIANE KOERS owns and operates All Business Service, a software training and consulting business formed in 1988 that services central Indiana. Her area of expertise has long been in the word-processing, spreadsheet, and graphics areas of computing, as well as providing training and support for Peachtree Accounting Software. Diane's authoring experience includes over 40 books on topics such as PC security, Microsoft Windows, Microsoft Office, Microsoft Works, WordPerfect, PaintShop Pro, Lotus SmartSuite, Quicken, Microsoft Money, and Peachtree Accounting, many of which have been translated into other languages, including Dutch, Bulgarian, French, Spanish, and Greek. She has also developed and written numerous training manuals for her clients.

Diane and her husband enjoy spending their free time fishing and RVing around the United States and playing with their four grandsons and their Yorkshire Terrier, Sunshine.

Table of Contents

Introduction

WELCOME TO THE WORLD of Microsoft Word 2010. This new *Picture Yourself* book from Cengage Learning will help you use the many and varied features of one of Microsoft's most popular products—Microsoft Word, part of the Microsoft Office Suite.

Microsoft Word 2010 is a powerful word processing program that will take your documents far beyond what you can produce with a typewriter. Whether you want to create a simple letter to a friend, produce a newsletter for a professional organization, or even write a complicated, multiple-page report containing graphics and tables with numerical data, you will find the information that you need to quickly and easily get the job done in *Picture Yourself Learning Microsoft Word 2010*.

This book uses a detailed approach with illustrations of what you will see on your screen, linked with instructions for the next mouse movements or keyboard operations to complete your task. Computer terms and phrases are clearly explained in non-technical language, and expert tips and shortcuts help you produce professional-quality documents.

Picture Yourself Learning Microsoft Word 2010 provides the tools you need to successfully tackle the potentially overwhelming challenge of learning to use Microsoft Word. Whether you are a novice user or an experienced professional, you will be able to quickly tap into the program's user-friendly integrated design and feature-rich environment.

Through this book you will learn how to create documents; however, what you create is totally up to you—your imagination is the only limit! This book cannot begin to teach you everything you can do with Microsoft Word, nor does it give you all the different ways to accomplish a task. What I have tried to do is show you the fastest and easiest way to get started with this fun and exciting program.

This book is divided into four parts. In Part 1, I show you how to create a basic document. While it's not the most exciting section of the book, it's certainly the most practical. Look out after that—things start to be lots of fun! In Part 2, you work with longer documents, and in Part 3, you learn how to enhance the appearance your documents with columns, tables, and graphics. Part 4 helps you to improve the quality of your documents and save you lots of time with Word tools.

Who Should Read This Book?

This book can be used as a learning tool or as a task reference. The easy-to-follow, highly visual nature of this book makes it the perfect learning tool for a beginning computer user as well as those seasoned computer users who might be new to Microsoft Word 2010. The only prerequisites are that you, the reader, know how to log onto Windows and how to use your mouse.

In addition, anyone using a software application always needs an occasional reminder about the details required to perform a particular task. By using *Picture Yourself Learning Microsoft Word 2010*, any level of user can quickly look up instructions for a task without having to plow through pages of descriptions.

Added Advice to Make You a Pro

You'll notice that this book keeps explanations to a minimum to help you learn faster. Included in the book are a couple of elements that provide some additional comments to help you master the program, without encumbering your progress through the steps:

▶ Tips often offer shortcuts when performing an action, or a hint about a feature that might make your work in Word quicker and easier.

▶ Notes give you a bit of background or additional information about a feature, or advice about how to use the feature in your day-to-day activities.

I hope you enjoy this book. Picture yourself learning the fastest and easiest way to use Microsoft Word 2010.

—Diane Koers

Part 1
Just the Basics

You are about to embark on a journey into the world of Microsoft Word 2010. In this life, there are a number of essential things we need. Air and water certainly fit the bill, and many of us consider chocolate and true love right at the top. If you are using a computer, a good word processing program is essential—and you have it. Microsoft Word is the most popular word processing program in the world. It's abundance of features and ease of use leaves it unmatched. Whether you're making a grocery list or writing the great American novel, Word is the program for you. This part of the book explains the fundamentals of working with Word, and even if you have worked with other word processing programs, I am sure you will find Word's ease of use enriching.

Getting Started with
Word

PICTURE YOURSELF AS A SMALL CHILD looking through a glass door. The world looks huge when viewed through the perspective of a toddler, but generally children aren't afraid to explore the world around them. That's how they learn. In this chapter, you'll begin exploring the world of Microsoft Word.

Microsoft Word is a powerful word processing program that takes your documents far beyond what you can produce with a typewriter. Whether you want to write a simple letter to a friend, produce a newsletter for a professional organization, or even write a complicated, multiple-page report containing graphics and tables with numerical data, you can create it in Word.

If this is your first opportunity to use Microsoft Word, you may be a little overwhelmed by all the buttons and items on the screen. Just remember that although Word is a powerful program, it's also very easy to use, which is why most businesses have adopted it as a company standard. Don't worry. You'll be creating your first document after just a couple of mouse clicks.

Opening Word

CHOOSE START > All Programs > Microsoft Office > Microsoft Word 2010. A blank document appears on your screen ready for you to begin entering your data.

Create a Desktop Shortcut

To place a Word application icon on your Windows desktop, right-click the Word icon (under the Start > All Programs > Microsoft Office menu) and choose Send To > Desktop (create shortcut).

Whenever you finish working with a specific application, you exit the program to release the program from your computer's memory. Click the File tab and choose Exit or click the Close button in the upper right corner of the application window. You may be prompted to save your file. Click Yes or No if prompted to save your file.

Tip

Optionally, click the File tab and choose Close. The current file closes, but the current program remains open.

Exploring the Word Window

DESIGNED TO ADJUST to the way you work, instead of the traditional Windows menu bar and standard toolbars, Word uses a Ribbon. Take a look at Figure 1-1, and let's take a stroll through a Word window and review some of its elements. These elements are common not only to Word, but also to most Office applications.

File tab   Quick Access Toolbar   Title bar   Ribbon

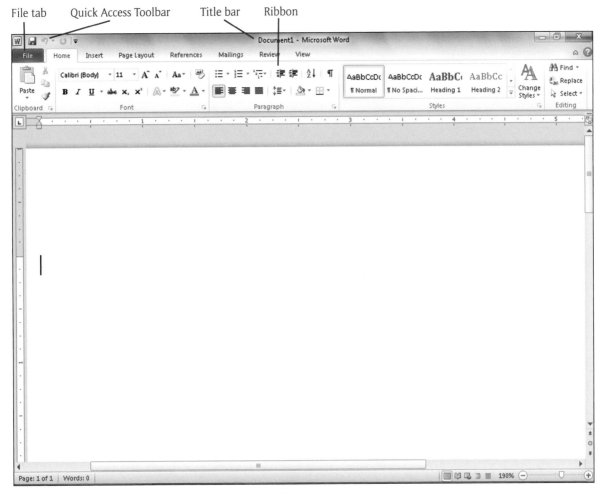

Figure 1-1
The Ribbon is designed to provide the right tool at the right time.

▶ **Title bar:** Across the top you see a title bar that shows the program title and the document title. If you are working with a document created in an earlier version of Word, you may see the words Compatibility Mode displayed. You'll learn about Compatibility Mode later in this chapter.

▶ **File tab:** Pause your mouse over the icon on the top-left screen corner. Microsoft calls this icon the File tab. As you stop your mouse over it, a description of the File tab functions appears. The File tab is where you see the Backstage view and access many common file functions, such as Open, Save, and Print.

▶ **Quick Access Toolbar:** The Word Quick Access Toolbar (QAT), which is the only toolbar, provides fast and easy access to basic file functions. Hover your mouse over any of the four icons above the File tab. By default, the Quick Access Toolbar functions include Save, Undo, and Redo. You can click the arrow next to the QAT and customize it to better meet your needs.

▶ **Ribbon:** If you hover your mouse over the Ribbon area containing tabs, which are task-orientated screens, a description of the feature appears in an Enhanced ScreenTip. The tabs are also broken down into subsections called groups, which break the tasks into smaller areas. Figure 1-2 shows the Page Layout tab, which includes the Themes, Page Setup, Page Background, Paragraph, and Arrange groups. As you click a different tab, the Ribbon changes to reflect options pertaining to the selected tab.

Tip

Beginning with Word 2010, you can now customize the Ribbon. See Chapter 17 for more information.

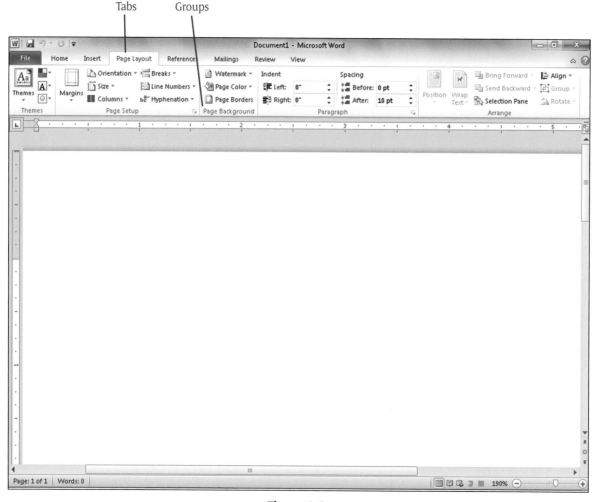

Figure 1-2
Related items appear in groups.

▶ **Dialog Box Launcher:** Many options include an icon at the bottom-right edge of the group option. Microsoft calls this the Dialog Box Launcher, and clicking it opens a related dialog box. In Figure 1-3, clicking the Page Layout > Paragraph Dialog Box Launcher, displays the Paragraph dialog box.

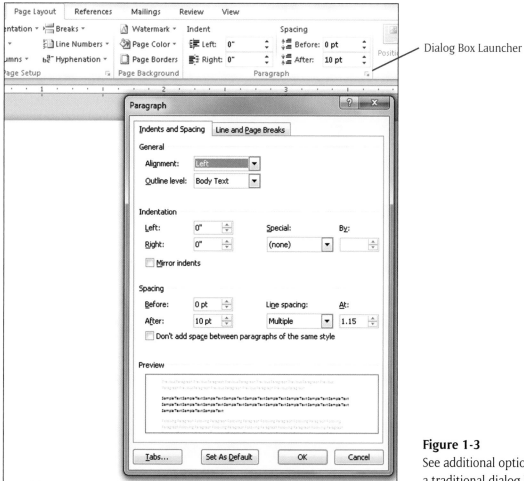

Figure 1-3
See additional options through a traditional dialog box.

Tip

Click the Cancel button to close a dialog box without making any changes.

▶ **Galleries:** Some Ribbon buttons display a down arrow, which means there are more choices available such as on the Insert > Illustrations > Shapes button. Click the arrow to display a shapes gallery. See Figure 1-4. (Click the arrow again to close the gallery.)

▶ **Status bar:** Along the bottom of the Word application window you see a status bar that tells what page of your document you are on and how many words are in the document. You can customize what displays in the status bar by right-clicking anywhere on the status bar. The application displays a list of options in the Customize Status Bar menu, similar to the one shown in Figure 1-5. Click any option without a checkmark next to it to activate the feature, or click any option with a checkmark to deactivate the feature.

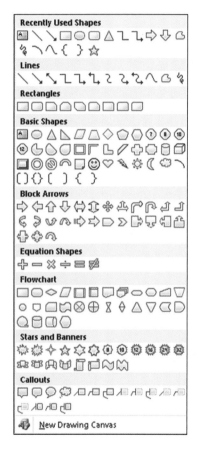

Figure 1-4
A gallery example.

Status bar

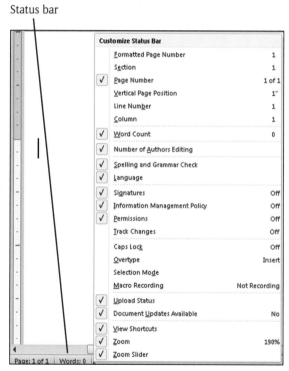

Figure 1-5
Display helpful information on the status bar.

Working with Word Elements

In the previous section, you saw elements common to most Office applications; however, Word includes many items that you'll see only in Word. Let's take a look at Figure 1-6.

Rulers   Insertion point   View controls

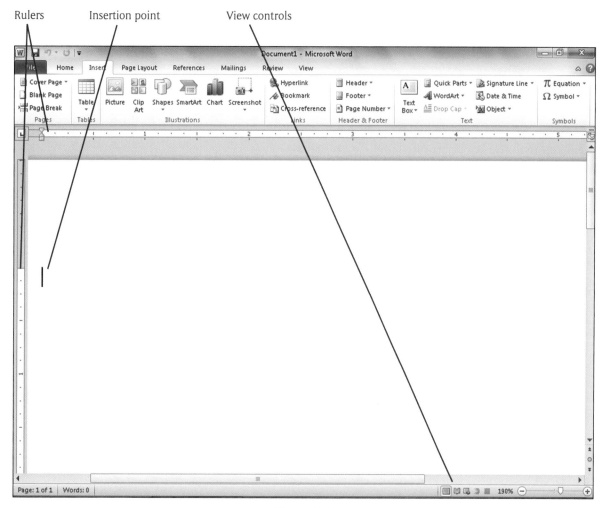

Figure 1-6
Word screen elements.

► **Mouse pointer:** The shape of the mouse pointer changes as you move it to different areas on the screen.

► **Ruler:** Use the rulers to measure the document settings within the page margins. (See Chapter 4 for information on setting margins.)

> ## Display Rulers
>
> Show or hide the rulers by choosing View >
> Show > Ruler.

▶ **Document screen:** The white area of the
screen is where your typed text appears.

▶ **Insertion point:** The blinking vertical line
in the document screen indicates where
text will appear when you begin typing.

▶ **View controls:** Buttons on the status bar
show you your document from various perspectives. (See Chapter 6 for more about
changing views.)

Selecting Commands with the Keyboard

Sometimes you don't want to take your hands off
the keyboard to make a choice from the Ribbon.
Fortunately, Word provides easy ways to select

commands using the keyboard instead of the
mouse. Follow these steps to make a keyboard
command selection:

1. If appropriate for the command you intend to
   use, place the insertion point in the proper
   word, paragraph, or cell.

2. Press Alt on the keyboard. Shortcut letters
   and numbers appear on the Ribbon. The letters control Ribbon commands, and the
   numbers control Quick Access Toolbar commands. See Figure 1-7.

3. Press a letter to select a tab on the Ribbon;
   for example, press N and you see options for
   the Insert tab. The application displays the
   appropriate (in this example the Insert) tab
   and letters for each command on that tab.

4. Press a letter or letters to select a command.
   The application displays options for the command you selected.

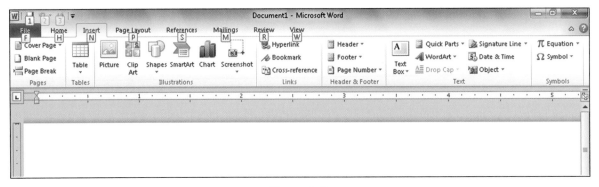

Figure 1-7
Make command selections using the keyboard.

Take a Step Backward

Press the Escape key to revert the keyboard controls back one step.

5. Press a letter or use the arrow keys on the keyboard to select an option. If you use the arrow keys, press the Enter key after making a selection. The application performs the command you selected, applying the option you chose.

Tip

Press F6 to change the focus of the program, switching between the document, the status bar, and the Ribbon.

Exploring the Backstage View

New to Word 2010 is the Backstage view. In older programs, you might have referred to this as the File menu in that it contains many file-related choices, such as Save, Open, or Print. But the Backstage view is more than just a menu. It's a full information center.

Take a look at Figure 1-8. With a document open, in this example a Word file called Surviving a Recession, you see three columns of information. The first column is where you see the file commands and represents actions you can select. The second column currently displays tasks relative to, in this case, the file Surviving a Recession. As you make selections from the first column, the choices in the second column change. The third column contains information about the current document, including the author, the file creation and modification dates, file size, and other document properties.

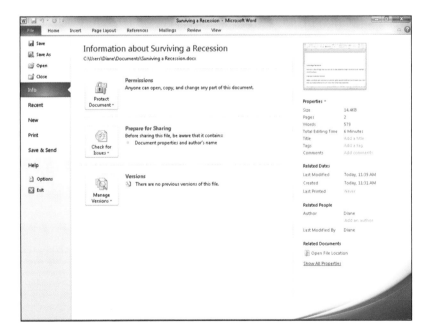

Figure 1-8
The File Information window.

Now click the Print option from the first column. As you see in Figure 1-9, the second column changes and now displays options related to printing. If you click the Recent option, you see a list of documents you recently worked with. You can click any document to open it. See "Opening an Existing File" file later in this chapter.

Click the File tab to close the Backstage view and return to your open file.

File tab

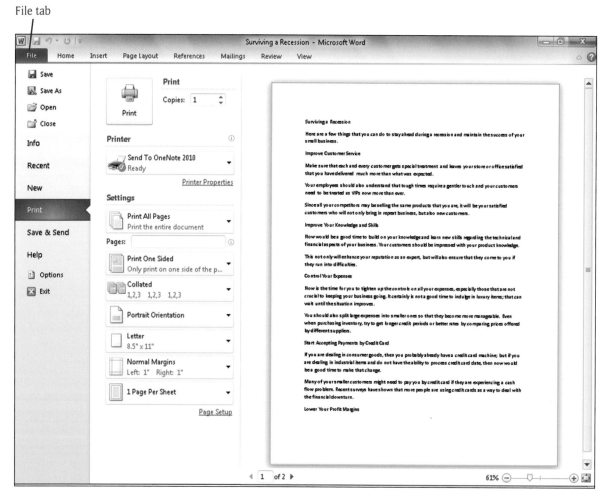

Figure 1-9
Viewing File Print options.

Working with Files

WHENEVER YOU WORK with Word, Word is creating a file, called a *document* file. You can create the file and just throw it away when you're finished, or you can save it on a disk drive for future reference.

Saving a File

The first time you save your file, Word prompts you for a name and a folder in which to save it. Click the File tab and choose Save or click the Save button on the Quick Access Toolbar. The Save As dialog box appears, as shown in Figure 1-10.

Tip

Optionally, press Ctrl+S to save your file.

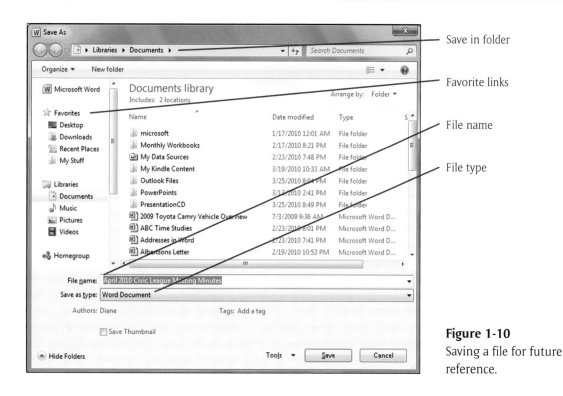

Save in folder

Favorite links

File name

File type

Figure 1-10
Saving a file for future reference.

From the Save As dialog box, you enter the following information:

- ▶ **Location:** By default, Word saves your files in your Documents folder. If you want to save your file in a different folder, use the Favorite Links pane to navigate to the folder or disk drive where you want to save the file.

- ▶ **Name:** In the File Name text box, type a descriptive name for the file. File names can contain any characters except an asterisk, slash, backslash, or question mark.

- ▶ **Type:** Word has a specific file type it uses as a default. Word 2010 and Word 2007 documents use a .docx file type. Most of the time you'll want to use the default file type, but if not, click the Save As Type down arrow and select a different file type. If someone who doesn't have Word 2010 or

Word 2007 will be opening your file, you might consider saving your file in a format that more closely matches their version, such as Word 97–2003. Older Word versions use a .doc file extension.

Click the Save button. Word saves the file in the location and with the name you specified. After assigning the file a name and a location, each time you click the Save button, the saved file is updated with any changes.

Depending on the file type you chose, Word may prompt you for additional information. In Figure 1-11, for example, you see a dialog box warning you of your document features used with Word 2010 that aren't available when saving a file in a Word XP or 2003 format.

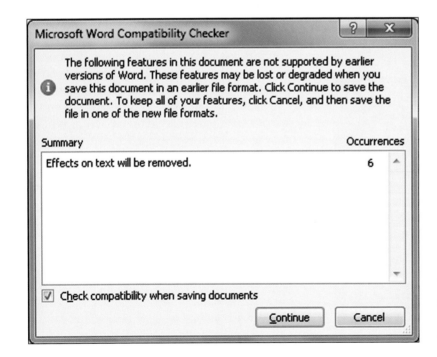

Figure 1-11
Some Word 2010 features are not available in earlier Word versions.

Save Often!

Don't wait until a project is finished to save it. A good rule of thumb is to save your work at least every 10 minutes.

Perhaps you want to make some changes to your file, but you're not sure if you will like the changes. Or maybe you wrote a proposal to a company, and you need a similar one for a different company. One way to work around the changes is to save the file with a different name or in a different location. Word then keeps the old version with the original name or location and keeps the modified file with a different name or in a different location.

Unique File Names

No two files can have the exact same name in the exact same folder. You can place them in different folders, save them as different file types, or vary the name by at least one character.

To save a revised file without overwriting the original file, click the File tab and choose Save As, which displays the Save As dialog box. From the Save As dialog box you can enter a new file name, select a different folder, or choose a different file type.

Creating a New File

As mentioned earlier in this chapter, when you open Word, a blank document appears. You can also generate a new document at any time by clicking the File tab and choosing New. The application then displays the New Backstage view, prompting you for more information. See Figure 1-12. You click the template you want to use, and then click the Create button. (Chapter 17 discusses templates.) By default, Word temporarily names each new file by the next numerical increment, such as Document2 or Document3.

Create button

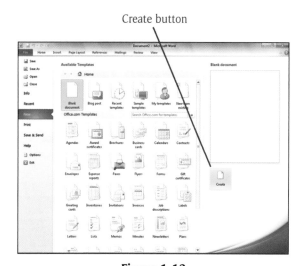

Figure 1-12
Create any number of new files.

Tip

Optionally, press Ctrl+N to create a new file without opening the Available Templates window.

Opening an Existing File

When you've worked on and saved a file previously, you can reopen it to review or modify the file. Following are several ways to open an existing file.

1. Click the File tab and choose Open. An Open dialog box similar to the one seen in Figure 1-13 appears.

File type arrow

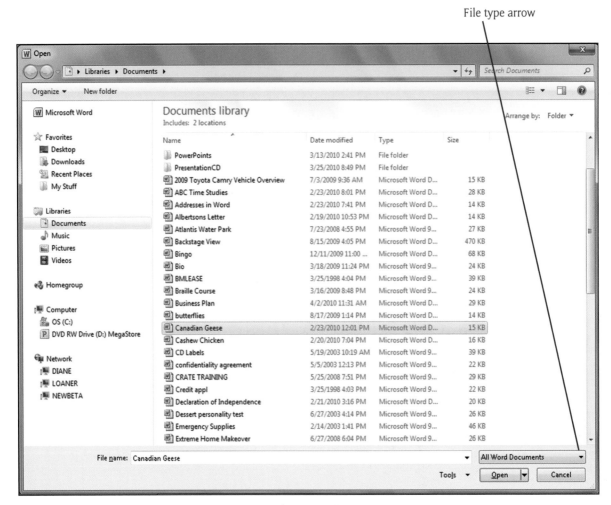

Figure 1-13
Open a previously saved file.

Tip

Optionally, press Ctrl+O to display the Open dialog box.

2. If needed, select the appropriate folder from the Folders pane.

3. Select the file you want to open.

Display Other File Formats

Click the file type arrow to display files saved in other formats.

4. Click the Open button. The document appears, ready for you to edit.

Compatibility Mode

If the file you open was created in a previous version of Word, the words Compatibility Mode appear on the title bar, next to the document name (see Figure 1-14).

Compatibility Mode

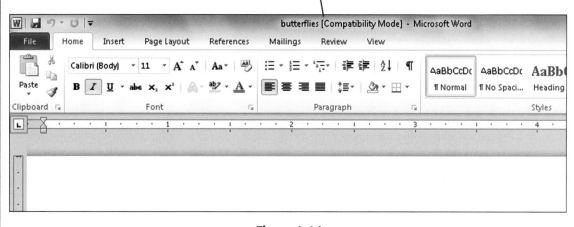

Figure 1-14
Some Word 2010 functions are not available when working in Compatibility Mode.

Converting a Prior Version File to Word 2010

If you originally created a file in a prior than 2007 version of Microsoft Word, you may find you want to convert it to a Word 2010 file so you can take advantage of the great new features provided by Word 2010. Begin by opening a file created in the earlier Word version. The application title bar indicates the document is in Compatibility mode. Click the File tab and from the Backstage view Info screen, choose Convert. Word displays a message indicating you are about to convert the current document. (See Figure 1-15.) Click OK. Word replaces the older version of the document, using the same name you used for the older version of the document. If the older version was a Word 97-2003 or earlier document, Word 2010 changes the file extension to .docx.

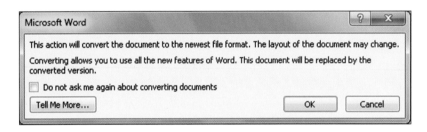

Figure 1-15
Converting a Word document.

Renaming a File

When you first save your file, you're prompted to name it. But perhaps you didn't give it a name intuitive enough to know what the file represents. If you click the File tab, choose the Save As command, and then save your file with a different name, you will have both the original file and the new file. If you just want to rename the existing file, you can use the Open or Save As dialog boxes. Follow these steps:

1. With the Word application open, but not the file you want to rename, click the File tab and choose Open. The Open dialog box appears.

Tip

Optionally, click the File tab, choose Save As, and then proceed using the Save As dialog box.

2. Locate and click once on the file you want to rename. Do not double-click the file, as double-clicking the file will open it.

3. Choose Organize > Rename (see Figure 1-16). The original file name becomes highlighted.

Organize

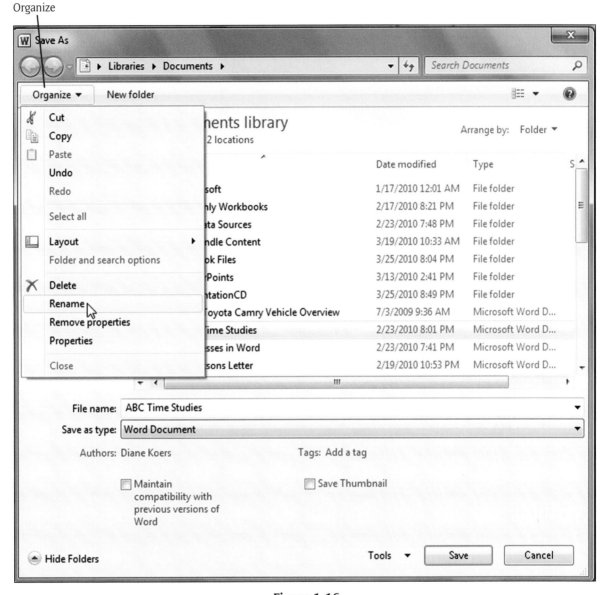

Figure 1-16
Choose a new file name.

4. Type the new file name and press Enter when you are finished typing. Word renames the file.

5. Click the Cancel button, or press the Escape key, to close the Open (or Save As) dialog box.

Deleting a File

Similar to renaming files, you can also use the Open or Save As dialog boxes to delete unwanted files. With Word open, but not the file you want to delete, click the File tab and choose Open or Save As. Either the Open or Save As dialog box appears. Locate the file you want to delete and choose Organize > Delete. A confirmation dialog box appears like the one shown in Figure 1-17. Choose Yes to delete the file, and then click the Cancel button (or press the Escape key) to close the dialog box.

Tip

Alternatively, from the Open or Save As dialog box, click the file you want deleted and press the Delete key.

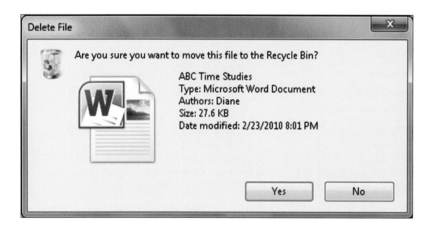

Figure 1-17
Delete unwanted files.

Previewing with Live Preview

WORD 2010 INCLUDES a feature called Live Preview where you can see how formatting choices look in your document before you actually apply them to the document. By pointing to formatting options with your mouse, such as fonts or styles, you can see the effect on your document. If you want a different look, you simply move your mouse to a different option to view its effect. Additionally, you can use Live Preview to view tables, shapes, and graphics.

Take a look at Figure 1-18, where you see the effect of selecting a different font immediately display on the Word document heading. If you decide you like the effect, just click the mouse on the font to actually apply it to the text.

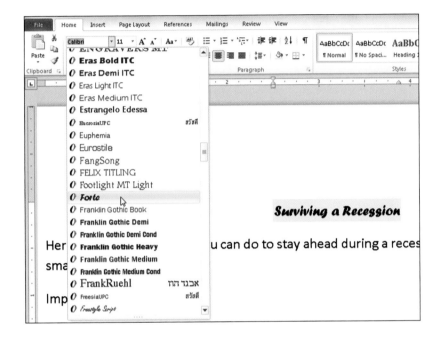

Figure 1-18
Preview how font changes will affect your document.

Creating a Word
Document

PICTURE YOURSELF WITH AN IDEA. Ideas begin with an intention and then progress into a plan. Whether you extend the idea verbally or though another medium, such as an e-mail or document, the plan typically involves developing a topic, transmitting the idea to a recipient, letting them comprehend and digest the information, and finally for the recipient to respond.

One of the most popular ways to transmit information is through Microsoft Word. You begin with a blank document, and then typically create a piece of writing containing the point you're making about a topic. And in that writing document, generally, each paragraph is a group of sentences dealing with one idea related to that topic.

You begin this chapter getting more acquainted with the Word screen, and then you begin your creation. Along the way, you'll probably make some mistakes. That's okay because you can edit your document. Editing and correcting documents are a snap with Word.

Moving Around the Screen

ONCE YOU HAVE CREATED a new Word document (see Chapter 1 for a refresher), you begin typing in a document at the location of the blinking insertion point (cursor). As you type a few lines of text, you'll notice that you don't need to press the Enter key at the end of each line. The program automatically moves down (or "wraps") to the next line for you. Word calls this feature *word wrap*. You need only to press the Enter key to start a new paragraph. In Figure 2-1, you see the text wrapped around to the next line.

To make changes to your document, you'll need to move the insertion point. Take a look at several methods Word provides for moving around the screen.

Now is the time for you to tighten up the controls on all your expenses, especially those that are not crucial to keeping your business going. It certainly is not a good time to indulge in luxury items; that can wait until the situation improves.

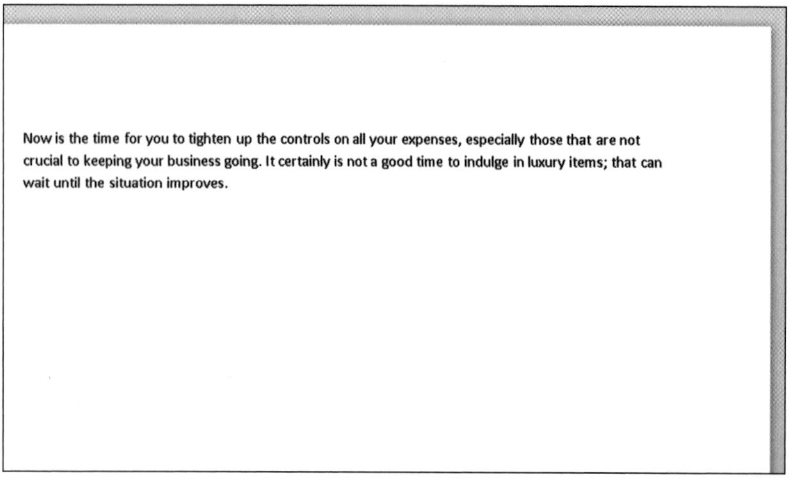

Figure 2-1
Word wrap takes care of adjusting the line for you.

Using Click and Type

You can position the insertion point anywhere on the document using the Click and Type feature. Double-click your mouse pointer where you want to type. Word determines and sets any necessary paragraph formatting based on where you double-click.

Tip

The Click and Type feature works only if you are using Print Layout or the Web Layout view. Chapter 6 covers the different Word views.

Before double-clicking the mouse, pay close attention to the appearance of the mouse pointer. If there are lines to the right of the I-beam pointer, the text you type will flow to the right of the insertion point. If the lines are to the left, the text will flow to the left of the insertion point, and if the lines are below the I-beam, the text will be centered at the insertion point (see Figure 2-2).

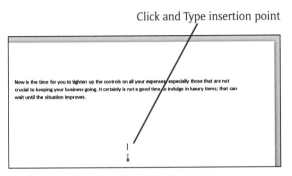

Figure 2-2
Using Click and Type.

Using the Scroll Bars

The Word document screen includes two scroll bars; a vertical scroll bar and a horizontal scroll bar; however, depending on the current view and the document zoom amount, you may not see the horizontal scroll bar. Figure 2-3 illustrates a document with both scroll bars visible.

Click the arrow at either end of the scroll bar to move the document up or down in the window, or click the arrow at either end of the horizontal scroll bar to move the document left or right. Displaying text by using the scroll bars does not move the insertion point. You still need to click the mouse wherever you want to locate the insertion point.

Tip

Optionally, drag the scroll box up or down to quickly move through a document.

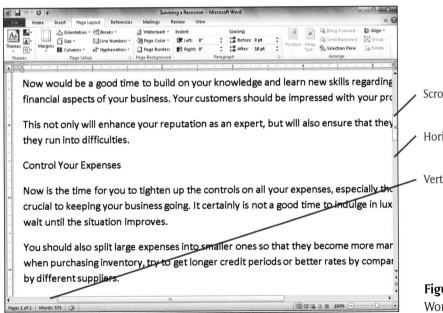

Figure 2-3
Word document scroll bars.

Using the Keyboard

As you've seen, you can work on any part of the document that appears on your screen simply by clicking the mouse pointer where you want to work. You can also move around in a Word document by pressing the Up, Down, Right, or Left arrow keys on the keyboard. Each press of the key moves the insertion point one character or one line at a time.

There are also a number of shortcut keys designed to speed up the process of moving around in a Word document. Table 2-1 illustrates these shortcut keys.

Using the Go To Command

If you have a lengthy document, use the Go To command to jump to a specific location in the document. Follow these steps:

1. Choose Home > Editing and click the Find button drop-down arrow.

2. Choose Go To. The Find and Replace dialog box appears with the Go To tab in front (see Figure 2-4).

Table 2-1 Shortcut Keys

To Move...	Do This
A word at a time	Press Ctrl+Right arrow or Ctrl+Left arrow
A paragraph at a time	Press Ctrl+Up arrow or Ctrl+Down arrow
A full screen up at a time	Press PageUp
A full screen down at a time	Press PageDown
To the beginning of a line	Press Home
To the end of a line	Press End
To the top of the document	Press Ctrl+Home
To the bottom of the document	Press Ctrl+End
To a specified page number	Press Ctrl+G, and then enter the page number

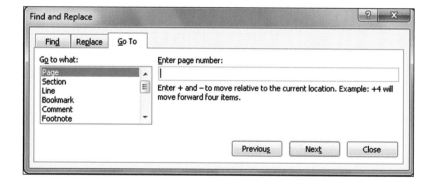

Figure 2-4
Quickly locate specific pages in your document.

Tip

Two optional methods for displaying the Go To option are to press the F5 key or press Ctrl+G.

3. Type the page number you'd like to display and then click Next, or press the Enter key. Word displays the specified page with the insertion point located at the beginning of the specified page.

Editing Text

UNLESS YOU'RE A PERFECT TYPIST, you'll probably make a few mistakes in your document. Or maybe you'll change your mind about some of the text in the document. In a word processing application such as Word, corrections and changes are easy to make, and in some instances, typing errors are even automatically corrected for you.

Adding New Text

When you want to add new text in the document, place the insertion point where you want to locate the new text and then begin typing. As you type, Word inserts the characters and pushes the existing characters to the right or to the next line if necessary. Notice in the bottom example of Figure 2-5 how the added word "business" is inserted after the phrase "on all your," which makes some of the words in the top line drop down to the second line.

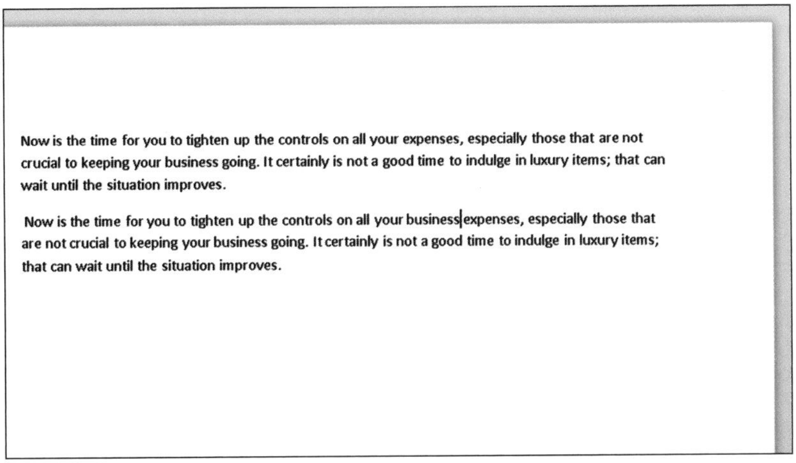

Now is the time for you to tighten up the controls on all your expenses, especially those that are not crucial to keeping your business going. It certainly is not a good time to indulge in luxury items; that can wait until the situation improves.

Now is the time for you to tighten up the controls on all your business expenses, especially those that are not crucial to keeping your business going. It certainly is not a good time to indulge in luxury items; that can wait until the situation improves.

Figure 2-5
Insert additional text wherever you want.

> ### Overstrike Mode
>
> If you notice the existing text doesn't move over, but seems to disappear, you may have accidentally pressed the Insert key, which takes you out of Insert mode and into Overtype mode. Press the Insert key to return to Insert mode.

Deleting Existing Text

You can delete unwanted text one character, word, or paragraph at a time. Two common keys used to delete text are the Backspace and Delete keys. Pressing the Backspace key deletes one character at a time to the left of the insertion point, while pressing the Delete key deletes one character at a time to the right of the insertion point. In Figure 2-6, in the bottom example, the word "non-essential" was deleted by pressing the Delete key repeatedly until the word disappeared.

> ### Which Key Is the Backspace?
>
> On most keyboards, the Backspace key shows a left-pointing arrow, which makes it an easy way to remember which direction the Backspace key deletes.

Optionally, make a selection in your document and press either the Backspace or Delete key to delete the selection. See the next section for more on selecting text.

Selecting Text

Before you can move, copy, delete, or change the formatting or placement of existing text, you must first select the text you want to edit. When text is selected, or highlighted, it appears on your screen showing through a colored (typically blue) shading. Word allows you to select contiguous or non-contiguous text for editing. The following list shows different selection techniques:

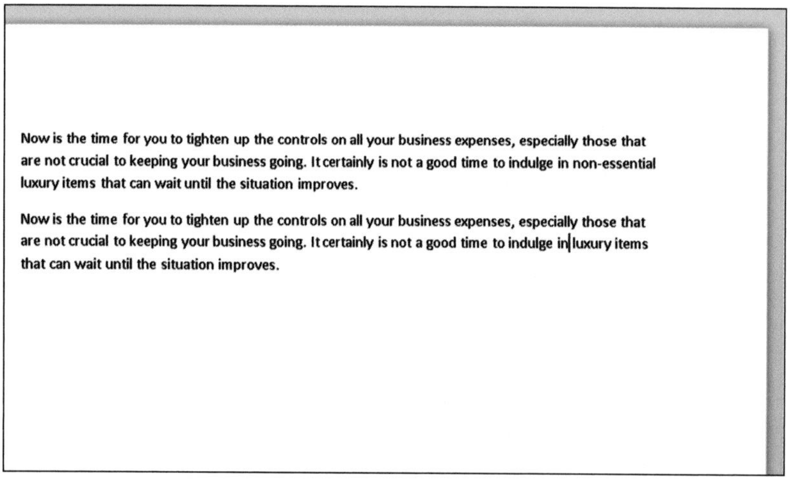

Now is the time for you to tighten up the controls on all your business expenses, especially those that are not crucial to keeping your business going. It certainly is not a good time to indulge in non-essential luxury items that can wait until the situation improves.
Now is the time for you to tighten up the controls on all your business expenses, especially those that are not crucial to keeping your business going. It certainly is not a good time to indulge in luxury items that can wait until the situation improves.

Figure 2-6
Deleting unwanted characters.

▶ To select a single word, double-click the word.

▶ To select a sentence, hold down the Ctrl key and click anywhere in the sentence (see Figure 2-7).

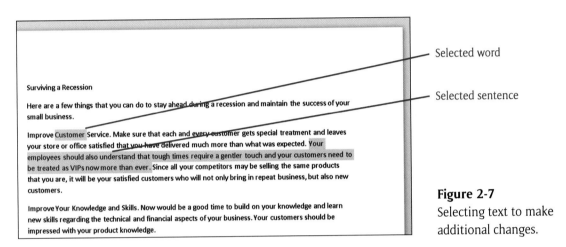

Selected word

Selected sentence

Figure 2-7
Selecting text to make additional changes.

▶ To select an entire paragraph, triple-click anywhere in the paragraph (see Figure 2-8).

▶ To select an entire document, hold down the Ctrl key and press the letter A.

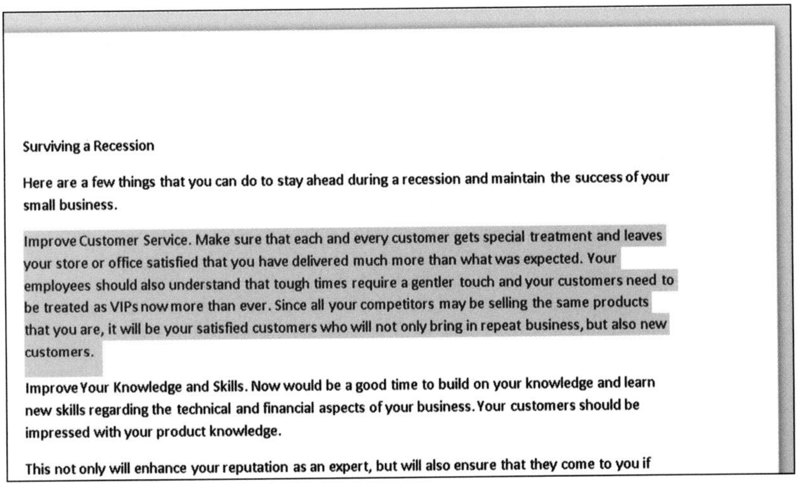

Surviving a Recession

Here are a few things that you can do to stay ahead during a recession and maintain the success of your small business.

Improve Customer Service. Make sure that each and every customer gets special treatment and leaves your store or office satisfied that you have delivered much more than what was expected. Your employees should also understand that tough times require a gentler touch and your customers need to be treated as VIPs now more than ever. Since all your competitors may be selling the same products that you are, it will be your satisfied customers who will not only bring in repeat business, but also new customers.

Improve Your Knowledge and Skills. Now would be a good time to build on your knowledge and learn new skills regarding the technical and financial aspects of your business. Your customers should be impressed with your product knowledge.

This not only will enhance your reputation as an expert, but will also ensure that they come to you if

Figure 2-8
Select an entire paragraph or the entire document.

- To select a single line of text, click once in the left margin with the mouse arrow pointing to the line you want selected.

- To select a contiguous text area, click at the beginning of the text you want selected, and then hold down the Shift key and click at the end of the text you want selected. Optionally, click and drag the mouse over the text you want to select.

- To select non-contiguous text areas, select the first area you want selected, then hold down the Ctrl key and use the preceding techniques for each additional text area you want included (see Figure 2-9).

Tip

To deselect text, click once anywhere in the document.

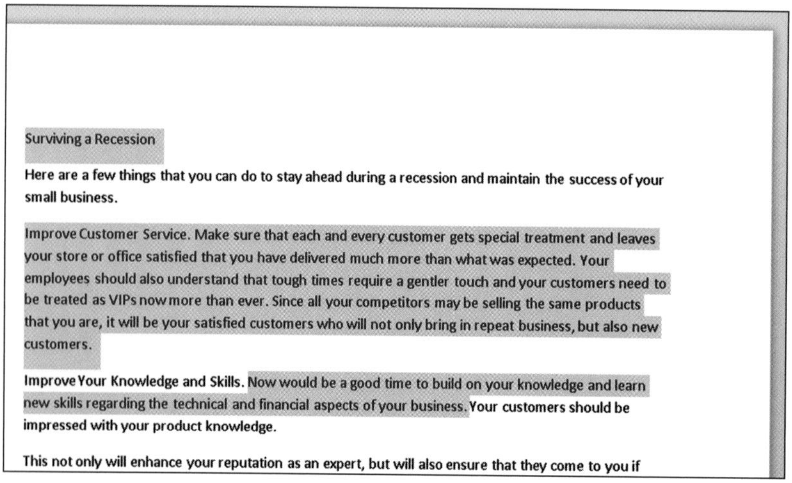

Surviving a Recession

Here are a few things that you can do to stay ahead during a recession and maintain the success of your small business.

Improve Customer Service. Make sure that each and every customer gets special treatment and leaves your store or office satisfied that you have delivered much more than what was expected. Your employees should also understand that tough times require a gentler touch and your customers need to be treated as VIPs now more than ever. Since all your competitors may be selling the same products that you are, it will be your satisfied customers who will not only bring in repeat business, but also new customers.

Improve Your Knowledge and Skills. Now would be a good time to build on your knowledge and learn new skills regarding the technical and financial aspects of your business. Your customers should be impressed with your product knowledge.

This not only will enhance your reputation as an expert, but will also ensure that they come to you if

Figure 2-9
Selecting non-contiguous areas in which to make changes.

Discovering AutoCorrect

Word includes a fabulous feature that makes us look like better typists than we really are! The feature is called AutoCorrect, and, in many cases, if you mistype a word or forget to capitalize a sentence, Word automatically corrects it. Or if you type something like "(c)," Word automatically understands that what you really want is a copyright symbol, and it changes the (c) to ©.

To take full advantage of the automatic correction feature, you have to understand how it works and how to customize it to better fit your needs. Follow these steps to review the AutoCorrect options:

1. Click the File tab and choose Options, which displays the Word Options dialog box shown in Figure 2-10.

2. On the left side, choose Proofing.

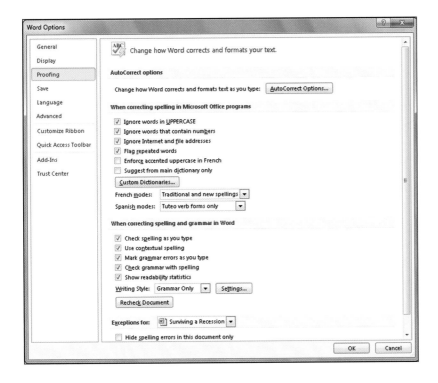

Figure 2-10
Setting Word options.

Tip

See Chapter 17 for information on other Word options.

3. Click AutoCorrect Options. The AutoCorrect Options dialog box opens (see Figure 2-11). On the AutoCorrect tab, you see the options Word automatically corrects for you.

But Wait! There's More!

Scroll down the list to see hundreds of predefined AutoCorrect words and symbols.

Figure 2-11
Create your own AutoCorrect items.

4. If you want to add your own common mis-spellings to the list, type your common mis-take in the Replace text box and then type the correction in the With box. Click the Add button to add the correction to the list.

Create Custom Entries

If you frequently use a lot of complex words, such as chemical names or medical terms, enter an abbreviation for the term in the Replace box and put the complete term in the With box. After adding the term, when you need to add the term in your document, you need only type the abbreviation followed by a space, a period, or other character. For example, enter hctz to have Word replace it with Hydrochlorothiazide.

---

5. Click OK twice to close both the AutoCorrect and the Word Options dialog boxes.

Changing Text Case

As you just discovered, Word automatically corrects many text case errors. For example, if you type "SPringtime," Word automatically changes it to "Springtime." If, however, you type the entire word in uppercase ("SPRINGTIME"), you can quickly change it to "Springtime" or "springtime." You can apply a text case change to a word, a phrase, or any amount of selected text. Just follow these steps:

1. Select the text you want to change. The text becomes highlighted.

2. Click Home > Font > Change Case. A drop-down list of options appears, as shown in Figure 2-12.

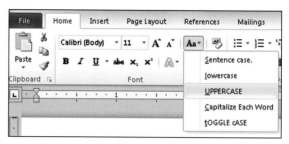

Figure 2-12
Quickly switch from lower- to uppercase lettering.

3. Select an option from the drop-down list.

Tip

Optionally, make a text selection and press Shift+F3. Each time you press Shift+F3, a different case option applies.

Adding Special Symbols

You may think the only characters you can type into a Word document are those that appear on your keyboard. That's just not the case. You can add many different special characters, such as the trademark symbol, diacritical marks, Greek letters, smiley faces, or foreign currency symbols.

Choose Insert > Symbols > Symbol. A list of 20 different symbols appears. If you want to use one of those symbols, just click it and Word inserts it into your document. But those 20 symbols are not the only ones you can insert. From the Symbol menu, choose More Symbols and the Symbol dialog box shown in Figure 2-13 appears.

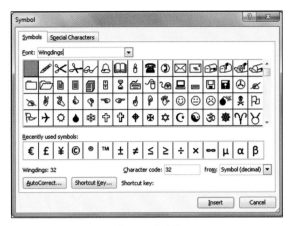

Figure 2-13
Insert special characters into your document.

Different fonts display different symbols. If you don't see the symbol you want, select a different font from the Font drop-down list. For a large variety of unusual characters, look at the Wingdings fonts. Additional special characters are available on the Special Characters tab.

When you find the symbol you want, click Insert. Word inserts the symbol into the document. Click the Close button when you are finished.

Creating Equations

If you write technical papers or scientific journals that need the use of equations, Word has a built-in support tool for writing and editing equations. The tool is designed so that when you type the basic equation, Word automatically converts it into a professionally formatted equation.

Not all equations require the use of the equation tool. For example, to show the makeup of water, you would simply type H2O, but then format the 2 as subscript by selecting it, and choosing Home > Font > Subscript, making the formula read H_2O. Another example of using regular text formatting is $E = mc^2$. But what if you wanted to insert the quadratic formula?

You would simply choose Insert > Symbol > Equation which displays a gallery of predefined equations. Hover your mouse over each formula to see its description, then choose the predefined equation you want, which in this example, is for the quadratic formula shown in Figure 2-14. Word inserts the equation as an object in your document. If you need to change a variable in the equation, simply click inside the equation box and make the necessary change.

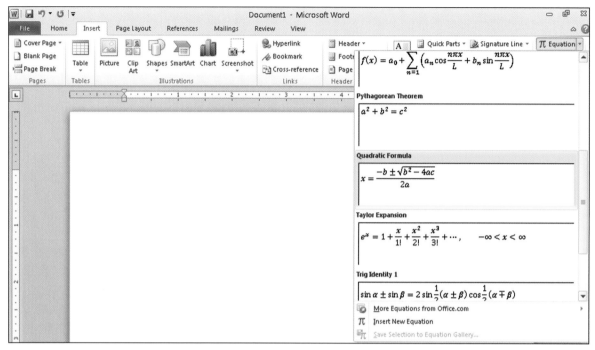

Figure 2-14
Using a predefined equation.

Tip

To delete an equation, select the entire equation and press the Delete key.

That's easy if you happen to be lucky enough to need one of the predefined equations. That's probably not going to happen though. . . . So for those times when the formula is more complex, such as for Newton's Law of Universal Gravitation, $F_g = G\frac{m_1 m_2}{r^2}$ follow these steps to use the Word Equation Editor:

1. Choose Insert > Symbol > Equation > Insert New Equation. An equation box with the words "Type equation here" appears on the screen. You also see the Equation Tools > Design tab, which contains a number of tools for creating equations. (See Figure 2-15.)

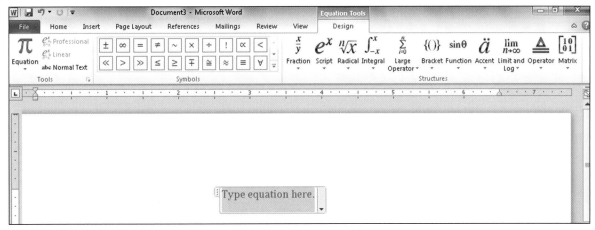

Figure 2-15
The Equation Tools > Design tab.

2. Begin by choosing the equation element you need first. In this example, I need a character with a subscript, so I choose Equation Tools > Design > Structures > Script > Subscript. Word places a small, dotted placeholder box in the equation. Type the characters you need in the appropriate box. In Figure 2-16, I need to type the letter "F" in the first box and the letter "g" in the smaller subscript box.

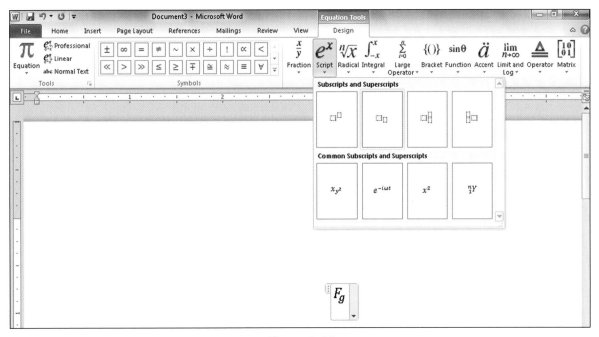

Figure 2-16
Beginning the equation.

3. Continue adding symbols, text, or structures as needed. For this example, I'll need to type an equals sign symbol, then a character (the letter G) followed by the fraction symbol. (I need a Stacked Fraction.) On the top of the fraction, I need two subscript structures, and on the denominator portion, I need a super-script structure. Now my formula structure looks as you see in Figure 2-17.

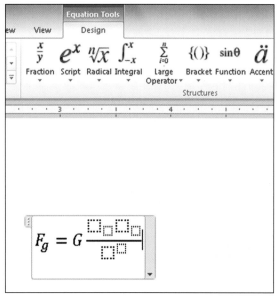

Figure 2-17
Placeholders in the equation.

4. Finally, type the desired characters in the placeholder boxes. See Figure 2-18 for the finished equation.

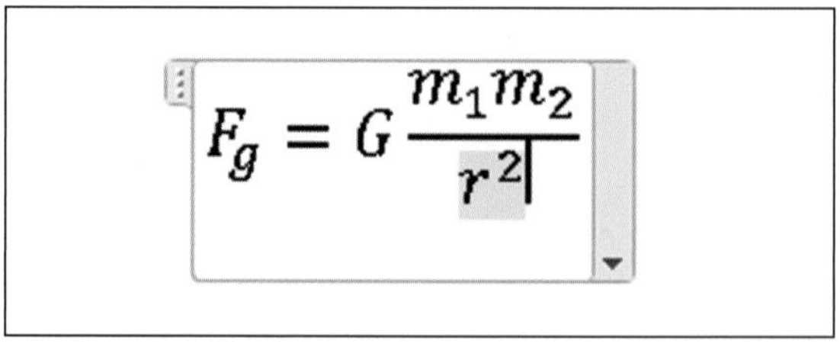

$$F_g = G\frac{m_1 m_2}{r^2}$$

Figure 2-18
The finished equation.

Save Your Equations

You can add your own equations to the Equation Gallery. Select the equation you want to add, then choose Equation Tools > Design > Tools > Save Selection to Equation Gallery. In the Create New Building Block dialog box, enter a name for the equation and click OK. When you exit Word, choose Save to keep the Equation.

Moving and Copying Text

WORD PROVIDES A NUMBER of different methods with which you can copy and move text. Moving or copying text usually involves the Windows Clipboard, which temporarily holds text you place on it. You use the Clipboard feature to move or copy text from one place to another, thereby avoiding the need to retype it.

Moving Text

When you want to remove text from one place and put it into another location, you cut and paste the text. With Cut and Paste, Word deletes the selected text, holds it, and then places it into a new location. Just follow these steps:

1. Select to highlight the text you want to move.

2. Choose Home > Clipboard > Cut. The text disappears from the document, but Word stores it on the Windows Clipboard.

Tip

Optionally, press Ctrl+X or right-click and choose Cut, which also moves the selected text to the Clipboard.

3. Click the mouse where you want to place the text. The blinking insertion point appears at the new location.

4. Choose Home > Clipboard > Paste, or press Ctrl+V. Word places the text at the new location. In Figure 2-19, the highlighted paragraph was originally the first paragraph, but through cutting and pasting, it is now the second paragraph.

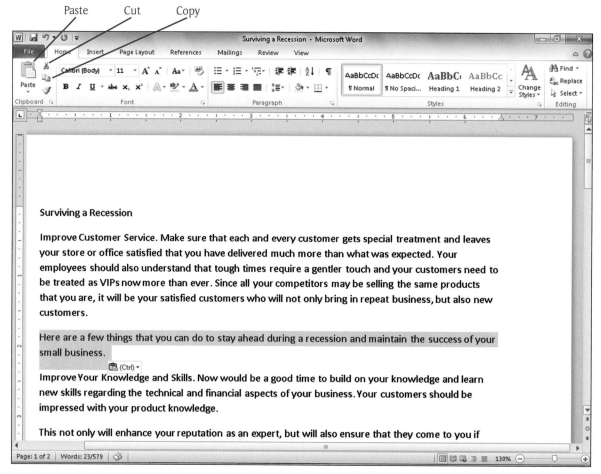

Paste   Cut   Copy

Figure 2-19
Save typing and editing time with Cut and Paste.

Paste Without Formatting

If you want to paste the text without the formatting, instead of clicking the Paste button directly, click the arrow beneath the Paste button and choose Paste Special. From the Paste Special dialog box (see Figure 2-20),

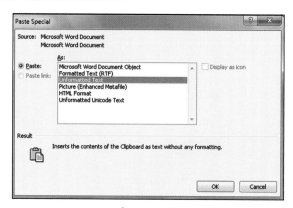

Figure 2-20
Paste without any formatting included.

Copying Text

The Copy and Paste features leave the selected text at its existing location and duplicate it into a new location. Working similarly to the Cut and Paste functions, Copy and Paste use the Windows Clipboard to temporarily store the text. Use the following steps to copy text to a new location:

1. Select to highlight the text you want to duplicate.

2. Choose Home > Clipboard > Copy or right-click and choose Copy. The text remains in the document, but Word also stores it on the Windows Clipboard.

Tip

Optionally, press Ctrl+C to copy selected text to the Clipboard.

3. Click the mouse where you want to place the text. The blinking insertion point appears at the new location.

4. Choose Home > Clipboard > Paste, or press Ctrl+V. Word places the text at the new location (see Figure 2-21). Notice that the second paragraph is repeated as the fourth paragraph.

Tip

When you paste text, you may see a small icon, called a Paste Options button, appear to the right of the pasted or moved text. See the section "Understanding Paste Options" later in this chapter.

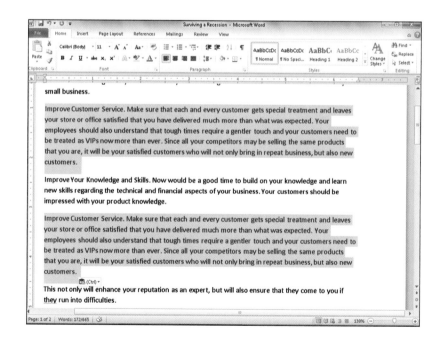

Figure 2-21
Duplicate text without retyping.

Using Drag and Drop

Another, sometimes faster, method to move text from one location to another is to use the drag-and-drop editing function. The drag-and-drop feature works best for moving a relatively small amount of text a short distance. The following steps show you how to use drag and drop.

1. Select the text you want to move.
2. Position the mouse pointer on top of the highlighted text. The mouse arrow should point to the left.
3. Hold down the mouse button and drag the mouse pointer to the desired location. As you drag, a small box appears at the bottom of the mouse arrow and a gray line indicates the text position (see Figure 2-22).
4. Release the mouse button to finish the text move.

Tip

To copy text instead of moving it, hold down the Ctrl key before dragging the selected text. Then release the mouse button before releasing the Ctrl key.

Copy Between Documents

If you want to move text from one document to another, open both documents and display them side by side by choosing View > Window > View Side by Side. Then highlight and drag the desired text from one document window to another (see Figure 2-23). Hold down the Ctrl key if you want to copy the text to the second document.

Surviving a Recession

Here are a few things that you can do to stay ahead during a recession and maintain the success of your small business.

Improve Customer Service. Make sure that each and every customer gets special treatment and leaves your store or office satisfied that you have delivered much more than what was expected. Your employees should also understand that tough times require a gentler touch and your customers need to be treated as VIPs now more than ever. Since all your competitors may be selling the same products that you are, it will be your satisfied customers who will not only bring in repeat business, but also new customers.

Improve Your Knowledge and Skills. Now would be a good time to build on your knowledge and learn new skills regarding the technical and financial aspects of your business. Your customers should be impressed with your product knowledge.

Improve Customer Service. Make sure that each and every customer gets special treatment and leaves your store or office satisfied that you have delivered much more than what was expected. Your

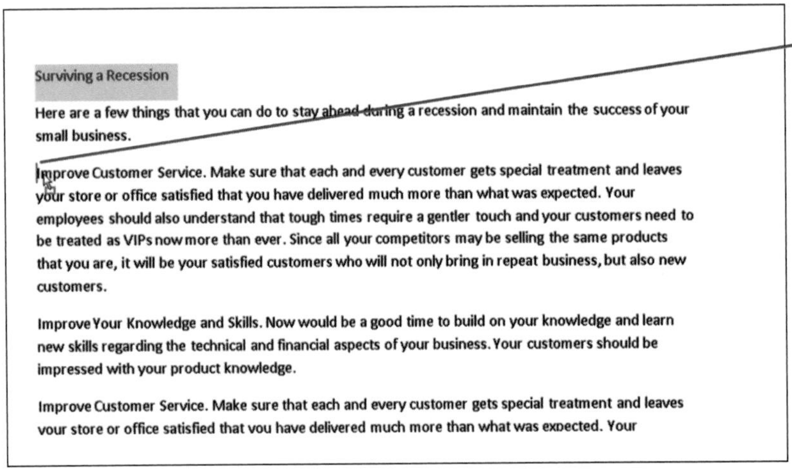

New position for text

Figure 2-22
Select and drag text to a new location.

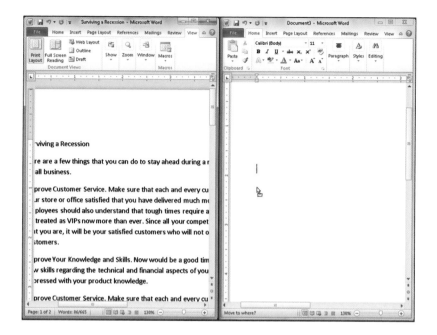

Figure 2-23
Move or copy text easily
between documents.

Understanding Paste Options

By default, when you paste text, Word includes any
formatting contained in the original text along
with the text. For example, if the original text is
underlined, the pasted text is underlined as well.

If the pasted text is a different font, size, or style
than the text near where you pasted, you'll see the
Paste Options button, which provides the option to
paste text with or without formatting. (You'll learn
more about formatting in Chapter 3.) Click the
arrow next to the Paste Options button, as shown
in Figure 2-24, which displays the Paste Option
Gallery and choose from the available choices:

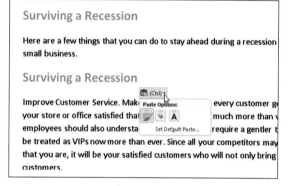

Figure 2-24
Select paste options.

> ▶ **Keep Source Formatting:** Leaves the pasted
> text formatted the same as the original text.

> ▶ **Match Destination Formatting:** Modifies
> the pasted text so it's formatted to match
> the closest existing text.

> ▶ **Keep Text Only:** Modifies the pasted text
> with the default document font.

Display Paste Options

After using the Ctrl+V shortcut to paste your
text, just press the Ctrl key one more time to
drop the new Paste Options gallery and
change to a different Paste option.

Using Undo and Repeat

I F YOU MAKE A CHANGE and then decide you really don't want to make that change after all, use Word's Undo function. You can use Undo to restore text that you deleted, to delete text you just typed, or to reverse a recently taken action. Word keeps track of several steps you've recently taken, so you can also undo your actions back several steps if you prefer.

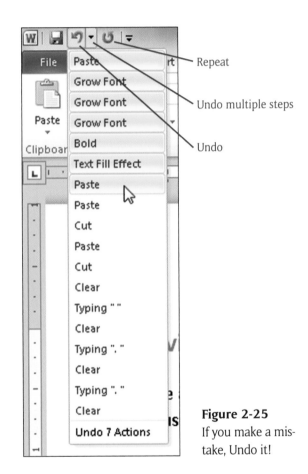

Figure 2-25
If you make a mistake, Undo it!

Cannot Undo a Save Command

Be aware that once you save your document, you cannot use Undo to "unsave" it. Also, if you close the document, when you reopen it, you cannot undo changes made in your previous editing session.

▶ To reverse the last action you took, click the Undo button on the Quick Access Toolbar.

▶ To repeat a previous action, click the Repeat button on the Quick Access Toolbar. If you just used the Undo button, the repeat button allows you to undo the previous Undo action.

▶ To undo multiple actions at once, click the arrow next to the Undo button and choose how far back you want to reverse your actions (see Figure 2-25).

Displaying Non-Printing Symbols

TO ASSIST YOU IN EDITING a document, Word can display hidden symbols it uses to indicate spaces, tabs, and hard returns, which are those created when you press the Enter key. These symbols do not print, but you can display them on your screen.

Choose Home > Paragraph > Show/Hide. As shown in Figure 2-26, you see the paragraph symbol where a paragraph ends, and you see dots that represent spaces and arrows that represent tabs. To turn off the display of hidden characters, click the Show/Hide button again.

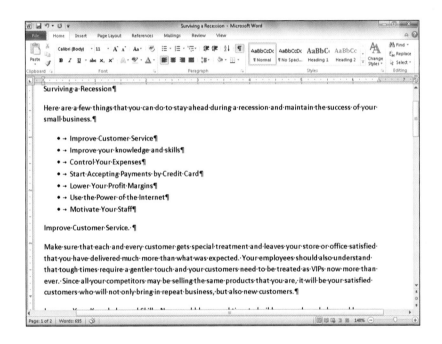

Figure 2-26
Viewing non-printing Word symbols.

Tip

Press Ctrl+Shift+* (asterisk) to display or hide the non-printing symbols.

Making a Word Document
Look Good

PICTURE YOURSELF GOING for an important job interview. You need to make a good impression, so you want to look your best. You make sure your clothes are clean and coordinated, your hair is combed, and your shoes are shined. You put on your best smile, assemble your thoughts, and go forward into the interview.

When you create a Word document, especially one that others review, you want it to look its best. Besides making sure you've dotted all the Is and crossed all the Ts, the document should have a clean, consistent, well-defined appearance. You use Word's formatting features when modifying your document's appearance.

Selecting Text Attributes

WHEN YOU SPEAK, the tone of your voice conveys how you feel. You can convey your enthusiasm (or lack of it), be friendly, or be sarcastic. In a similar way, *fonts*, which are families of design styles for the numbers, letters, and symbols that make up text, can provide additional information to the reader. Fonts can, for example, make your document appear mature and businesslike or young and casual.

Choosing a suitable font size can make a document easier to read. Other text attributes you might use to set the document tone include style settings, such as bold, underline, italics, or even color.

For many text attributes, Word offers a chance to "try before you buy" with its Live Preview feature. By pointing to various formatting choices, you can see the effect the option has on your document before you actually choose the format option. If you like it, you can simply click your mouse to choose the option. For example, if you pause your mouse over a font choice, the text appears deselected (it isn't) and displays with the font you are pointing to. Live Preview works with most font and paragraph formatting choices as well as styles and picture formatting changes.

Tip

If you don't like the Live Preview option, you can turn it off. Click the File tab and choose Options. Click General and remove the check mark from Enable Live Preview.

Choosing a Font

In addition to the many fonts you already have on your machine, Word comes with additional fonts. The default font used with Word 2010 is called Calibri. Fonts generally fall into two different categories: serif and sans serif. Serif fonts usually have details on the ends of some of the strokes that make up letters and symbols. A font that has serifs is called a serif font and a font without serifs is called sans-serif, from the French word *sans*, meaning "without."

Changing fonts is a very simple process. Select the text you want to modify and choose Home > Font, and from the Font drop-down list select the font you want to use (see Figure 3-1).

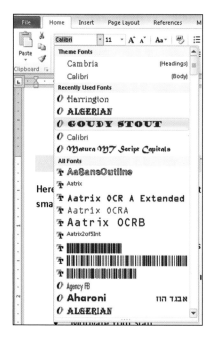

Figure 3-1
Choose a font from the list.

Start Typing the Font Name

If you know the font name you want, you can quickly jump to that font by typing the first few characters of the font name. For example, if you want a Tahoma font, from the font list, type **Ta**, or for Arial, type **Ari**.

Tip

The keyboard shortcut for Grow Font is Ctrl+> and for Shrink Font it's Ctrl+<. (Hold down the Shift key to access the > or < key.)

Selecting a Font Size

You can use any size for any font. Font sizes are measured in *points*, where a point is approximately 1/72 of an inch tall. Therefore, a 72-point font is approximately 1 inch tall.

Select the text you want to format and then choose Home > Font. Click the Font Size drop-down list arrow. You see a drop-down list of available sizes similar to those shown in Figure 3-2. Choose the size you want from the drop-down list, or type your own measurement in the Font Size box. While you can enter a value between 1 and 1638, don't expect to be able to read a 1-point font, and a character as large as 1638 points won't even begin to fit on a standard page!

Optionally, you can click the Grow Font or Shrink Font button to increase or decrease your font size. Figure 3-2 illustrates a document with a title font size of 24 points.

Applying Formatting Attributes

Applying formatting attributes such as **bold**, *italic*, or underline calls attention to particular parts of your text. Additionally, you can assign a superscript or subscript notation to any text that makes it appear above or below the standard text, such as a copyright or trademark symbol. You can easily access these choices and others with the Home tab of the Ribbon.

Select the text you want modified and from the Home tab (see the Font group shown in Figure 3-3) choose the attribute you want to apply.

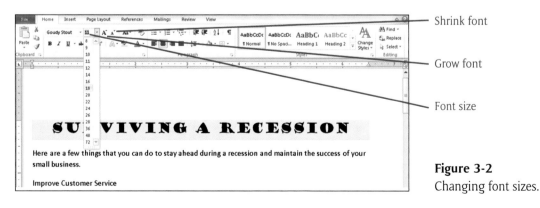

Shrink font

Grow font

Font size

Figure 3-2
Changing font sizes.

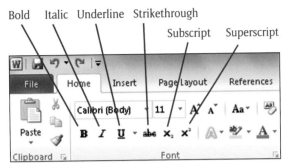

Figure 3-3
Applying special text attributes.

Formatting Shortcut Keys

Some formatting shortcuts include Ctrl+B for bold, Ctrl+I for italic, and Ctrl+U for a single underline.

If you want your text underlined, you can click the down arrow next to the Underline button and select an underline style and color from the drop-down list shown in Figure 3-4.

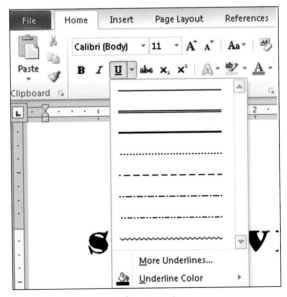

Figure 3-4
Choosing an underline style.

Adding Color

Another way to add impact to your document is by adding color to your text. Color becomes very effective when printing to a color printer or viewing your document on screen. Follow these steps to apply color to your text:

1. Select the text you want formatted.

2. Choose Home > Font > Font Color, or if you want to select a specific color, click the down arrow next to Font Color and make a choice from the resulting gallery, as shown in Figure 3-5.

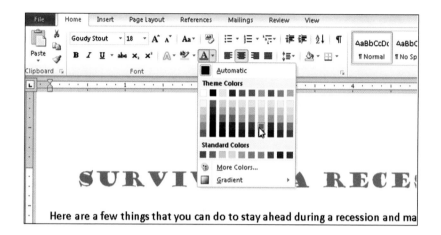

Figure 3-5
Add WOW to a document with color.

Polish Your Documents

Do you notice how the gallery colors are grouped together in themes? Office document themes, available in Word, Excel, and PowerPoint, contain colors, fonts, and other formatting options, all designed to give your documents a polished, professional appearance. See "Working with Themes" later in this chapter.

Highlighting Text

You can highlight text in your document in the same manner you highlight text with a marker in a book. You can even choose the color of highlighter you want to use. While on a monitor or with a color printer, you see the highlight color, on a black and white printer, highlighting prints as gray shading over the text. Highlighting calls attention to specific areas of your document.

Select the text you want to format with highlighting and then choose Home > Font > Text Highlight Color, or if you want to select a specific color, click the down arrow next to Text Highlight Color and

make a choice from the resulting gallery. Word deselects the text and applies the highlighting. Figure 3-6 shows text with pink highlighting.

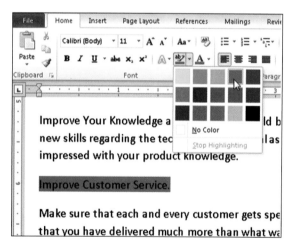

Figure 3-6
Call attention to special areas with highlighting.

Tip

To remove highlighting, choose No Color from the available highlight color selections.

Adding Text Effects

New to Word 2010, you find the ability to add spectacular special effects to your text. With just a few mouse clicks, your text can illustrate shadows, glows, reflections, bevels and many other great formatting features.

Select the text you want to work with, and then choose Home > Font > Text Effects. A gallery of text effects appears as you see in Figure 3-7. Select the effect you want, or click one of the options at the bottom for even more text enhancements.

Using the Mini Toolbar

Word (along with Excel and PowerPoint) contains a semitransparent Mini Toolbar designed to provide quick access to many text and paragraph formatting features so you don't have to move your mouse so far to select the commands from the Ribbon.

The Mini Toolbar appears whenever you select some text. As your mouse points to the selected text, the transparent toolbar appears. As you move your mouse pointer so it rests on top of the toolbar, the Mini Toolbar appears in full opacity (see Figure 3-8).

Tip

If you are working in Compatibility Mode, the Text Effects option is not available.

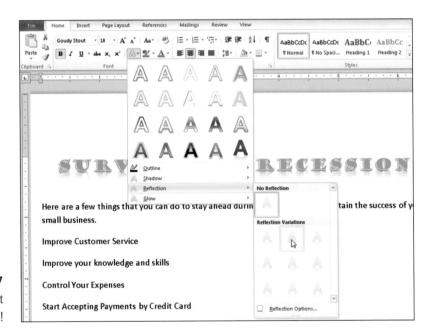

Figure 3-7
Add lots of pizzazz with text effects!

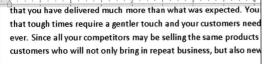

Figure 3-8

Save mouse movement by using the Mini Toolbar.

Available choices on the Mini Toolbar include the following:

- ► Font
- ► Font Size
- ► Grow Text
- ► Shrink Text
- ► Increase Indent
- ► Decrease Indent
- ► Bold
- ► Italic
- ► Underline
- ► Center
- ► Text Highlight Color
- ► Font Color
- ► Format Painter

Using the Font Dialog Box

Another way to apply formatting to your selected text is through the Font dialog box, where you can make all your font choices via a single box. Also, you'll find that the Font dialog box offers additional attribute options not available on the Ribbon. Use the following steps to work with the Font dialog box:

1. Select the text you want formatted.

2. From the Home tab, click the Fonts group Dialog Box Launcher or press Ctrl+Shift+F. You see the Font dialog box displayed in Figure 3-9.

Figure 3-9
The Font dialog box.

3. Make any desired text attribute changes. The preview box at the bottom of the dialog box illustrates your choices. Live Preview isn't available from the Font dialog box.

4. Click the OK button.

Removing Formatting

If you decide you really liked the original formatting in your document, you can easily return it to the default document settings. After selecting the text from which you want to remove formatting,

choose Home > Font > Clear Formatting. (See Figure 3-10.) All text and paragraph formatting choices return to the default setting with the exception of highlighting. Any applied highlighting remains on the selected text.

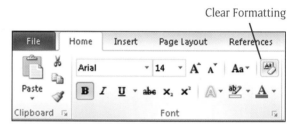

Figure 3-10
Easily remove unwanted formatting.

Changing the Default Font

As mentioned earlier in this chapter, Word 2010 begins with an 11-point Calibri font. If your company has a different font as its company standard, or you just prefer a different font for most documents, you can change the default font for any new Word documents that you create. Changing the default font does not affect any existing documents.

Tip

The document body font is actually determined by the theme you use. See "Working with Themes" later in this chapter.

You can set the default font from any blank document, or any currently open document. Just follow these steps:

1. From the Home tab, click the Fonts group Dialog Box Launcher or press Ctrl+Shift+F.

2. Select the font and size you want as your default.

3. Click the Default button. A confirmation message like the one shown in Figure 3-11 appears.

4. Click All Documents Based on the Normal Template, and then click OK.

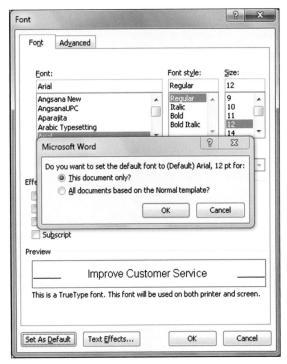

Figure 3-11
Confirm the Default font change.

Formatting Paragraphs

WORD INCLUDES MANY FEATURES designed to assist you in placing text on the page just the way you want it. You can align text left to right using tabs or alignment options, or you can adjust your text vertically using line spacing options. Following are some of the available paragraph formatting choices.

Aligning Text

Alignment arranges the text to line up at one or both margins, or centers it between the margins. Alignment applies to entire paragraphs. In other words, you can't center align part of a paragraph and left align another part of the same paragraph.

You can align text to the left, right, or center, or you can *justify* your text, which means that the text becomes evenly spaced across the page from the left margin to the right margin. Apply alignment options by selecting the text you want to align, then choosing Home > Paragraph and clicking one of the following alignment buttons:

▶ **Align Text Left:** The text aligns evenly at the left margin. This is the default choice.

▶ **Center:** The text centers evenly between the left and right margins.

▶ **Align Text Right:** The text aligns along the right document margin.

▶ **Justify:** The text fills with micro spaces so it aligns evenly on both the left and right margins.

Figure 3-12 illustrates a document with text matching each alignment option.

Adding Paragraph Borders

Word includes borders that you can apply to any size block of text, which draw the reader's eye to specific areas for a "quick read." Use a border to place a frame around a word, phrase, paragraph, or group of paragraphs to frame the text and call specific attention to the areas. A border can encase the entire area or be any combination of lines around the text, such as above and/or below the text. Select the text you want bordered and choose Home > Paragraph. Click the drop-down arrow next to the Borders button, which displays a list of options like the one you see in Figure 3-13. Choose the border option you want.

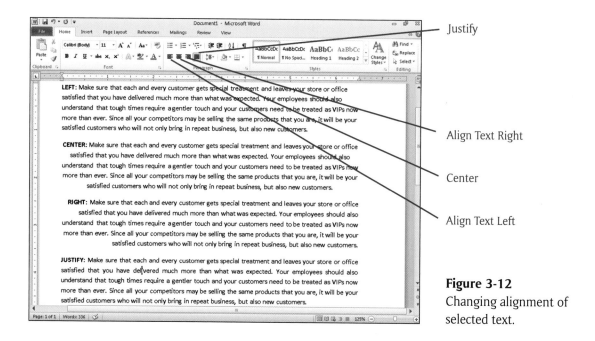

Figure 3-12
Changing alignment of selected text.

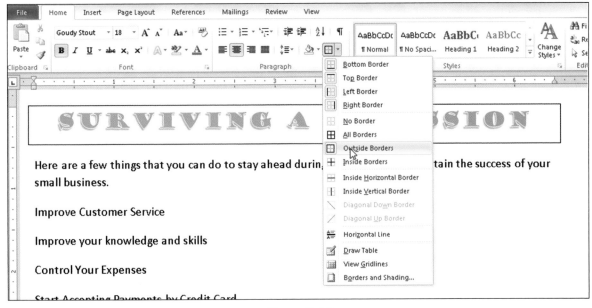

Figure 3-13
Adding borders around text.

Automatic Borders

Word automatically adds a thin single-line border if you type three dashes in a row and then press the Enter key. Typing three underscore characters in a row and pressing Enter automatically creates a thicker border line.

You may be wondering what the difference is between shading and highlighting. Highlighting only covers the selected text and not the entire paragraph. Also, you typically use a light color for highlighting so you can still see the black text through it. When you add shading, the shading covers the entire paragraph, and if you choose a darker color, Word automatically changes the text color to one that coordinates so you can still effectively read the text.

Shading Text

Shading helps you distinguish headlines and important passages, such as sidebars, by creating a *screen*, which is typically light gray shading against the standard black text. Screens can add contrast to and enhance the readability of your document. Shading especially looks good when used in combination with a border.

Tip

A great way to add enhancement is to use black or dark gray shading with white text.

Click anywhere in the paragraph you want shaded and choose Home > Paragraph > Shading. Choose a color from the resulting Shading gallery, as shown in Figure 3-14. In this figure, adding dark blue shading caused Word to change the font color to white.

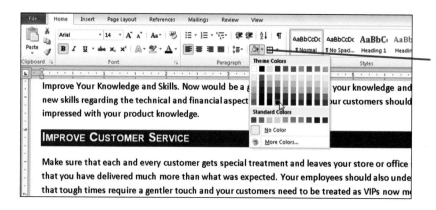

Paragraph Shading

Figure 3-14
Adding shading to your paragraphs.

Optionally, if you want to add a shading pattern ranging from a light 5% shade to patterns, such as diagonal stripes or polka dots, you can choose Home > Paragraph, and then click the Borders drop-down arrow. From the list, select Borders and Shading, which then displays the Borders and Shading dialog box. Click the Shading tab then click the Fill drop-down arrow to select a fill color. Choices are available in themes or standard colors. You can then click the Style drop-down list to select a pattern.

Tip

Use caution with patterns. Using a busy pattern can be distracting or make your text very difficult to read.

Indenting Text

Typically, text runs between the left and right margins, but you may want to indent particular paragraphs. Surprise! Word contains a tool for indenting. Click anywhere in the paragraph you want to indent, and then choose Home > Paragraph > Increase Indent. Each click of the Increase Indent button indents the text one-half inch from the left margin. Click the Decrease Indent button to move the text back one-half inch.

If you want to indent from the right margin or you want to manually set how much indentation Word applies, you can use the Format Paragraph dialog box. Click the Paragraph Dialog Box Launcher, which displays the Paragraph dialog box shown in Figure 3-15.

Indented paragraph   Increase indent   Decrease indent   Paragraph Dialog Box Launcher

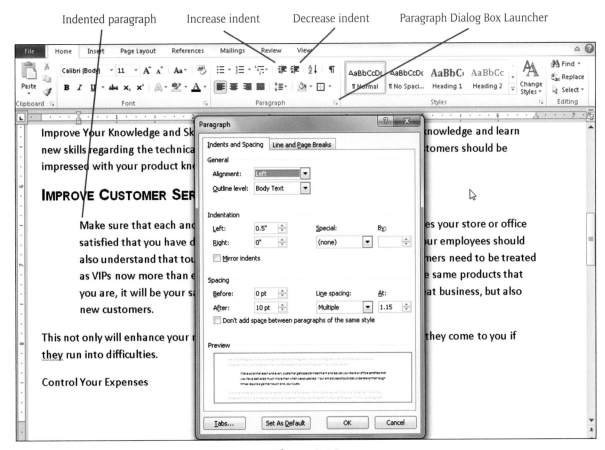

Figure 3-15
Set text apart by using indentation.

Click the spinner arrows for the Left or the Right text boxes to specify the number of inches to indent the left and right edge of the paragraph. The Preview box at the bottom shows the effects of your settings. Optionally, click the Special drop-down list and select an indenting option:

▶ **First line:** This option indents only the first line of the paragraph and leaves the rest of the paragraph even with the left margin.

▶ **Hanging:** This option indents all lines except the first line of the paragraph.

Click OK after you finish making selections. Word applies the paragraph indentation settings you selected.

Another way to control indention is by dragging the indentation icons on the ruler:

Tip

If you don't see the ruler, choose View > Show > Ruler.

▶ ⬚ Left Indent

▶ ⬚ Hanging Indent

▶ ⬚ First Line Indent

▶ ⬚ Right Indent

Tip

You can also change indentation by choosing Page Layout > Paragraph > Indent.

Working with Tabs

By default, each time you press the Tab key, Word moves the insertion point a half inch to the right. However, you can set tab stops at desired points along the ruler so that when you press the Tab key, the insertion point moves to that point automatically, instead of stopping every half inch.

Do not try to line up text by pressing the space bar. Even if the text looks evenly aligned on the screen, it won't be lined up when printed. Use tabs instead.

The following steps show you how to set your own tab settings:

1. Click the mouse pointer at the location you want to create a tabbed paragraph.

Tip

If you want to set tabs for multiple previously typed paragraphs, select the paragraphs before proceeding to Step 2.

2. Make sure the ruler display is turned on. If you don't see your rulers, choose View > Show > Ruler.

3. Click the Tab button located at the left end of the horizontal ruler as often as needed until you see your desired tab alignment icon (see Figure 3-16). Some tab choices include:

   ▶ ⬚ **Left:** The Tab button defaults to the left tab symbol, which looks like an "L." When using a left tab, text appears with the left edge of the text at the tab.

   ▶ ⬚ **Center:** When you select a center tab symbol, the Tab button looks like an upside-down "T." When using a centered tab, text centers at the tab stop.

   ▶ ⬚ **Right:** When you select the right tab symbol, the tab button looks like a backward "L." When using a right tab, text appears with the right edge of the text at the tab stop.

   ▶ ⬚ **Decimal:** If you display the decimal tab, the Tab button appears as an upside-down "T" with a dot on the right. When writing out dollar and cent amounts, for example, decimal points align to the tab.

   ▶ ⬚ **Bar:** Bar tabs are very different from the previous four tabs. Text doesn't position around bar tabs. Instead, Word inserts a vertical bar at the top position and runs through the depth of the paragraph.

Tab button   Indent markers

Figure 3-16
Setting manual tabs.

4. Click on the horizontal ruler to set the tab for the current paragraph or the currently selected paragraphs. Depending on the tab type you selected, a left, right, center, decimal, or bar tab symbol appears where you clicked the ruler.

5. Click in the paragraph and press the Tab key. Notice how the insertion point moves to the tab setting you created.

6. Type some text. The text you type appears on the page. In Figure 3-17, you see examples of left, right, center, and decimal align tabs as you might use them in a document. (To make the tabs easier to see, I've also displayed the hidden characters.)

Tip

Pressing Enter continues the tab settings to the next paragraph.

Moving a Tab

If you're not happy with the position of your tab stop, you can easily move it. Select to highlight the paragraphs that have a tab you want moved, and then drag the tab to a new location on the ruler bar. As you drag the tab, a vertical dotted line like the one shown in Figure 3-18 illustrates the new tab position. When you release the mouse button, the text moves to the new tab position.

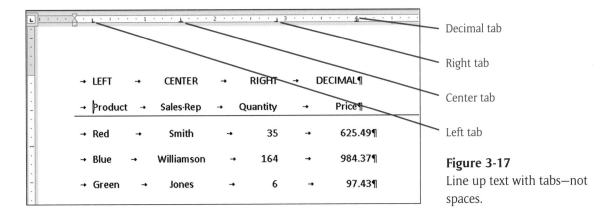

Decimal tab

Right tab

Center tab

Left tab

Figure 3-17
Line up text with tabs—not spaces.

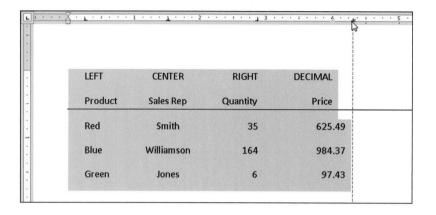

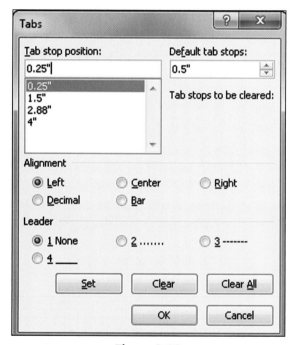

Figure 3-18
Easily move manual tabs to a different area.

Deleting a Tab

Like moving a tab, using the ruler makes deleting a tab a very simple process. Select the paragraphs that have a tab you want to delete and then drag the current tab setting off the ruler, into the body of the document. A vertical dotted line appears. When you release the mouse button, the tab disappears from the ruler and text realigns according to your new tab settings. If there is no previous manual tab stop, the default tab settings take effect.

Using the Tabs Dialog Box

If you want your tab stops at more precise positions than you get by clicking the ruler, or if you want a dot leader before the tab, use the Tabs dialog box. Select the text where you want to set the tab. From the Home tab, click the Paragraph Dialog Box Launcher. Click the Tabs button, which displays the Tabs dialog box shown in Figure 3-19.

Figure 3-19
The Tabs dialog box.

Tip

Double-click any manual tab stop on the ruler to open the Tabs dialog box.

In the Tab Stop Position text box, type the location you want for the new tab and choose an Alignment and optional Leader style for the tab. Click the Set button. Repeat this action for each tab you want set. Click OK to close the Tabs dialog box.

Changing Line Spacing

Line spacing is the amount of vertical space between each line of text. You might want to change line spacing when you want to make a document easier to read, such as a contract, or to make room for changes when writing a document draft. Like text alignment, line spacing applies to complete paragraphs. Use the following steps to change line spacing:

Default Line Spacing

Word 2010 and 2007 use a default line spacing of 1.15. Earlier versions of Microsoft Word used single spacing (1.0) as the default setting.

1. Select the text you want to change.

2. Choose Home > Paragraph > Line Spacing. A list of options appears (see Figure 3-20).

3. Select a line spacing option. Word applies the spacing you select to the highlighted text.

Adjusting Spacing Between Paragraphs

Paragraph spacing is the amount of vertical space between each paragraph of text. Remember that whenever you press the Enter key, you start a new paragraph. In early versions of Word, the default was no spacing between paragraphs, so, traditionally, you would press the Enter key a second time to leave space between two paragraphs. Word 2010 and Word 2007 use a different default setting. The default setting allows for 10 points of blank space at the bottom of every paragraph, thereby eliminating the need to press the extra Enter key.

However, you have complete control over how much spacing, if any, you want between two paragraphs. Similar to indentation, paragraph spacing is controlled through the Paragraph dialog box. From the Home tab, click the Paragraph Dialog Box Launcher, which displays the Paragraph dialog box (see Figure 3-21).

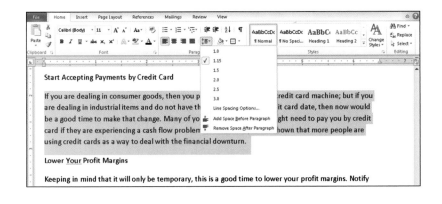

Figure 3-20
Choosing a line spacing option.

Paragraph spacing

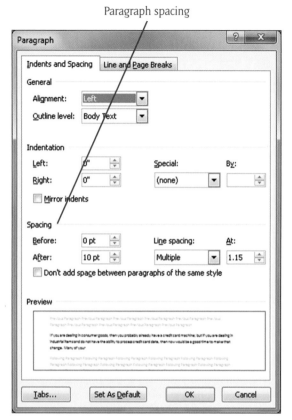

The Spacing section is where you determine the amount of space you want before or after each paragraph. Settings are measured in points and range from −1 to 1584.

Tip

You can also change paragraph spacing by choosing Page Layout > Paragraph > Spacing.

Figure 3-21
Manually setting the desired amount of spacing between paragraphs.

Copying Formatting

IF YOU SPEND several minutes setting up just the right text and paragraph formatting, and you know you'll need the same formatting several more times in your document, you don't want to have to remember all your settings and repeat them over and over again. Instead, you can copy formatting from one area to others by using the Format Painter tool. Follow these easy steps to copy formatting:

1. Select some of the text containing the formatting you want to use elsewhere. Your selection could include just a few characters or an entire paragraph.

2. Choose Home > Clipboard > Format Painter. Your mouse pointer changes to the shape of a paintbrush.

3. Press and hold the mouse button and drag over the text you want formatted.

4. Release the mouse button. Notice, as shown in Figure 3-22, how the next heading takes on the formatting attributes of the first heading.

Tip

To keep the Format Painter function active for repeated use, double-click the Format Painter button. When you finish using the Format Painter function, click the Format Painter button again, which turns it off.

Format Painter

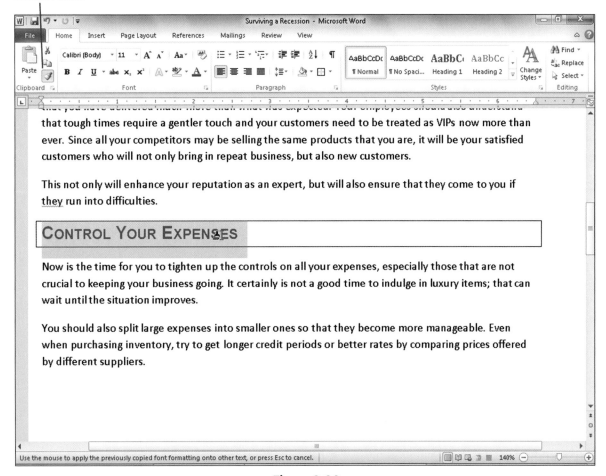

Figure 3-22
Save formatting time by using the Format Painter tool.

Working with Lists

YOU CAN USE BULLETS or numbers to call attention to lists in your documents. Traditionally, you use bullets when the list items do not follow any particular order (such as a list of options), and you use numbers when you want the items to follow each other in numerical order (such as the steps in this book). Select the text for which you want to add bullets or numbers. Then choose Home > Paragraph and click either the Bullets button or the Numbering button. Both items have a drop-down arrow from which you can select a bullet or number style (see Figure 3-23). You can preview the options with Live Preview by hovering your mouse over any option before selecting.

Bullets vs. Numbering

If you choose bullets and then decide you want numbering, or vice versa, select the text, and then choose the other option. If you decide you don't want a bulleted or numbered list, select the text and click the Bullets or Numbering button again, which removes the selected option.

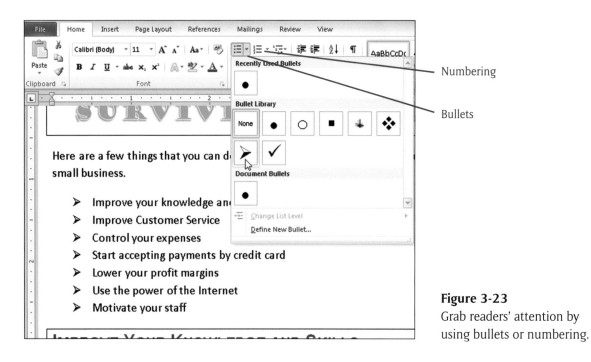

Numbering

Bullets

Figure 3-23
Grab readers' attention by using bullets or numbering.

If you have not already typed your list, Word monitors your keystrokes and, depending on what you type, automatically converts a list to a bulleted or numbered list. If you type a 1 followed by a period and then either a space or tab, Word automatically converts the item to a numbered list. If you type an asterisk (*) followed by a space or a tab, Word automatically changes the asterisk into a bullet. When you finish typing and press the Enter key, Word creates the next numbered item or adds another bullet.

Tip

Other features Word monitors and automatically changes include changing fractions to fractional characters like 1/2 to $1/2$ or applying ordinals, such as changing 1st to 1st.

Tip

See Chapter 8 for information on creating a multi-level list.

When Word formats the entry as a list, you see an AutoCorrect Options button next to the bullet or number (see Figure 3-24). If you don't want Word to change the list formatting, click the AutoCorrect Options button and choose Undo Automatic Numbering or Undo Automatic Bullets.

Figure 3-24
Word's AutoFormat as You Type feature.

Disable Automatic Settings

To permanently turn off the automatic numbering or bullet formatting, choose File tab > Word Options. In the Proofing section, click AutoCorrect Options. Click the AutoFormat As You Type tab and turn off Automatic Bulleted Lists and Automatic Numbering.

Working with Themes

YOU SPEND A LOT OF TIME preparing the content in your documents, making sure you are getting your point across to the recipient clearly. Throughout this chapter, you've seen how you can add a little extra "oomph" to your document by adding formatting.

All Microsoft applications include a feature that saves you boatloads of time by providing expertly designed *themes*, which can give all of your Office documents a unified and professional appearance. Themes include a set of colors, fonts, and other formatting details that coordinate together, and since the themes are shared across all the Office programs, all your Office documents can now have the same look.

By default, when you create a new Word (or Excel, PowerPoint, and so forth) document, Office begins with the Office theme. As you've already seen, it starts with the Calibri 11 point font, and you've also seen the default paragraph settings. Microsoft Office includes 43 other themes with names such as Apex, Civic, or Metro. You can also download additional themes from Microsoft Office Online.

All of the document content links to the theme, so if you change the theme, a complete set of new colors, fonts, and effects is applied to your entire document. You can still, however, make any individual formatting changes to the document. Themes also save time when it comes to adding tables, charts, or diagrams to your documents because those elements can also include the matching theme settings.

To apply a different theme to your document, click Page Layout > Themes > Themes. A gallery appears of the different themes, as shown in Figure 3-25. As you pause your mouse over any theme, you can immediately see how the fonts and colors change in your document. Click the theme you want to use.

Theme Color Strategy

Theme colors have 12 color positions. The first four colors are for text and backgrounds. The next six are accent colors, and the last two colors are used for hyperlinks. The folks at Microsoft built visibility rules into the themes so that usually you can switch colors at any time, and all your content will remain legible and still look good.

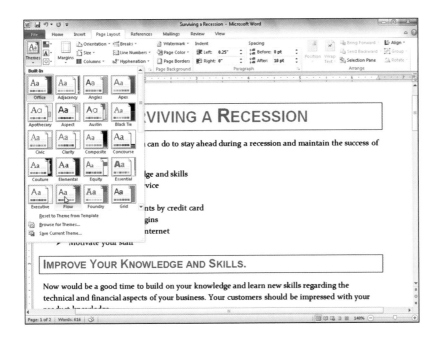

Figure 3-25
Provide a unified appearance in documents by using Office themes.

Working with Styles

THIS ENTIRE CHAPTER is about making your document look good by using Word's many formatting tools. You've already worked with direct formatting, which is where you apply the formatting directly, such as bold, underline, or a different font.

In the previous section, you discovered themes. You discovered that themes change the overall colors, fonts, and effects used in your document. However, there is a faster way to quickly apply formatting: working with styles. Styles are a saved collection of formatting steps. You can apply styles to characters, paragraphs, lists, and tables.

Using Quick Styles

Quick Styles are predefined sets of font and paragraph formatting settings, each designed to coordinate with each other. For example, a Quick Style might include styles for headings, titles, body text or even quotations. Some include color changes and some do not. Quick Styles change how the different colors, fonts, and effects are combined and which color, font, and effect is dominant.

Quick Styles are tied to themes and help maintain design and consistency in your document without actually changing the entire document theme. Use the following steps to work with Quick Styles:

1. Select the text to which you want to apply formatting.

2. Choose Home > Styles and click the More button next to the Styles scroll bar. A gallery of style options appears, as shown in Figure 3-26.

3. As you position your mouse over the styles, Live Preview shows you the effect on your selected text. Select the option that best suits your text.

Tip

Optionally, choose Home > Styles > Change Styles > Style Set to view additional style options, which are named after and originate from the different themes. (See Figure 3-27.)

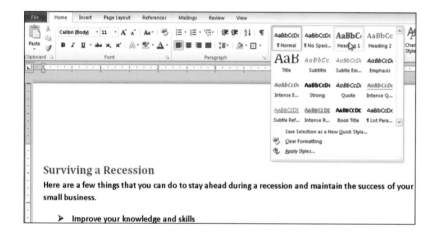

Figure 3-26
Choose from Word's predefined styles.

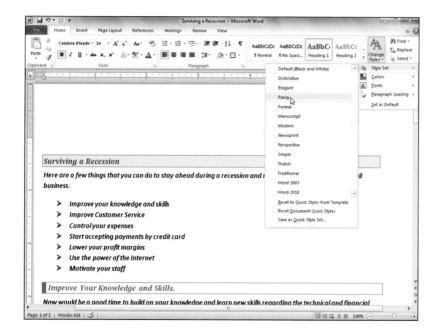

Figure 3-27
More Word predefined style formats.

Working in the Styles Task Pane

Every new Word document includes styles; however, the exact styles the document includes vary with the document template you use. (See Chapter 17 for more information about templates.) The Quick Styles you worked with in the previous section are the ones available with the standard blank Word document.

Many companies have a complete series of styles they use to standardize the look of company documents. In the next section, you discover how to create your own styles. You can use the Styles task pane for easy access to the standard and your custom styles.

From the Home tab, click the Styles group Dialog Box Launcher. On the right side of your screen, the Styles task pane appears like the one you see in Figure 3-28. The styles that have a paragraph mark (¶) next to them are *paragraph* styles, and the ones that have an "a" next to them indicate they are *character* styles, and there are some that are marked with both. Word calls these *linked* styles. Paragraph styles apply to entire paragraphs (such as alignment, spacing, or tab settings), and character styles can apply to the text itself (such as bold, italics, or font). Paragraph styles also include everything that a character style contains. You mostly use paragraph and character styles in your documents.

Styles Dialog Box Launcher   Paragraph style indicator

Character style indicator

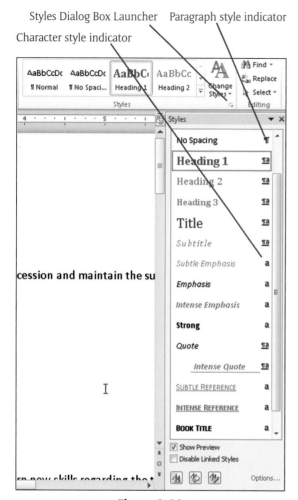

Figure 3-28
The Styles task pane.

Linked styles work as either a character style or a paragraph style, depending on your selection. For example, if you simply click in a paragraph or select a paragraph and then apply a linked style, Word applies the style as a paragraph style. However, if you select specific words in the paragraph and then apply a linked style, Word applies the style as a character style with no effect on the overall paragraph. Word also has table styles, which you apply to tables. (See Chapter 12.) From here you can click in or select your text and apply a style by clicking the desired style from the Styles task pane.

Creating Customized Styles

If your company has a standard format it likes to use for document areas, you can create your own Quick Style and quickly apply it whenever you need it. For example, suppose your company likes proposals to have a heading in a 24-point bold Harrington font with the Gradient Fill – Blue, Accent 1 text effect and a shadow.

You can save all that formatting in a style and save it for use in future documents. Follow these steps to save the formatting to a Quick Style.

1. Format and select some text the way you want it.

2. Choose Home > Styles and click the More button.

3. Choose Save Selection as a New Quick Style, as shown in Figure 3-29. The Create New Style from Formatting dialog box appears.

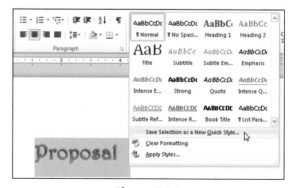

Figure 3-29
Create your own quick style.

4. Enter a name for your style, "Proposal," for example.

5. Click Modify. The dialog box expands. See Figure 3-30.

New documents based on this template

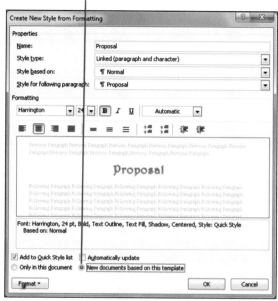

Figure 3-30
The expanded Create New Style from Formatting dialog box.

6. Select New Documents Based on This Template.

7. Click OK. The new Quick Style appears in the Quick Style box. See Figure 3-31.

Managing Styles

Sometimes the styles you already have, whether standard or custom styles, aren't quite right for the current document. For example, say the Heading 1 style is a 14-point bold Veranda font, but for this document, you want it as an 18-point font.

You could select every occurrence of the Heading 1 style and change them individually to an 18-point size, or you can modify the style. When you modify a style, you decide if you want it changed for only the current document, or if you want to change it also for future documents based on the same template.

Fortunately, Word has a Manage Styles box you can use for quick, efficient style management. Just follow these steps:

1. Display the Styles task pane by clicking the Home > Styles Dialog Box Launcher.

2. Along the bottom of the Styles task pane are three small icons, the third of which is the Manage Styles icon.

3. Click Manage Styles. The Manage Styles dialog box appears, as shown in Figure 3-32.

New Quick Style

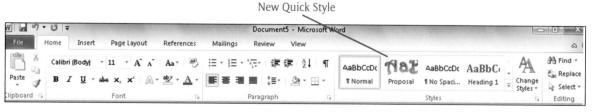

Figure 3-31
The newly saved Quick Style.

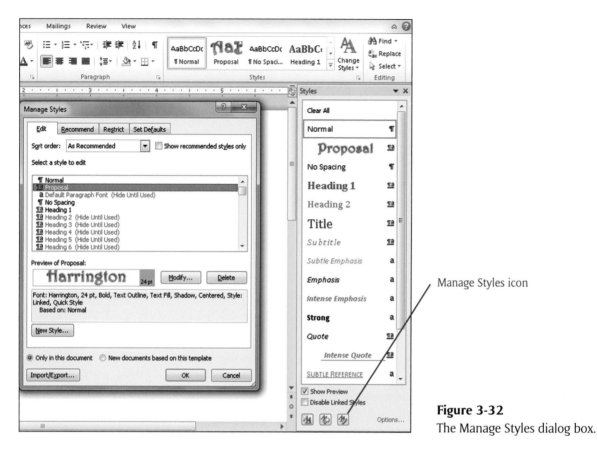

Figure 3-32
The Manage Styles dialog box.

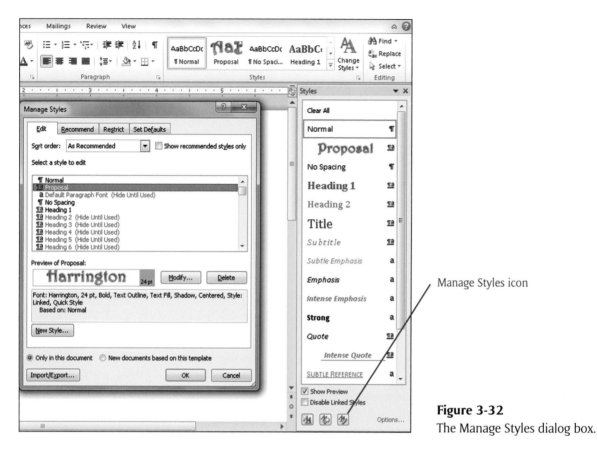

Manage Styles icon

4. From the Manage Styles dialog box, select the style you want to modify.

5. Select whether the change you are planning should apply to the current document or to any new documents based on the template.

6. Click the Modify button and make changes to the style.

7. Click OK when you are finished.

Deleting Styles

In the previous section, you worked with the Manage Styles dialog box where you discovered how you can modify a style. You may have noticed a Delete button on the Manage Styles dialog. If you

click the Delete button, you are only temporarily deleting the style—not permanently.

If you want to permanently delete a customized style, you must do so through the Style Organizer window. For whatever the reason, Microsoft made the Style Organizer window a little difficult to get to, but the following steps show you the way:

1. Click the File tab and choose Options. The Word Options dialog box appears.

2. On the left side, choose Add-Ins. The right side displays options related to Add-Ins.

3. Click the Manage drop-down list and choose Word Add-ins. See Figure 3-33.

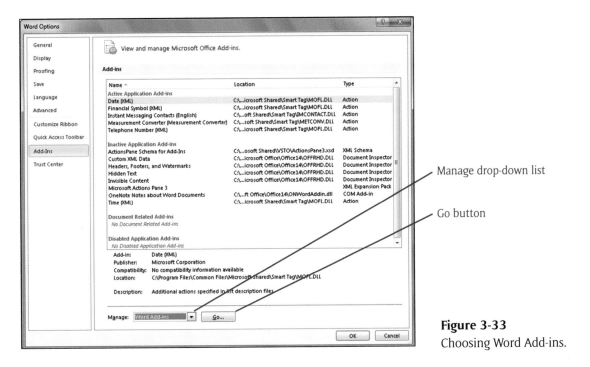

Manage drop-down list

Go button

Figure 3-33
Choosing Word Add-ins.

4. Click the Go button. The Templates and Add-Ins dialog box appears.

5. Click the Organizer button located in the lower-left corner. The Organizer dialog box appears, as shown in Figure 3-34.

6. From the right column (In Normal:) select the style you want to delete.

7. Click the Delete button. A confirmation box appears.

8. Click Yes, and then when you are finished, click the Close button.

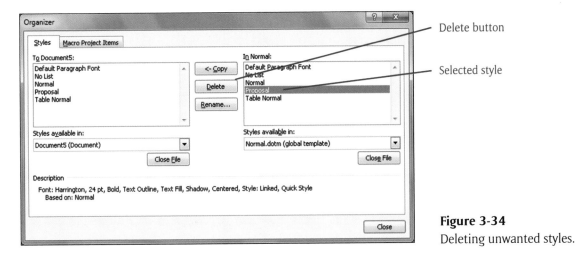

Delete button

Selected style

Figure 3-34
Deleting unwanted styles.

Revealing Formatting

Word has a really cool feature that lets you quickly see all formatting applied to selected text. Called Reveal Formatting, you can review the font formatting, paragraph formatting, and section formatting all at once.

To see the text formatting, first select the text you want to inspect, then open the Style task pane by clicking the Home > Styles Dialog Box Launcher.

From the bottom of the Styles task pane, click the Style Inspector icon, which is the middle icon. The Style Inspector pane shown in Figure 3-35 appears.

From the bottom of the Style Inspector pane, click the Reveal Formatting icon (the one on the left). The Reveal Formatting pane appears on the right side of your Word window. See Figure 3-36. From here you can see all formatting applied to the selected text.

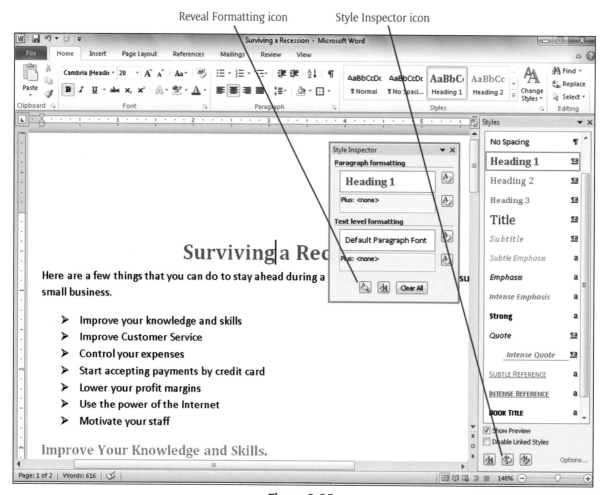

Figure 3-35
The Style Inspector.

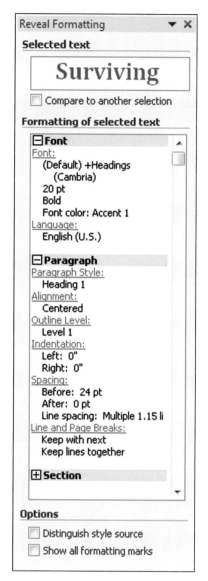

Figure 3-36

The Reveal
Formatting
task pane.

If you want to change any of the options, click the applicable underlined link. A dialog box relative to that option appears where you can change the settings for the selected text.

When you are finished, click the Close box (x) on the Reveal Formatting task pane, the Styles task pane, and the Style Inspector task pane.

Managing Word

Page Layouts

PICTURE YOURSELF TAKING YOUR FAMILY to an amusement park. The older children want to go this way, and the younger children want to go another way. Grandpa just wants to sit and rest and watch. How will you manage everything?

Balancing a document's *white space*—the amount of blank space on a page—is an important aspect of designing professional-looking pages. You can increase or decrease white space by adjusting margins and the amount of text you place on a page. Additionally, Word provides the ability to work with multiple documents at the same time, as well as methods for quickly comparing information between two documents. When multiple windows are active, you'll need a way to manage them all. That's what this chapter is about—managing a Word document.

Creating Page Breaks

WORD AUTOMATICALLY INSERTS a page break when text fills the page. This page break sometimes doesn't fall where you want it to. You can override Word's automatic page break by creating your own page break. You can make a page break at a shorter position than Word chooses, but you cannot make a page longer.

A manual page break is sometimes called a hard page break because, unlike the page breaks that Word inserts, a manual page break doesn't move if you delete text above it, adjust the margins, or otherwise change the amount of text on the page. Insert a manual page break by positioning the insertion point where you want the new page to begin and choosing one of the following methods:

- ▶ Choose Insert > Pages > Page Break
- ▶ Choose Page Layout > Page Setup > Breaks > Page
- ▶ Press Ctrl+Enter

If you are in the default Print Layout view, you see the text below the insertion point move down to the next page of the document. However, if you have the Show/Hide characters active, you see the words "Page Break," along with a dotted line, where the new page begins, as shown in Figure 4-1. (Document views are discussed in Chapter 6.)

Tip

You can show or hide the hidden characters by choosing Home > Paragraph > Show/Hide ¶.

You cannot delete Word's automatic page breaks, but you can delete the manually inserted hard page breaks at any time. Simply click the mouse pointer at the beginning of the text after the page break indication, and then press the Backspace key. Word deletes the manual page break, and the document text readjusts to fit on the pages correctly.

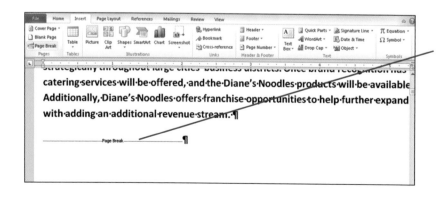

Page break indicator

Figure 4-1
Manually starting a new page.

Using Section Breaks

WHEN YOU NEED TO APPLY different page formatting options to only a portion of the document, you need to break the document into *sections*. For example, when page 1 requires different margin settings from the rest of the document, you must break page 1 into its own section. If only pages 16–18 need to be printed in landscape orientation, you can break pages 16, 17, and 18 into a section. Other uses for section breaks are when you need a different header or footer for a section of your document or you want to separate the chapters in your document so that the page numbering for each chapter begins at 1.

Most section breaks involve entire pages; however, if you need different columns, they don't necessarily have to be on different pages. Word allows for four different types of section breaks:

- ▶ **Next Page:** Inserts a section break and starts the new section on the next page.
- ▶ **Continuous:** Inserts a section break and starts the new section on the same page.
- ▶ **Odd Page:** Inserts a section break and starts the new section on the next odd-numbered page.
- ▶ **Even Page:** Inserts a section break and starts the new section on the next even-numbered page.

Section formatting options include the following, many of which are covered in this chapter:

- ▶ **Margins:** The amount of space between the text and the paper edge.

- ▶ **Paper Size:** The paper size you intend to use when printing.
- ▶ **Paper Orientation:** The direction the text prints on the paper edge.
- ▶ **Paper Source:** When printing, which paper tray the printer should pull paper from.
- ▶ **Page Borders:** Bordered lines that appear around the entire document page.
- ▶ **Vertical Alignment:** The placement of text between the top and bottom margins.
- ▶ **Headers and Footers:** Text that appears at the top or bottom of every document page.
- ▶ **Columns:** How text in newsletter-style columns flows from one column to the next on the same page.
- ▶ **Page Numbering:** Sequential numbering for each document page.
- ▶ **Line Numbering:** How Word automatically counts the lines in a document and displays the appropriate number beside each line of text.
- ▶ **Footnotes and Endnotes:** A note of text placed at the bottom of a page or at the end of the document typically citing a reference used in the document.

To insert a section break, position the mouse where you want the new section to begin, choose Page Layout > Page Setup > Breaks, and select the desired section break type from the drop-down list as shown in Figure 4-2. A section break controls the formatting of the text that precedes it.

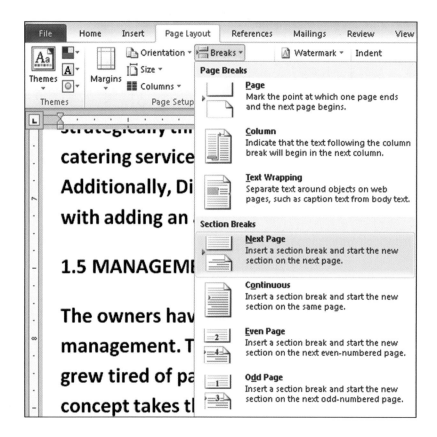

Figure 4-2
Types of page and section breaks.

Depending on the type of section break you choose, from the default Print Layout view, you see the text below the insertion point remain at the same location or move down to the next page of the document. However, if you are in Draft view or you have the Show/Hide characters active, you see the words "Section Break" and the type of section break in action, along with a dotted line, where the previous section ends (see Figure 4-3). Chapter 6 covers the different Word views.

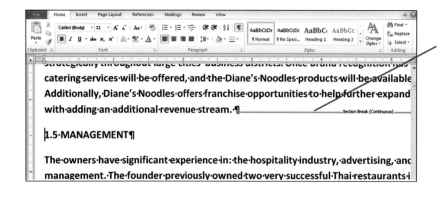

Section break indicator

Figure 4-3
Adding a section break.

Managing Page Layouts

SOMETIMES WORKING WITH a long document can feel a bit overwhelming. Fortunately, Word contains many features designed to assist you, such as those that allow you to set the page size and layout, mixing and matching them as needed.

Setting Margins

Margins are the space between the edges of the paper and where the text actually begins to appear. Word allows you to set margins for any of the four sides of the document and also allows you to mix and match margins for different pages. Word sets the default margins as 1 inch on each of the top, bottom, left, and right sides. You can set the document margins before you begin entering text into a document, after you've completed the entire document, or at any time in between.

Choose Page Layout > Page Setup > Margins and select from the choices you see in Figure 4-4, or click Custom Margins, which displays the Page Setup dialog box where you can set your own choices. By default, Word applies the new settings to the entire document.

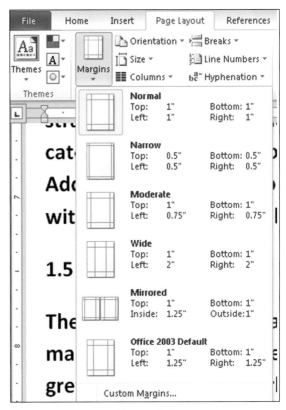

Figure 4-4
Choosing from standard margin options.

If you want to change margins for only part of the document, select the portion you want to change. From Page Layout > Page Setup > Margins, choose Custom Margins. Set the margins you want and, from the Apply To drop-down list, choose Selected Text (see Figure 4-5). Word creates section breaks and applies the new margin settings.

Apply To

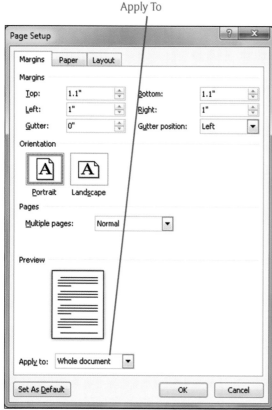

Figure 4-5
Applying margin settings to only
part of a document.

Changing Document Orientation

Webster's dictionary describes orientation as a position in relation to a specific place or object. In word processing, orientation refers to how the text is positioned in relation to the top of a page. Two orientations exist: Portrait, the default orientation, prints the text beginning along the short edge of the paper, and Landscape orientation prints along the long edge of the page.

Choose Page Layout > Page Setup > Orientation and choose Portrait or Landscape, as shown in Figure 4-6.

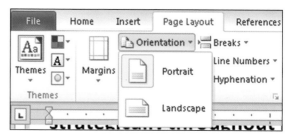

Figure 4-6
Choosing a document orientation.

Sections Required

Similar to margin settings, if you want to change the orientation for only part of the document, select the portion you want to change and, from the Page Setup dialog box, choose your orientation and from the Apply To section, choose Selected Text. Word creates section breaks and applies the new settings to the selected section.

Setting the Paper Size

Word assumes you want your document printed on standard paper 8.5 inches wide by 11 inches long, but you may want some or all of your document printed on a different paper size. Although Word can work with many different sizes of paper, often the selections available to you depend on the printer you have. In many situations, you can even create your own custom paper size.

Word provides a number of different ways to manage document paper sizes:

▶ To change the paper size for the entire document, choose Page Layout > Page Setup > Size and select a size from the resulting drop-down list (see Figure 4-7).

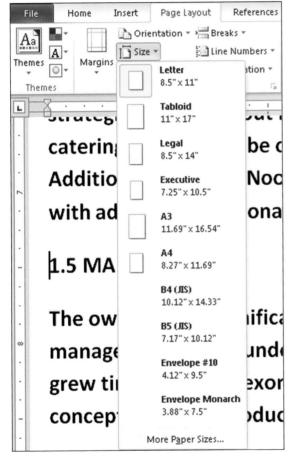

Figure 4-7
Selecting the desired paper size.

▶ To change the paper size from a certain location through the rest of the document, position the insertion point where you

want the new paper size to take effect, and then choose Page Layout > Page Setup > Size and select More Paper Sizes. From the Paper tab of the Page Setup dialog box, select the paper size you want and then, in the Apply To drop-down list, choose This Point Forward.

▶ To change the paper size for a particular section, create the section breaks where needed and click anywhere inside the section you want to change, or select the text area. Choose Page Layout > Page Setup > Size and select More Paper Sizes. From the Paper tab of the Page Setup dialog box, select the paper size you want and then, from the Apply To drop-down list, choose This Section or Selected Sections.

Adding Line Numbering

Sometimes, especially with legal documents, you need to place line numbering. Word has a feature that can automatically count the lines in a document and display the appropriate number beside each line of text. Word gives you a number of different line numbering options. For example, you can number every line in a document, number every line in only a part of the document, or display line numbering at specific intervals such as 2, 4, 6, 8 or 10, 20, 30, 40, and so forth.

Word also has a few rules about how it counts special items:

▶ Blank lines are included. Paragraph spacing is not included.

▶ A table counts as one line. (See Chapter 12 for information about tables.)

▶ Graphics count as one line. (See Chapter 13 for information about graphics.)

► A text box counts as one line if it is positioned in-line with the text on the page. If text on the page wraps around the text box, the lines of text on the page are counted. Lines of text inside a text box are not counted. (See Chapter 13 for information about text boxes.)

► Footnotes, endnotes, headers, and footers are not included.

To add line numbering, choose Page Layout > Page Setup > Line Numbers. You see the menu as shown in Figure 4-8.

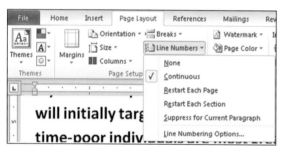

Figure 4-8
Line numbering choices.

Line Numbering Sections

If your document has sections, and you want to number the entire document, before applying line numbering, you must select the entire document by pressing Ctrl+A.

By default, Word numbers every line in a document as 1, 2, 3, 4, and so on. You can choose to number continuously through the entire document, or you can have the numbers restart at each page or section.

Line numbering does *not* show up on your screen document. It appears only in the printed document or in Word's Print Preview window. To see how the line numbering looks, click the File tab and choose Print. You see the document with its line numbering on the left side of the screen. Figure 4-9 illustrates a document numbered continuously throughout the entire document.

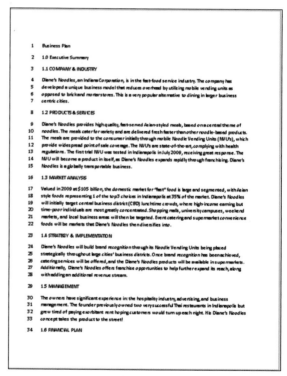

Figure 4-9
A document with line numbering.

If you want a different numbering scheme than the default sequential 1, 2, 3, 4, choose Page Layout > Page Setup > Line Numbers > Line Numbering Options. The Page Setup dialog box appears. Click the Line Numbers button on the Page Setup dialog box. You see the Line Numbers dialog box shown in Figure 4-10.

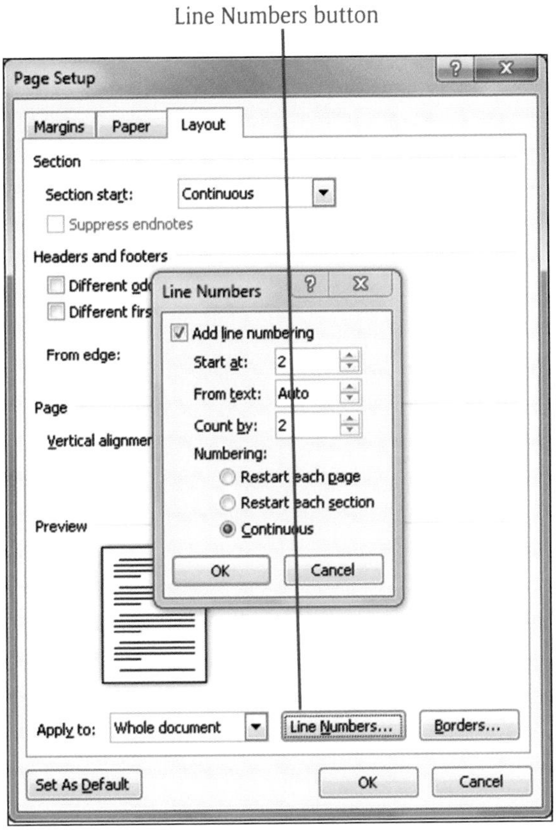

Check the Add Line Numbering option, and then select any other desired options. Click OK twice.

Tip

To remove line numbering, choose Page Layout > Page Setup > Line Numbers > None.

Line Numbers button

Figure 4-10
Setting the line number pattern.

Adding Headers and Footers

HEADERS AND FOOTERS are features used for placing information at the top or bottom of every page of a document. As you'd expect, a header prints at the top of every page, and a footer prints at the bottom. You can place any information in headers and footers, such as a company logo, the document title, page numbering, and so forth.

Using Header and Footer Styles

In keeping with the themed concept of Office 2010, the predefined headers and footers contain elements designed to make your document more visually appealing. Choose Insert > Header & Footer > Headers (or Footers) which displays a gallery of 27 unique header (or footer) styles, as shown in Figure 4-11. If you were not already in Print Layout view, Word automatically switches you to it.

From the Header or Footer gallery, select the style you want. The document header area becomes visible, the body of the document fades, and Word displays one or more additional tabs on the ribbon. You can now use the Header & Footer Tools > Design tab for creating your personalized header or footer.

In the header example shown in Figure 4-12, Word inserts a placeholder for the document title. Click the placeholder and enter the desired text. Also in the same figure, you see a placeholder that says Pick the Date. If you click the down arrow, Word displays a calendar from which you can select the date you want in the header. Optionally, you can just type a date in the date field. The actual choices you see depend on which header or footer style you select.

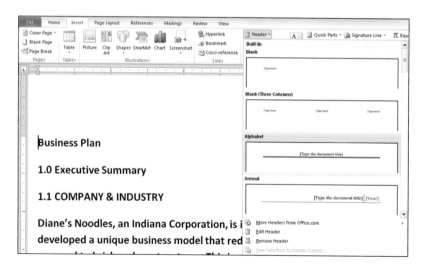

Figure 4-11
Creating a header or footer.

Title placeholder   Click here to select a date

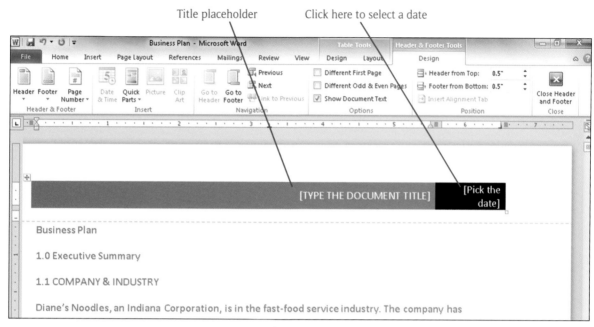

Figure 4-12
Working with text placeholders.

Tip

If you don't want the predefined place-holder, click the small tab above the placeholder and press the Delete key.

Now take a brief look at some of the tool groups on the Header & Footer Tools > Design tab, as shown in Figure 4-13.

Figure 4-13
The Header & Footer Tools > Design tab.

▶ **Header & Footer:** Use this group to change the header or footer style, or to insert the page number in the header or footer.

▶ **Insert:** From this group you can insert the current date or time, a picture, or a piece of clip art. You can also select from Quick Parts and choose one of the document properties shown in Figure 4-14.

▶ **Position:** This group contains settings for exact header and footer placement in relation to the top or bottom of the document paper edges.

▶ **Close:** Use this button to close the header or footer and return to the document body. You can also double-click anywhere in the document body to close the header or footer.

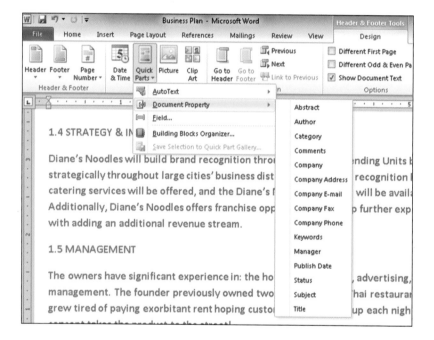

Figure 4-14
Adding document Quick Parts.

▶ **Navigation:** Use the tools in this group to move between the document headers and footers.

▶ **Options:** The Options group allows you to choose whether the first page of your document should have a different header or footer from the rest of the document. You can also choose different headers for the odd or even numbered pages.

Every page of the document displays the header and/or footer you created (see Figure 4-15). Remember, however, that documents displayed in Outline or Draft view do not reveal any headers or footers.

Changing the Header or Footer

If you don't like the header or footer you selected, double-click the header or footer, and then from the Header & Footer Tools > Design tab, click the Header or Footer button and choose a different header or footer.

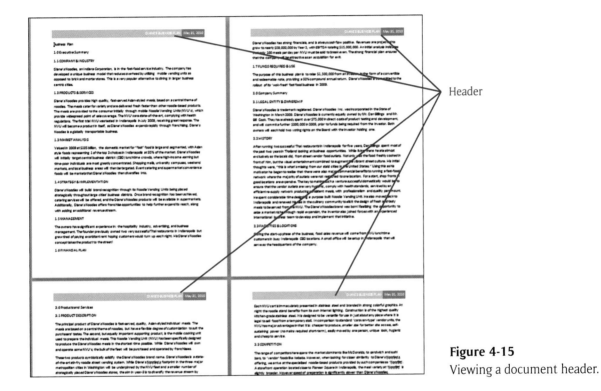

Header

Figure 4-15
Viewing a document header.

Tip

To further edit the header or footer, either double-click in the header or footer area, or choose Insert > Header & Footer > Header (or Footer) > Edit Header (or Footer). To remove the header or footer, choose Remove Header (or Footer) from the same menu.

Creating a Custom Header or Footer

If none of the predefined headers or footers suits your needs, you can certainly create your own. You can add text, fields (such as date, time, or author), or page numbers, and you can add graphics (such as logos, lines, and other art). Just follow these steps:

1. Choose View > Document Views > Print Layout.

Tip

If you want to work on the footer instead of the header, click Go To Footer to jump to the footer area.

2. Double-click in any desired header or footer section and type the text you want for the header (or footer). As you see in Figure 4-16, you can format the header and footer text just as you would any cell data.

3. Insert any other options from the Header & Footer Tools > Design tab:

   ▶ **Page Number:** Insert a code that indicates the page number.

   ▶ **Date & Time:** Insert the print date or time of day.

   ▶ **Picture:** Insert a graphic image such as a company logo.

   ▶ **Clip Art:** Insert a clip art image.

4. Click in the document body, outside of the header (or footer) area, to close the header or footer.

Adding Page Numbering

Although Word automatically numbers your pages as you type them, it doesn't print the page numbers; it simply displays them in the screen status bar. You can easily tell Word you want to print them. Typically, the page numbers appear in the header or footer area, but they don't have to. You can place them wherever you want. What you do need to remember, though, is to use the Page Number feature provided by Word—don't try to

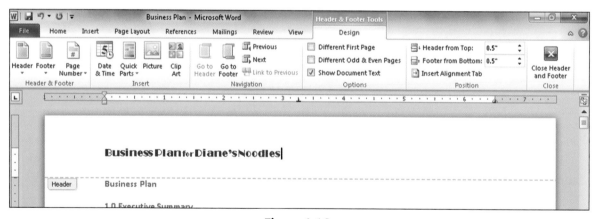

Figure 4-16
Creating your own header or footer.

type the page numbering yourself. If you type Page 1 of 6 in the footer, every page will say Page 1 of 6. If you use one of Word's Page Number features, the page numbering will change as needed, such as Page 2 of 6 or Page 3 of 6.

To insert a page number, choose Insert > Header & Footer > Page Number. A menu of placement options appears. You can put the page number at the top of the page in the header, at the bottom of

the page in the footer, in the page margins outside of the header or footer, in the margin area, or you can put the page numbering at the current document position of your cursor.

Choose the position you want, and then a gallery of prefabricated page number styles appears (see Figure 4-17). Select the page numbering style you want to use. Word adds the page numbering to your document, as shown in Figure 4-18.

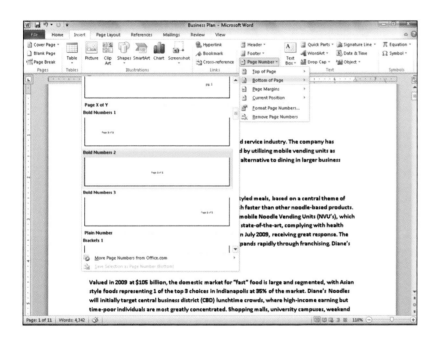

Figure 4-17
Select a page numbering style.

Page numbering

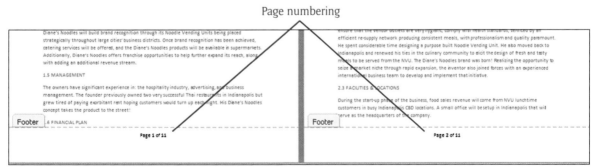

Figure 4-18
Page numbering added to the document.

Understanding Security
and Printing

PICTURE YOURSELF WORKING AWAY on an employee evalua-tion. You don't want anyone to see it, and people are constantly coming in and out of your office, even when you're not there. How can you protect your work from those of whom you don't want to see it? And if you decide to pass the file on to others, is there any way you can lock the contents to keep others from changing it? The answer is yes. Word contains a number of ways to keep your files safe.

This chapter is about security. It's also about printing. When you want to share the document in a printed form, you have quite a few choices as to what to print. In this chapter you'll learn how to keep your documents secure and how to share them when you want to.

Keeping Documents Secure

MANY DOCUMENTS CONTAIN data that is confidential in nature, such as business plans or personal diaries. In today's world of electronic snooping, it's up to you to protect your work against prying eyes. Even if you allow others to view your documents, you may want to prevent accidental or intentional changes. Fortunately, Word provides several security tools, including password protection.

Making Backups

Prepare yourself. I'm going to nag at you here. Okay, this section doesn't really have anything to do with Microsoft Word. It's more of a personal plea. Back up your files. *I repeat*: Back up your files. You know the silly, but popular, little saying, "Stuff happens." (That's not exactly how it goes, but you get the idea.) Well, it's true. Things happen. Now, I don't mean to sound pessimistic, but computers do fail, files get deleted or corrupted, and disasters (such as fire or theft) can occur.

Well, you can always get another computer and reload your Microsoft Word program. But even millions of dollars can't buy back all the documents and the hundreds of work hours you have in them and that you have stored on your computer. That's why backing up your files on a *regular* basis is important. Then, if disaster strikes, you can restore them.

Whether you copy your images using Windows Explorer to a flash drive, a CD, or a DVD, or you use a special backup program, don't procrastinate. Do it!

Officially, Microsoft Word doesn't have any specific function for backing up your files, but refer to the Windows Help system on how you can copy files from your Documents folder (or wherever you store your documents) to your backup flash drive, CD, or DVD. Trust me—you won't regret it.

Inspecting for Personal Information

Many Word documents contain *metadata*, which is somewhat hidden information that others could see—data such as the names of people who have previously edited the document, file locations, and even e-mail addresses. You may not want others to have access to this information. Fortunately, you can eliminate the metadata by using the Document Inspector.

If you are collaborating with others using features like comments or tracked changes, you may not want to remove the metadata until the collaboration is complete. Typically, you run the Document Inspector just prior to publication. (You'll discover comments and tracked changes in Chapter 16.)

First save your file and then click the File tab. From the document Information panel, choose Check for Issues and then choose Inspect Document. You see the Document Inspector dialog box shown in Figure 5-1.

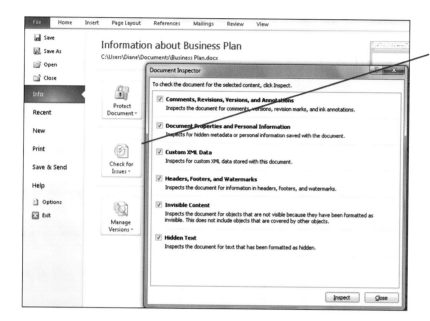

Check for Issues

Figure 5-1
Inspecting your document for personal information.

Deselect any options you do not want to check and click the Inspect button. Word inspects the document for various types of potential personal information. When the inspection is complete, the Document Inspector reappears with information, as shown in Figure 5-2.

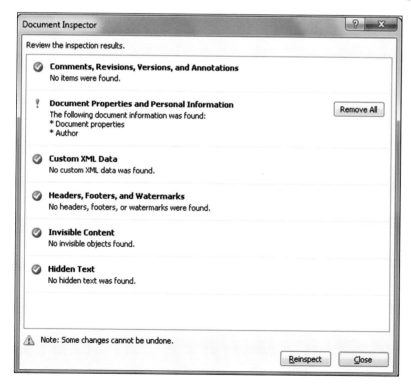

Figure 5-2
The Document Inspector reveals potential problem areas.

Click the Remove All button next to any option you want removed. Word removes the selected information and the Remove All button next to the option disappears. Repeat this for any additional items you want to remove. When finished, click the Close button and resave your file.

Restricting Formatting Changes

If you apply a file password (which you'll see how to do later in this chapter), with the right password you or others can open or modify the document. If you can modify a document, you can modify any portion of it—content or formatting. One method of protection you can apply is to protect the document against formatting changes. Then before someone can change the document appearance, they must first enter a password. Follow these steps to lock-in document formatting:

1. Choose Review > Protect > Restrict Editing. A Restrict Formatting and Editing task pane opens on the right side of the screen, as shown in Figure 5-3.

2. Click the Limit Formatting to a Selection of Styles check box.

3. Click the Settings link. The Formatting Restrictions dialog box appears (shown in Figure 5-4). By default, changes to any styles are allowed.

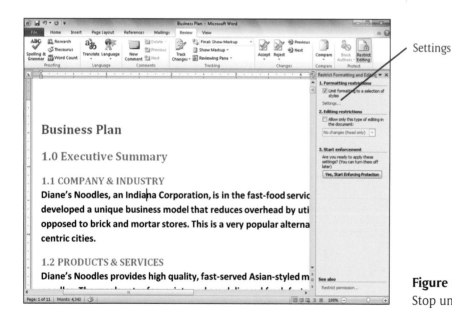

Settings

Figure 5-3
Stop unwanted formatting changes.

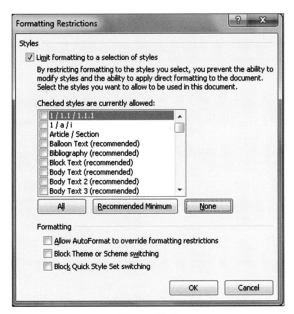

Figure 5-4
Setting formatting restrictions.

4. Click the None button. All choices are deselected; however, if you do want to allow formatting changes to a particular style, you can recheck that style name.

5. Click the OK button. Click No if you get a message box saying, "This document may contain formatting or styles that aren't allowed. Do you want to remove them?"

6. From the Restrict Formatting and Editing task pane, click the third option: Yes, Start Enforcing Protection. The Start Enforcing Protection dialog box appears.

7. Enter an optional password, and then reenter the password to confirm it. The password you type appears as a series of black dots.

8. Click OK. Notice in Figure 5-5 how any Ribbon option that affects formatting, including Quick Styles, becomes unavailable.

If you want to make any formatting changes, you must first click the Stop Protection button at the bottom of the Restrict Formatting and Editing task pane. If you don't see the Restrict Formatting and Editing task pane, choose Review > Protect > Restrict Editing. You must then enter the password to stop the protection and allow formatting changes.

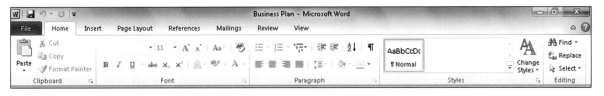

Figure 5-5
The Word Ribbon with formatting restricted.

Marking a Document as Final

To protect your document against accidental changes, Word includes a feature called Mark as Final. After choosing the option, the document cannot be changed unless you choose the Mark as Final option again, which then allows document changes.

Click the File tab and from the document Information panel, in the first section, click the Protect Document button and choose Mark as Final (shown in Figure 5-6). A confirmation message appears. Click OK. Next, another confirmation message appears. Click OK to that message also, and then click the File tab to return to the document.

Marking a document as final disables every option in the Ribbon that could change the document in any way. A bar appears across the top of the window (see Figure 5-7) indicating the document is marked as final; if you attempt to make any changes, Word simply ignores you. The document title bar also shows the document as (Read-Only).

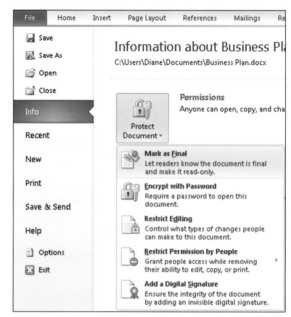

Figure 5-6

Disable editing by marking a document as final.

Edit Anyway button

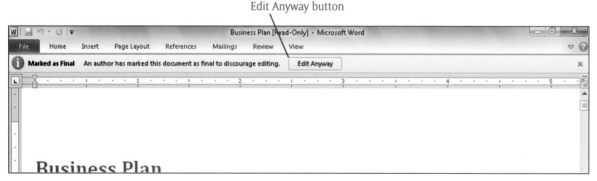

Figure 5-7

Opening a document marked as final.

This feature is easily bypassed. Suppose you need to change a date in the document, or you forgot to list a particular item. You can "unmark" the document from being final by simply clicking the Edit Anyway button.

Saving a File as Read-Only

If your goal is to prevent accidental changes, either by you or others, one of the easiest methods is to save the file with a read-only recommendation. When a file is read-only, you can still make changes to the document, but the only way you can save those changes is to save the file to a different file name or folder.

1. Click the File tab and choose Save As.

2. Optionally, select a different folder in which to save the file.

3. Enter a file name if you haven't already assigned a name.

4. Choose Tools > General Options (see Figure 5-8).

5. From the General Options dialog box, click the Read-Only Recommended check box.

6. Click the OK button, which returns you to the Save As dialog box.

7. Click the Save button.

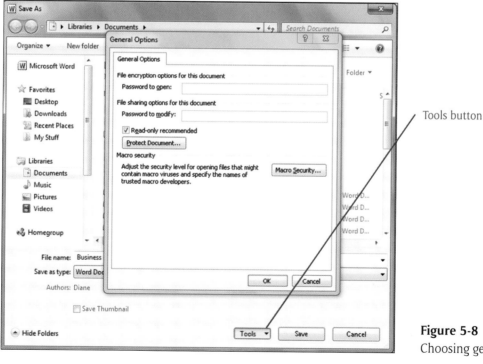

Tools button

Figure 5-8
Choosing general file options.

When you or another user attempts to open the file, the message shown in Figure 5-9 is displayed. Click Yes to open the document as a Read-Only file. If you choose No, Word again recommends you open the file as Read-Only, but if you click No again, the file finally opens as a standard file where changes can be made.

Figure 5-9
The read-only recommendation box.

Assigning a File Password

Another method to protect your documents, and probably one of the safest methods, is to assign a password. When you assign a file password, the application uses a key to encrypt the document's contents. Word, Excel, and PowerPoint all allow you to assign passwords. There are two levels of password protection you can use. One forces anyone who attempts to even open the file to supply a password. Of course, if they cannot open the file, they cannot view it or modify it. The second level is where you could allow others (with or without password protection) to open the file and view it, but not allow them to edit the file in any way without first providing another password.

To create file passwords, click the File tab and choose Save As. Select a folder for your file and enter a file name. Choose Tools > General Options. The General Options dialog box appears. Type a password in the Password to Open text box if you want users to enter a password before they can open and view the document. Word displays passwords with a black dot for each character, like those shown in Figure 5-10.

Figure 5-10
Assigning a file password.

The Perfect Password

Good passwords should be at least eight characters and should contain a mixture of numbers as well as upper- and lowercase letters. Passwords are case sensitive. Don't, however, make your passwords so difficult you can't remember them. If you lose the password to your Word, Excel, or PowerPoint document, it cannot be recovered!

Optionally, you can leave the Password to Open box empty and enter a password in the Password to Modify text box. Using this option allows others to open the file, but they cannot make any changes without keying in the password. Click OK, and a message box appears prompting you to reenter the password just in case you typed it incorrectly the first time. Reenter the password as prompted and click OK; then, click the Save button to save the password security.

Tip

If you want to use both a password to open and a password to modify, it's a good idea to use different passwords for each function.

When you or anyone opens the file, Word prompts you for the password (see Figure 5-11).

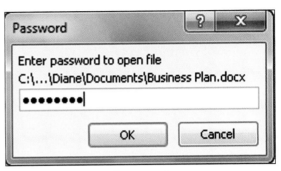

Figure 5-11
Enter the required password to open the file.

Tip

To remove file passwords, from the General Options dialog box, delete the characters from the Password to Open or Password to Modify text box and resave the file.

Understanding Protected View

In today's world, we must be very careful when we open documents created by others. It's too easy to open a virus along with the document, and we all know by now what havoc a virus can cause.

If you have an up-to-date anti-virus program on your computer, you shouldn't have too much of a problem. However, not everyone has an up-to-date anti-virus, and we have to face it—the bad guys are out there everywhere. To lessen the worry, Word now comes with an extra security feature called Protected View.

Protected View is a way for Microsoft to show Word (and other Office applications) files to you, but without all of the worry about those files being dangerous. When a file is detected to originate from the Internet, Word opens the file in a read-only view, which has minimal access to your system, and no access to your other files and information. Even if the file is malicious, it can't get out and do harm to your computer or data.

Tip
_____

Occasionally, Word also opens files that originated on a network server in Protected View.

Once you indicate that you trust the file, the next time you open the file, Word remembers when you chose to trust it, so you don't have to re-trust it next time. That's Word's way of making security strong, but still smart enough to get out of the way when its job is done.

When you open a potentially dangerous file, Word displays the file in read-only mode (look, but don't touch) with a yellow bar across the Ribbon indicating the file is in Protected View. (See Figure 5-12.) If you trust the file origin, click the Enable Editing button, and you can then work on the document. If you don't click Enable Editing, Word ignores any action you take to alter the document.

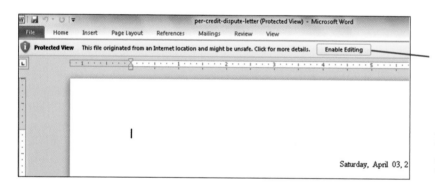

Enable Editing button

Figure 5-12
A document in Protected View.

Printing and Sharing

YOU DID IT! You created a great document, and now it's time to use it. With the adoption of e-mail within most corporations and homes, many documents today might never be printed on paper—they may only ever exist in an electronic form; however, there may still be times when you need a paper copy. This section shows you how to distribute your document both electronically and on paper.

Using Print Preview

Before you print your document, you should preview it on the screen so you can look at how document layout settings (such as the margins) will look in the printed document. In Print Preview, although you can only view the document and cannot edit it, you can tell quite a bit about it from a different perspective. The following steps walk you through the Print Preview process:

1. Click the File tab and, from the Backstage view that appears, choose Print. A Print Settings section appears on the left and a preview of the worksheet appears on the right.

2. From the Preview area (shown in Figure 5-13), select from the following options:

    ▶ If you have multiple pages, click in the page number box, then click the Next Page or Previous Page buttons to view additional pages.

    ▶ Use the Zoom controls at the lower right to enlarge or reduce the view, or click anywhere in the Preview window to zoom in or out.

Page number box   Next Page   Zoom controls

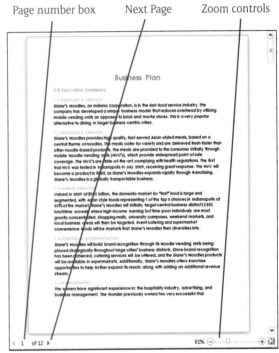

Figure 5-13

Previewing your document before printing it.

3. If you're ready to print your document, continue to the next section, but if you want to return to the document, click the File tab.

Printing a Document

When your document is complete and you've reviewed it for any changes, you may want to make a hard copy of it to file away or to share with others. Click the File tab and, from the Backstage view that appears, choose Print. A Print Settings section appears on the left and a preview of the worksheet appears on the right. The Print Settings section shown in Figure 5-14 illustrates the many printing options. Take a look at a few of them:

▶ **Copies:** Select the number of copies you want to print.

▶ **Printer:** If you are connected to more than one printer, you can select which printer you want to use from the drop-down list.

▶ **Settings:** Determine which pages you want to print. If you highlight a document area before you display the Print dialog box, you can choose Selection to print only that area. If you want to print only selected pages, enter into the Pages text box the page numbers separated by a comma or a dash. For example, to print only the first three document pages, enter 1, 2, 3 or 1-3. Other settings include options such as margins, paper size, or collating options. The last option (Page Per Sheet) determines how many document pages you want to print on a single sheet of paper. The formatting and document page layouts do not change; Word simply reduces the size of each printed page to fit the number of pages that you select. This feature is helpful as an overview or handout document.

Choose any desired options and then click the Print button to begin printing.

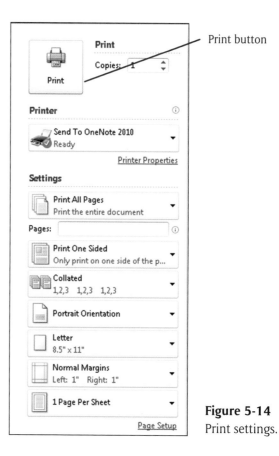

Figure 5-14
Print settings.

E-Mailing a Document

If you have e-mail access, you can send a document directly to another person. Word copies the content of the document as an attachment to an e-mail message. While many e-mail applications work fine with this feature, Office works best with Outlook and Outlook Express.

With the document open and ready to send, click the File tab and choose Save & Send > Send Using E-Mail. Then click the Send as Attachment button shown in Figure 5-15.

Send as Attachment

Figure 5-15
The Save & Send screen.

Word launches your e-mail application with the file listed as an attachment. Type the recipient's e-mail address or click the To button to select from your Outlook Contact List. Word automatically adds the document name as the subject, but you can click the Subject text box and change the subject. Optionally, type a message in the message body (see Figure 5-16). Click the Send button when you are finished.

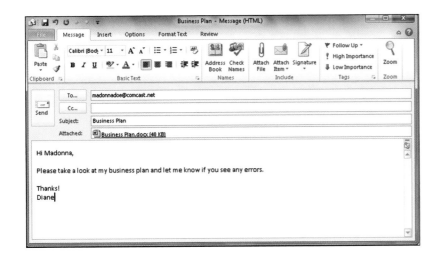

Figure 5-16
E-mailing a Word document as an attachment.

Part 2
Longer Documents

There's more to Word than short letters and memos. Now that you are more comfortable with the basics of Word, I'll show you how you can view your documents from different perspectives and generally work with longer documents. In this part, you'll discover outlines, mass mailings, and adding referencing information such as bibliographies, footnotes, tables of contents, and indexes. Using features like these makes creating legal briefs, annual reports, catalogs, and other complex documents much easier.

Working with Document
Views

PICTURE YOURSELF GOING OUTSIDE on a beautiful spring day. If you look up, you see the sky and the birds. If you look down, you see the grass and pavement, and if you look around, you see flowers, shrubs, cars, and people. The general view is of the outside, but as you move around, your perspective changes.

Word provides several different view perspectives to use when displaying a document, each having its own purpose. There is Print Layout view where you can see all elements in your document up close. Full Screen Reading view limits the distractions, and you can focus strictly on reading the document content. Web Layout view shows you how your document might appear on a website. Draft view hides margins, graphics, headers and footers, so you can concentrate on editing the document content.

Viewing your document from different angles is what this chapter is about. You'll discover when and how to use each of the views, as well as how to zoom in for a closer look or zoom out for an overall look.

Viewing a Document

WORD PROVIDES SEVERAL different view perspectives to use when displaying a document, each having its own purpose. For each of the following views (except Print Preview), choose View > Document Views and select an option.

Tip

Word also displays icons along the status bar that allow you to choose most of the view options.

Print Layout View

Print Layout (the default view), allows you to see how text, pictures, graphics, and other elements will be positioned on the printed page. This view is especially helpful if you are working with text columns. In Print Layout view, you'll see the document's top and bottom margins, as well as the headers and footers. The top and bottom margins appear, and page breaks between pages are indicated by a darker area.

If you are not already in Print Layout view, you can easily switch to it by clicking View > Document Views > Print Layout or click the Print Layout icon on the status bar. In Figure 6-1, you see a document in Print Layout view.

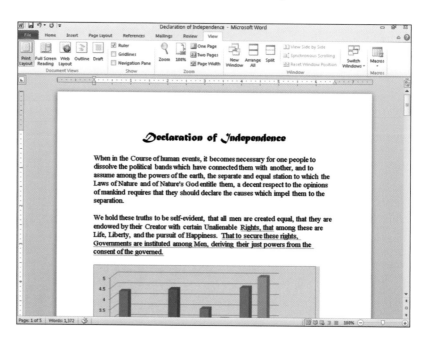

Figure 6-1
View document pictures in
Print Layout view.

Full Screen Reading View

Using the Full Screen Reading view hides most of the Ribbon and other screen elements and displays your document two pages at a time, usually in a larger font size, scaling the contents of your document to pages that fit comfortably on your screen, making it easy to read. When in Full Screen Reading view, the page breaks are not necessarily the same page breaks as those in the printed document, although you can change the settings so you are reading the document as it appears when printed.

To switch to Full Screen Reading view, choose View > Document Views > Full Screen Reading or click the Full Screen Reading icon on the status bar. See Figure 6-2 for an example of a document in Full Screen Reading view.

If your document has multiple pages, you see the document in two-page view, similar to reading a book. However, if you have trouble reading the document, you can adjust the reading font size without actually affecting the document itself. Choose View Options > Increase Text Size or hold down the Ctrl key and roll your mouse scroll wheel forward until the font is large enough for you to read.

Word provides several methods to move from page to page in a document:

▶ Click the navigation arrows at the top center of the screen

▶ Click the arrows in the lower corners of the pages.

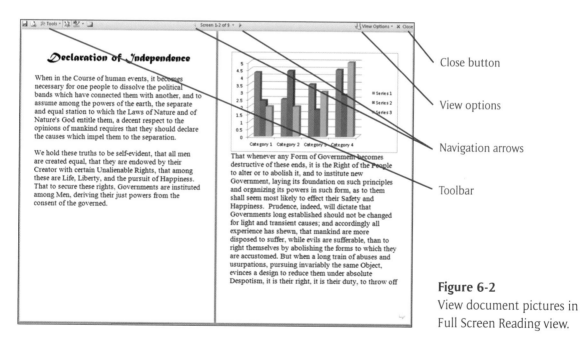

Close button

View options

Navigation arrows

Toolbar

Figure 6-2
View document pictures in Full Screen Reading view.

▶ Press the left or right arrow keys to view the next or previous pages.

▶ Press the Page Down key or the spacebar to view the next pages.

▶ Press the Page Up key or backspace to view the previous pages.

> ## Jump to a Screen
>
> To quickly display the last screen of the document, press the End key or press the Home key to quickly display the first document screen.

The Full Screen Reading view has a toolbar along the top left of the screen. (See Figure 6-3.) From here you can save, print, highlight document areas, or add comments to the document. There is also a tool to translate selected words or phrases from your document into a different language. The Tools arrow on the toolbar provides options to research document selections, choose a text highlight color, add a comment, or locate document words or phrases.

Figure 6-3
Full Screen Reading view toolbar.

At the top right of your screen, you see a View Options button. Clicking the View Options button displays a menu. From the View Options menu (shown in Figure 6-4), you can select from a number of choices. Let's take a look at a few of them:

▶ **Don't Open Attachments in Full Screen:** If you are using Microsoft SharePoint Services, you can view your e-mail in a Word document. When selected, this item blocks the attachments to protect your document security. This option is active by default.

Tip

Active menu items have a border around them.

▶ **Increase Text Size or Decrease Text Size:** As mentioned earlier, you can choose one of these options to zoom in or out on your document.

▶ **Show One Page or Show Two Pages:** Select one to determine how many screen document pages you want to see at a time. Two pages is the default option.

▶ **Show Printed Page:** Choose this if you want to see your document as it will look when printed.

▶ **Margin Settings:** Allows you to see the document margins. This feature only becomes available if you have Show Printed Page activated.

▶ **Allow Typing:** By default, you cannot edit your document while in Full Screen Reading view, but click this feature and you can then add or remove text from your document. You cannot access Ribbon tools for formatting features, but you can use keyboard shortcuts. For example, select your text and press Ctrl+B to add bolding to the selected text.

▶ **Track Changes, Show Comments and Changes, and Show Original/Final Document:** All three of these changes pertain to using Word's document tracking feature. See Chapter 16 for more information.

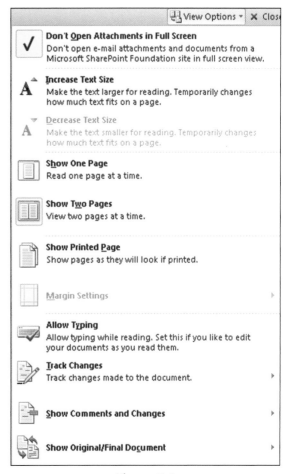

Figure 6-4
View Options menu.

✕ Close Click the Close button to return to the previously used view.

Web Layout View

If you are designing a document you plan on publishing to the Web, the Web Layout view is very helpful because it imitates how you see the document if it were viewed in a Web browser. Web Layout view hides page breaks and displays the document as if it were one long page.

Choose View > Document Views > Web Layout. Figure 6-5 shows a document in Web Layout view.

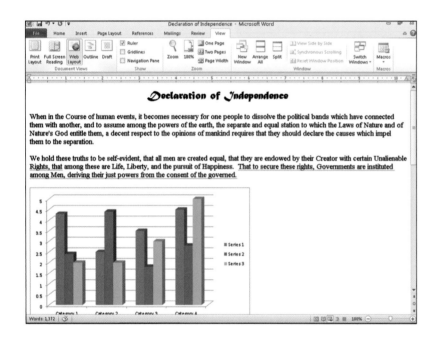

Figure 6-5
Web Layout view.

Outline View

Outline view displays your text in an expandable and collapsible view by heading levels. It includes an outlining tab from which you can display levels as well as promote and demote headings. (See Chapter 8 for information on outlines.)

Choose View > Document Views > Outline or click the Outline icon on the status bar. Figure 6-6 shows a document in Outline view. Notice that when switching to Outline view, Word displays an additional Ribbon tab. From the Ribbon tab, you can make outlining modifications. In order for you to use Outline view effectively, your document must contain heading styles. Refer to Chapter 3 for a refresher on using Word styles.

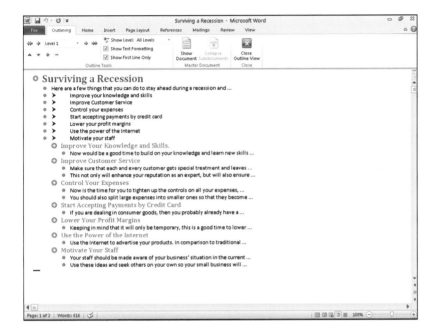

Figure 6-6
Outline view.

When you are finished using the Outline view, choose Outlining > Close > Close Outline View or click a different view button from the View controls on the status bar.

Draft View

Draft view is a general purpose (mostly) text-only view used for typing, editing, and formatting text. It simplifies the layout of the page so that you can type and edit quickly. In Draft view, Word indicates page breaks or section breaks by a dotted line. Headers, footers, page margins, backgrounds, and some other objects do not appear in Draft view. It's my personal favorite.

Change your document to Draft view by choosing Views > Document Views > Draft or by clicking the Draft view icon on the status bar. Figure 6-7 shows you a document in Draft view.

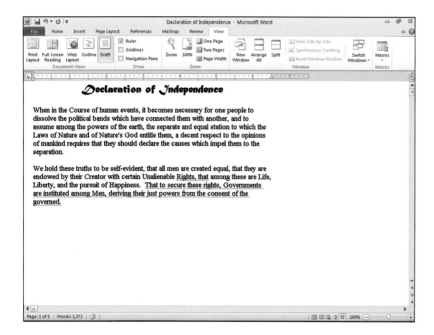

Figure 6-7
Draft view.

Tip

One other perspective you will find helpful is Print Preview. See Chapter 5 for more information.

Using the Zoom Feature

USING WORD'S ABILITY to zoom in on a document allows you to examine your document more closely or in greater detail through a close-up view of your text. You can also zoom out to see more of the page at a reduced size. Zoom settings do not affect the arrangement of text when you print the document.

Choose View > Zoom, and you see that Word provides a number of different ways you can zoom in or out of your document:

Zoom and Print

Using the Zoom feature does not alter the size at which the document will print.

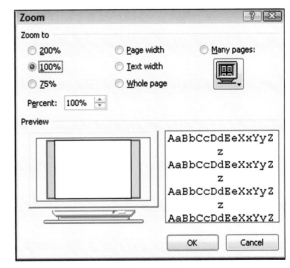

Figure 6-8
The Zoom dialog box.

▶ **100%** Click the Zoom button to display the Zoom dialog box (see Figure 6-8) where you can choose the zoom percentage you want. Alternatively, click the Zoom Level icon on the status bar.

▶ Choose View > Zoom > One Page to view the entire page (see Figure 6-9).

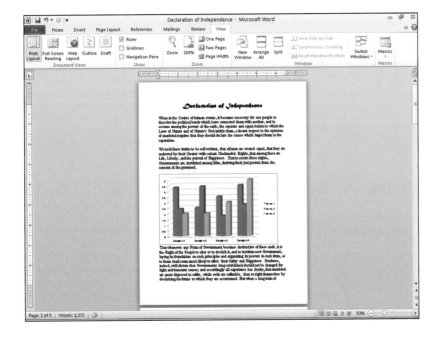

Figure 6-9
Viewing the full page.

▶ Choose View > Zoom > Two Pages to view two pages side by side. Use the scroll bar to scroll down through the document two pages at a time.

▶ Choose Page Width to view the page by page width.

▶ Choose 100% to return to the normal zoom rate of 100%.

▶ Drag the Zoom slider located on the status bar to zoom in and out as desired. The current zoom rate appears next to the Zoom slider.

Working with Split Windows

IF YOU WANT TO SEE two parts of a document, but you can't get them on the screen at the same time, you can split a window. Doing so enables you to view part of a long document in the upper window while you view another part of the document in the lower window.

When you split a window, each window panel contains its own scroll bar. Choose View > Window > Split. A horizontal line with a double-headed arrow appears at the mouse pointer. Click the mouse where you want the window divided, which then locks in the split. The window divides into two sections with each section having its own scroll bar and rulers. Take a look at Figure 6-10, which shows page 1 in the top section and page 5 in the bottom section.

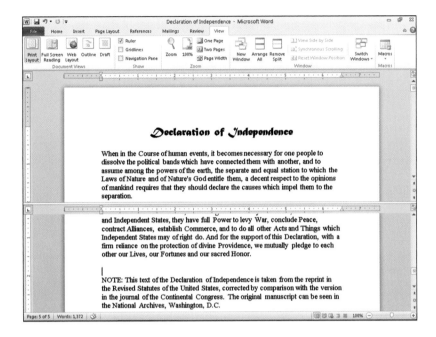

Figure 6-10
Splitting the window.

Resize Split Windows

To resize the windows, position the mouse at the top, bottom, or side of the either window until the mouse pointer becomes a double-headed arrow, and then drag the line until the windows are the desired size.

When you want to remove the window split, choose View > Window > Remove Split. Your document reappears in a single window.

Comparing Documents Side by Side

CCASIONALLY, YOU MAY want to view two documents side by side, perhaps to compare one version to another. Word provides the ability to view any two open windows next to each other.

Choose View > Window > View Side by Side. If you have more than two Word documents open, Word first requests which window you want to compare to the top current window (see Figure 6-11). If you have only two open Word documents, you do not see this Compare Side by Side dialog box.

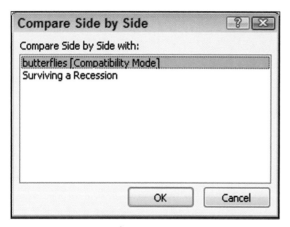

Figure 6-11
Which documents do you want to compare?

Tip

To edit a document, click anywhere in the document window.

By default, the two windows are synchronized so that, as you scroll through one window, the other one scrolls with it. If you want to scroll through the windows independently, you need to turn off Synchronous Scrolling. From either window, choose View > Window > Synchronous Scrolling. See Figure 6-12.

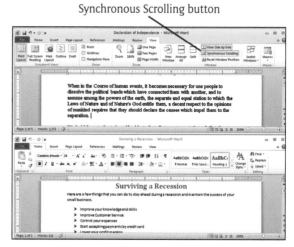

Figure 6-12
Viewing multiple document windows.

To return to a single document window, deactivate the feature by choosing View > Window > View Side by Side.

Using the Navigation Pane

IF YOUR DOCUMENT is quite lengthy, it can be difficult and time consuming to navigate through the document. However, if your document contains heading styles, you can use the Navigation pane feature to ease navigation. The Navigation pane also allows you to examine the document flow for completeness and ensure that formatting is consistent. Think of a Navigation pane as a simple table of contents. Choose View > Show > Navigation Pane. A Navigation pane, like the one shown in Figure 6-13, appears on the left side of the screen.

Each item in the Navigation pane represents a heading in your document; you can click any item to move the insertion point to that place in the document. You can click the plus sign (+) to expand a heading or click the minus sign (–) to hide subheadings.

To hide the Navigation pane, choose View > Show > Navigation Pane, which removes the checkmark from the Navigation pane option and closes the Navigation pane.

Blank Navigation Pane

If the document does not contain any heading styles, the Navigation pane will be blank.

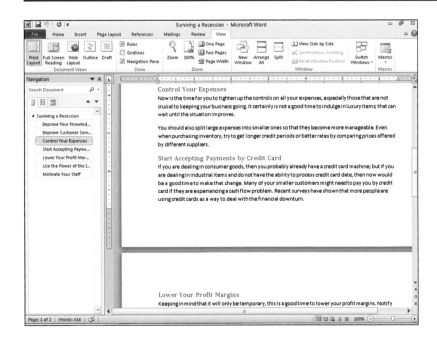

Figure 6-13
The Word Navigation pane.

Adding Supplementary
Elements

PICTURE YOURSELF ORGANIZING antiques and collectibles to prepare for an auction. You create a tag for each item to identify it. You also take a photo and write a brief description—including the provenance—so that you can create a listing for each item in the auction catalog. You need to be really organized to pull it all together in time and make it easy for buyers to find the items they want.

Longer documents, such as sales proposals, annual reports, and catalogs, usually include pictures or illustrations that need to be identified, information from other sources, references to legal statutes, and key terms or jargon. Packing more content into a document gives the reader much more to navigate. That's why learning about Word's tools for referencing information will pay off. You'll be able to create documents that not only meet professional or academic standards for referencing sources, but also enable readers to find and jump to key information with ease.

Working with Pages

IN CHAPTER 4, you learned about creating manual page breaks in a document. Manual page breaks can come in particularly handy for long documents, for example, when you want to move a heading or picture to the top of the next page. You can use additional page-oriented features to add necessary or decorative information to any document, long or short. This section shows you what some of those features are and how to use them in Word.

Creating a Cover Page

Most formal documents like reports and proposals do not launch right into the text. Instead they include a title page or *cover page* that provides basic information about the document. The information contained on a cover page can include the document title, a subtitle, a brief summary of the document (called an *abstract*), the year or date it was created, the author's name, a company name and address, or even an image that illustrates the document's contents.

Word 2010's Building Blocks Organizer offers 19 preformatted cover pages that you can add to any document. Each cover page has preformatted placeholders that prompt you to add applicable text. The more simple cover page designs include design elements like rules and blocks of color, while the more advanced designs include other graphic elements like photos and drawn objects.

To add a cover page to the current document, choose Insert > Text > Quick Parts > Building Blocks Organizer. In the Building Blocks Organizer dialog box, scroll down the Building Blocks list and click one of the choices with Cover Pages in the Gallery column. As shown in Figure 7-1, a preview of the selected cover page appears at the right side of the dialog box. When you've found the cover page you like, click Insert.

Word inserts the cover page as the first page in the document. You can go there and replace the placeholder information in the square brackets. Of course, you can substitute information other than that suggested by a placeholder. You also can delete a placeholder by clicking it, then clicking the tab that appears, and then pressing Delete to remove it.

Tip

Clicking a date placeholder displays a drop-down list arrow. Click it to open a calendar from which you can select a date.

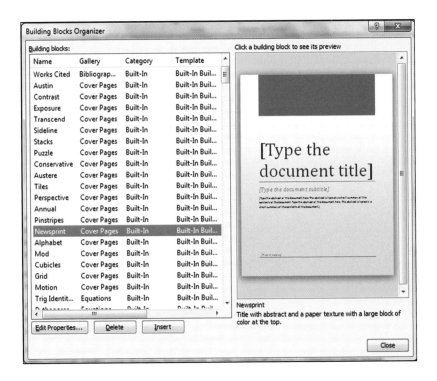

Figure 7-1
Selecting a cover page design.

Displaying a Watermark

Paper with a watermark has a semi-transparent imprint that's visible only when you hold the document up to the light. For some types of documents, such as checks, the watermark provides a way to verify a document's legitimacy. In Word 2010, a watermark is a lightly printed background image, often used to signal a document's status, such as CONFIDENTIAL or COPY. Word includes a few predefined watermarks that you can add to a document by choosing Page Layout > Page Background > Watermark, and then clicking one of the choices at the top of the menu that appears, shown in Figure 7-2.

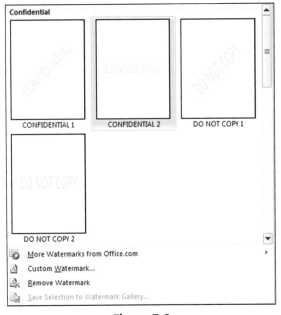

Figure 7-2
Predefined watermarks.

However, Word doesn't limit you to using its watermarks. You can create a picture watermark, such as if you want to include a logo behind the text on every page. Choose Page Layout > Page Background > Watermark > Custom Watermark. In the Printed Watermark dialog box, click the Picture Watermark option button, and then click the Select Picture button. Select the desired picture in the Insert Picture dialog box, click Insert, and then click OK.

You also can create your own text watermark that uses the word or phrase that you want and formatting that you specify. Choose Page Layout > Page Background > Watermark > Custom Watermark, and this time click the Text Watermark option button. You choose one of the predefined words from the Text drop-down list in the Printed Watermark dialog box, or type your own word or phrase into the text box, as shown in Figure 7-3. If needed, you can choose an alternate Font, Size, and Color in the dialog box, and change the layout between Diagonal and Horizontal. You also can use the Semitransparent check box to control the watermark's opacity. When you finish making your choices, click OK.

To remove a watermark, choose Page Layout > Page Background > Watermark > Remove Watermark.

Different Page, Different Watermark

Any watermark you apply appears on every page of the document and is anchored to the header area. If you need a watermark to appear on limited pages in the document, create a new section and apply the watermark in that section. Then, edit the header for the new section, choosing Header & Footer Tools > Design > Navigation > Link to Previous to unlink the header. You can then add and remove a watermark in the new section. See Chapter 4 for more on section breaks and footers.

Changing Page Color

If you plan to publish a document as a Web page or a document's recipient will be viewing it onscreen, you can add a page background to all the pages in the document. (By default, page backgrounds do not print.) You can see the page background when you view the document in Print Layout, Full Screen Reading, and Web Layout views. To apply one of the current theme colors or a standard color as the page background, choose Page Layout > Page Background > Page Color, and then click a color in the gallery that appears, as shown in Figure 7-4. The No Color choice removes any previously applied page background.

Custom text entry

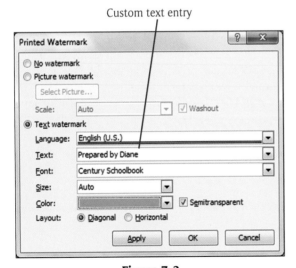

Figure 7-3
Custom text watermark settings.

126

Tip

To print your Page background, choose File > Options. From the Display section (under Printing options), check Print Background Colors and Images, and then click OK. Many printers do not print to the edge of the paper, so you may still see a white border around the page.

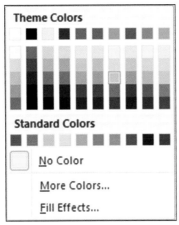

Figure 7-4
Page colors.

If a plain color doesn't provide the look you want, you can instead fill the page background with a gradient, texture, pattern, or picture. Choose Page Layout > Page Background > Page Color, and then click Fill Effects at the bottom of the gallery. In the Fill Effects dialog box that appears, click the tab for the type of background you want to create, use the tab's settings to select the desired fill (such as gradient colors or a texture), and then click OK. To remove a page background fill effect, choose Page Layout > Page Background > Page Color > No Color.

Adding Page Borders

A page border surrounds all of the text and other contents on a document page. In the Borders and Shading dialog box, you can select a line style, color, and width for the border, or even select decorative art to serve as the border. You also can use the choices in the Apply To drop-down list to control where the page border appears:

▶ **Whole Document:** Adds the page border to all pages in the document.

▶ **This Section:** Adds the page border only to pages in the current section.

▶ **This Section – First Page Only:** Adds the page border only to the first page in the section.

▶ **This Section – All Except First Page:** Adds the page border to all pages except the first page in the section.

To add a page border, choose Page Layout > Page Background > Page Borders. In the Borders and Shading dialog box (shown in Figure 7-5), first choose Style, Color, and Width settings in the center area of the Page Border tab. Alternately, choose a decorative border style from the Art drop-down list. Then click one of the Setting choices on the left, such as Box or Shadow, to apply the border. Finally, make a choice from the Apply To drop-down list to control which pages in the document show the border. Then click OK.

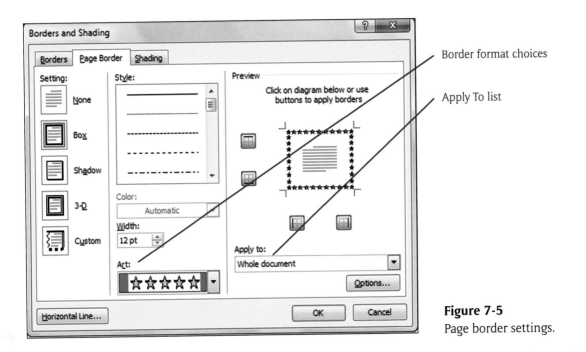

Border format choices

Apply To list

Figure 7-5
Page border settings.

Tip

If Word's predefined cover pages are too elaborate for you, you can create your own cover page by adding a border to the first page of the first section of the document and type the needed information on that page.

Creating Footnotes and Endnotes

WHEN YOU QUOTE or heavily reference information from another source, as when writing an article or report, you should indicate the source of the information. Word enables you to identify sources using either footnotes or endnotes. Each *footnote* appears at the bottom of the page holding the cited information, while *endnotes* appear together at the end of the document.

Know Your Footnote Style

The information and punctuation used in a footnote or endnote is defined by its style. Teachers, instructors, publishers, and some other organizations often require you to use a particular style, such as the MLA style established by the Modern Language Association.

Back in the typewriter era, you had to change the carriage position to create the superscript footnote number, and then leave room at the bottom of the page for the footnote itself. If you planned wrong and didn't leave room for a subsequent footnote on the page, you would have to retype the entire page.

That's what makes Word's automated footnote and endnote capabilities so beneficial. Word properly numbers and formats footnotes and endnotes, adjusts the page break based on the number of footnotes on the page, and compiles endnotes in the correct order for you.

Creating a Footnote or Endnote

It takes mere moments to create a footnote or endnote. Start by typing in the quoted or paraphrased text from the source. With the insertion point directly to the right of the last character in the information or closing quotation mark, choose References > Footnotes > Insert Footnote or References > Footnotes > Insert Endnote. Word inserts the number for the footnote or endnote in the text, and then moves the insertion point to the location for the corresponding footnote or endnote. Type the text for the note in the proper style. Figure 7-6 shows an example footnote.

Number inserted in text ⎯⎯

Corresponding footnote with text entered ⎯⎯

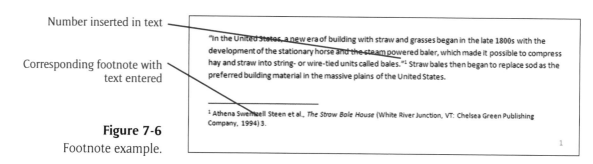

"In the United States, a new era of building with straw and grasses began in the late 1800s with the development of the stationary horse and the steam powered baler, which made it possible to compress hay and straw into string- or wire-tied units called bales."[1] Straw bales then began to replace sod as the preferred building material in the massive plains of the United States.

[1] Athena Swentzell Steen et al., *The Straw Bale House* (White River Junction, VT: Chelsea Green Publishing Company, 1994) 3.

1

Figure 7-6
Footnote example.

Copying Notes

If a source is really good, you might quote or paraphrase its contents multiple times in the same document. Word saves you the need to retype the same footnote or endnote information by enabling you to reuse an existing note. To do so, you copy and paste the note number that's placed just after the sourced text (not the footnote or endnote itself).

Drag over the note number to select it, and then copy it with either Ctrl+C or Home > Clipboard > Copy. Then click just to the right of the next quotation or paraphrased material, and paste using Ctrl+V or Home > Clipboard > Paste. That's it. Word automatically assigns the correct number to the pasted note both in the text and in the note itself.

Moving Notes

If you move text marked with a footnote or endnote in the document, the note "travels" with the text. That means Word automatically renumbers all notes as needed to reflect the new location of the sourced text relative to other sourced text.

If you inserted a footnote or endnote at the wrong location, a simple cut and paste solves the problem. Drag over the note number to select it, and then cut it with either Ctrl+X or Home > Clipboard > Cut. Then click in the correct location for the note and paste using Ctrl+V or Home > Clipboard > Paste.

Converting Between Note Types

Back in the typewriter era, it was extremely important to understand whether footnotes or endnotes were required for a particular document. If you used the wrong type of note, you would have to retype the entire document. Word's reference capabilities don't lock you in to one note type or the other. You can convert a footnote to an endnote and vice versa at any time. To do so, right-click anywhere in the footnote or endnote itself. In the shortcut menu that appears (see the example in Figure 7-7), and click Convert to Endnote (or Footnote).

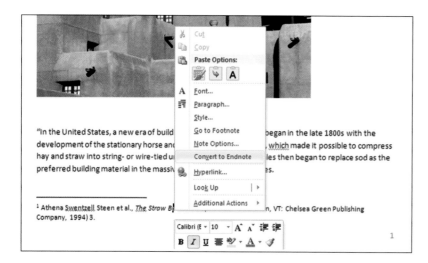

Figure 7-7
Converting a note.

Creating a Table of Contents

INCLUDING A *TABLE OF CONTENTS* (TOC) at the beginning of a long document provides a nice roadmap to the document's contents. The reader can identify a topic of interest and go right to the page that discusses the topic. If the document includes a title page or cover page, in most cases you should insert the table of contents on the page directly after the title or cover page. In many cases, you should also insert a hard page break after the table of contents to separate it from the following text. This ensures that the first page of information in the document starts at the top of a new page.

Word offers both a gallery of built-in table of contents styles and a dialog box where you can choose more specific settings for your table of contents. No matter which of these methods you use, you need to start by formatting the headings in the document using the appropriate Quick Styles. (The section called "Using Quick Styles" in Chapter 3 introduced how to apply styles in Word.) The Table of Contents feature in Word identifies which items to list based on the style applied. Text formatted with the Heading 1 and Heading 2 Quick Styles become the top-level and second-level entries in the table of contents.

Tip

Word actually offers nine heading level styles, and three of them are used in a TOC by default. To find the other styles, click the Dialog Box Launcher in the Styles group of the Home tab. Then click the Manage Styles button at the bottom.

After you have applied the heading styles to the headings in your document and have created the page where you want to insert the TOC, use one of these methods to generate the TOC:

▶ Choose References > Table of Contents > Table of Contents. Then click one of the two Automatic Table choices at the top of the gallery shown in Figure 7-8.

Figure 7-8
Generating an automatic TOC.

► Choose References > Table of Contents > Table of Contents > Insert Table of Contents to display the Table of Contents dialog box shown in Figure 7-9. Among the settings you can change here are whether or not to Show Page Numbers or Right Align Page Numbers. If your document has more than three heading levels that you'd like to include in the TOC, change the Show Levels value. You can use the Formats drop-down list to choose an alternate style for the TOC. If you plan to publish the document to the Web, leaving a check in the Use Hyperlinks Instead of Page Numbers box changes the TOC to a hyper-linked format in Web Layout view. Click OK to finish adding the table of contents.

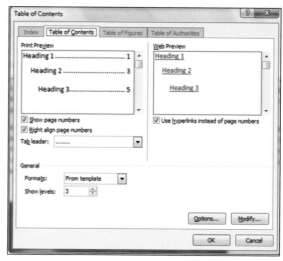

Figure 7-9
Selecting TOC settings.

If the text of the document changes, if you add or delete headings, or if you create a separate page to hold the table of contents after creating it, you'll need to update the table of contents. You can update just the page numbers of the table of contents, but the safest choice is usually updating the entire table, which ensures that the TOC reflects any heading changes made since you generated it.

To update a table of contents, click within it. Then click Update Table in the tab above the table. As shown in Figure 7-10, the Update Table of Contents dialog box appears. Choose either Update Page Numbers Only or Update Entire Table, and then click OK.

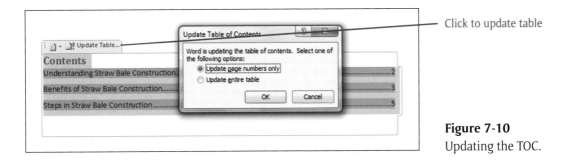

Click to update table

Figure 7-10
Updating the TOC.

Figure Captions

CHAPTER 13 WILL GIVE YOU a detailed look at how to use pictures, clip art, SmartArt diagrams, and more to illustrate the information in a document. Let's just say for this discussion that you've already mastered those techniques. When you include graphics of any type in a document, adding captions explains exactly what each illustration shows. Word's References tab includes a tool for adding a caption to any graphic that you select. Word automatically numbers the captions so that you can refer to them by number in the text. This helps the reader immensely if you need to refer back to a graphic on a much earlier page in the document, because the reader can identify the correct figure according to its number.

Follow these steps to add a caption:

1. Select the picture or other graphic by clicking it.

2. Choose References > Captions > Insert Caption. The Caption dialog box appears.

3. If you want to change the label that appears with the caption number, make another choice from the Label drop-down list or click the New Label button, enter another label, and click OK to create the alternate label. It is important to use the same label for all captions in the document, not only for style reasons, but also for reasons you'll learn more about in the next section.

4. You can click the Numbering button, choose another Format list option in the Caption Numbering dialog box, and then click OK to change the caption's numbering style.

5. Click back in the Caption text box at the top of the Caption dialog box and type the caption.

6. Click OK. Figure 7-11 shows a caption and the Caption dialog box settings used to create it.

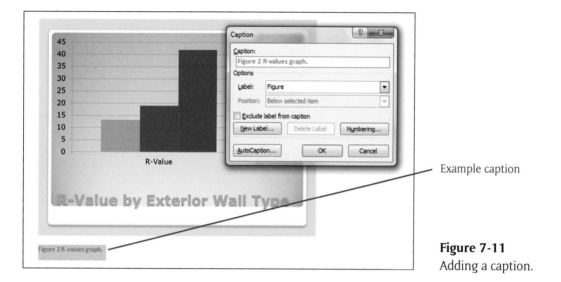

Example caption

Figure 7-11
Adding a caption.

Consistency Counts

Try to use consistent structure and punctuation for captions. For example, use all complete sentences, or only one- or two-word labels. Either use a period at the end of all captions, or none at all. As always, check the standards for the course, school, or organization to learn the proper caption style.

Adding a Table of Figures

A TABLE OF FIGURES is a list identifying the document page number on which each graphic for which you've added a caption appears. Some academic and technical environments prefer or require a table of figures to identify all illustrations in a document. Generally, a table of figures appears at the end of the document, along with other resources, such as the bibliography and endnotes; although in some circumstances, placing the table immediately after the table of contents makes the figures easier to find and reference.

Follow these steps to create a table of figures:

1. First create a separate page for the table, if needed, and then position the insertion point at the top of the page.

2. Choose References > Captions > Insert Table of Figures. The Table of Figures dialog box shown in Figure 7-12 appears. The settings it offers are similar to those for the Table of Contents dialog box shown in Figure 7-9. One important difference is the Caption Label drop-down list. The setting you choose there must correspond to the Label option you selected in the Caption dialog box when creating captions. Only captions using the selected caption label will be listed in the finished table of figures. You can clear the Include Label and Number check box if you prefer to identify captions by their text alone.

Caption label

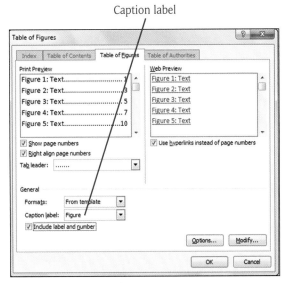

Figure 7-12
Creating a table of figures.

3. Click OK to tell Word to generate the table of figures.

4. You can finish the table by adding a heading above it, if desired.

If you left Use Hyperlinks Instead of Page Numbers checked in the Table of Figures dialog box, each item in the table of figures list is a hyperlink that you can use to move to the referenced graphic. Ctrl+click on any listed figure to jump to that figure in the document.

As for a table of contents, if the contents of your document change—such as if you move, delete, or add more graphics with captions—you'll need to update the table. To do so, click in the table, and then choose References > Captions > Update Table. Choose either Update Page Numbers Only or Update Entire Table in the Update Table of Figures dialog box, and then click OK.

A Table of Tables?

Some styles also require you to list tables in the document. To include both graphics and tables in a single table of figures list, assign them all the same Label in the Caption dialog box (such as Figure or a custom label). Then choose that caption label in the Table of Figures dialog box. Or to list different elements separately, use different caption label choices (such as Figure versus Table), and then generate separate tables of figures by changing the caption Label setting.

Creating a Bibliography

A BIBLIOGRAPHY LISTS SOURCES cited indirectly in a document (that is, sources you do not directly quote or paraphrase but from which you have drawn key conclusions, ideas, or concepts). You first must insert each citation, or reference, to the sources in the text where appropriate. Like footnotes and endnotes, citations follow a particular style, such as MLA or the *Chicago Manual of Style*, so you need to find out which style to use for your class, school, professional discipline, or organization. Word formats each citation you add according to the selected style. For example, a citation in the MLA style might have just the author last name or author last name and cited page number in parentheses, as in (Smith) or (Smith 235).

To also include other sources that you've drawn on even more indirectly in the bibliography, you have to add those sources separately. Note that you should also check on the style of your school or organization with regard to including footnoted/endnoted sources in the bibliography. Most styles call for you to also include footnoted/endnoted sources in the bibliography, in which case you must add the sources manually, while some instructors may consider footnotes/endnotes and a bibliography separate elements. Some styles frown on using both footnotes/endnotes and parenthetical citations, so you should use citations and a bibliography only in that instance.

Once you've completed all the citations and sources, you can compile the bibliography.

Adding Citations

Start by selecting the citation style and inserting citations in the document, like this:

1. Choose References > Citations & Bibliography > Style, and then click the style you want in the list, as shown in Figure 7-13.

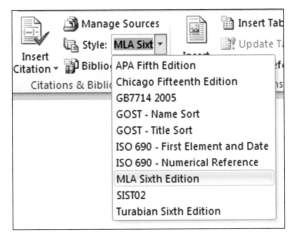

Figure 7-13
Citation styles.

2. Click to position the insertion point where you want the citation to appear in the document.

3. Choose References > Citations & Bibliography > Insert Citation > Add New Source. The Create Source dialog box appears.

4. Select the type of publication or source that you're citing from the Type of Source list. Then, fill in the rest of the text boxes with the information about the source. The dialog box will automatically adjust to prompt you for different information based on the citation style you selected in Step 1 and the Type of Source choice. For example, Figure 7-14 shows information for a book using the MLA Sixth Edition citation style.

5. Click OK to finish adding the source and creating the citation.

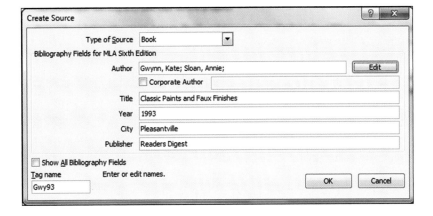

Figure 7-14
A new citation source.

6. To add a page number for the citation, right-click it and click Edit Citation. In the Edit Citation dialog box, type a page number or range in the Pages text box, as shown in Figure 7-15. To suppress information from appearing in the citation, click the appropriate check box under Suppress. Click OK to finish editing the citation.

Figure 7-15
Adding a page number.

7. Repeat Steps 2 through 6 to add citations from new sources. Or, if you've already added the source, choose References > Citations & Bibliography > Insert Citation, and then click the source name in the menu, as shown in the example in Figure 7-16. You can then add a page number to the subsequent citation as described in Step 6.

Figure 7-16
Using an existing source.

Adding a Source

You also can include sources in the bibliography that you haven't directly cited. Doing this is a good practice, as it both ensures you've given proper credit to other authors whose ideas you've drawn upon, as well as providing your peers and readers a comprehensive reading list so they can verify the information you presented or learn more about a particular topic.

Use these steps to create additional sources for the bibliography:

1. Choose References > Citations & Bibliography > Manage Sources. The Source Manager dialog box appears.

2. Click the New button to open the Create Source dialog box. It looks and works just like the Create Source dialog box shown in Figure 7-14.

3. Select the type of publication or source that you're citing from the Type of Source list. Then fill in the rest of the text boxes with the information about the source and click OK.

4. Repeat Steps 2 and 3 to create additional sources. They will be added to the Current List area at the right (see Figure 7-17). Note that you also can click a source in the Current List area and use the Delete or Edit buttons to remove or change it.

Tip

Sources you cited in other documents appear in the Master List area at the left side of the Source Manager dialog box. To add a source to the current document so that you can use it in citations, click the source in the Master List at the left, and then click the Copy button.

5. Click Close to finish working with sources.

Generating the Bibliography

Once you've added and edited all the citations and have included additional sources that you did not specifically cite, you can create the finished bibliography. Once again, Word properly formats the bibliography based on the style you selected in the Citations & Bibliography group of the References tab.

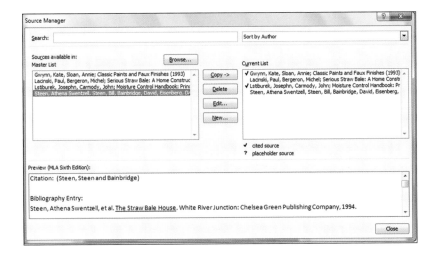

Figure 7-17
Managing sources.

Follow these steps to finish creating the bibliography:

1. Press Ctrl+End to go to the end of the document (assuming you haven't already created the index, in which case you should insert the bibliography on a new page before the index).

2. Press Ctrl+Enter to insert a hard page break.

3. Choose References > Citations & Bibliography > Bibliography, and click the Bibliography choice under Built-In. (See Figure 7-18.) The Bibliography immediately appears in the document.

To update a bibliography after you change sources, click in the bibliography, then click Update Citations and Bibliography in the tab above it, as shown in Figure 7-19.

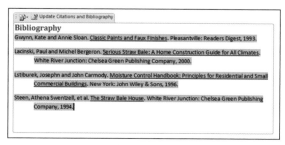

Figure 7-19
Updating the bibliography.

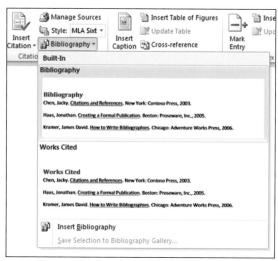

Figure 7-18
Adding the bibliography.

Ditching the Underlining

Notice that Word uses underlining for book titles in the bibliography. Most styles have migrated to using italics for book titles in footnotes and a bibliography. You can simply reformat each book title in the bibliography as needed by dragging over the title and pressing Ctrl+U to remove the underlining and Ctrl+I to add italics.

Adding a Table of Authorities

LEGAL DOCUMENTS OFTEN REQUIRE a *table of authorities*, which is a list of all of the cases, statutes, rules, treatises, regulations, constitutional provisions, and other types of authorities cited in the text. Creating a table of authorities works much like creating a bibliography, except that you type the citation into the text using the appropriate format for the type of citation and citation style that you're following. For example, you might type in (James v. Jones, 48 Wn. 3d 405 (1963)) for a legal case citation or (NCGS § 131A-247(6)) for a statute citation. You then select and mark all the citations, and create the table of authorities.

Use this process to mark citations and create the table of authorities:

1. Type in and select the citation to mark. If the style that you are using calls for parentheses surrounding the full citation, do not select the outermost pair of parentheses.

2. Choose References > Table of Authorities > Mark Citation. The Mark Citation dialog box opens.

3. Choose the proper Category for the citation, as shown in Figure 7-20.

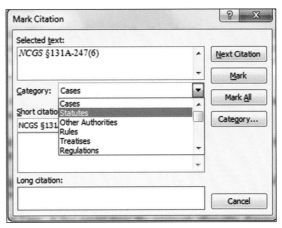

Figure 7-20
Marking a legal citation.

4. If there is a shorter version of the citation that appears elsewhere in the document, edit the Short Citation text box entry to match the shorter version.

5. Click Mark to mark only the current instance of the citation, or click Mark All to mark all instances in the document. Word inserts a field code that identifies the citation and turns on the display of nonprinting characters.

6. Click Close.

7. Repeat Steps 1 through 6 to create and mark additional citations.

8. Click to position the insertion point where you want the table of authorities to appear in the document, creating a new page first, if desired.

9. Choose References > Table of Authorities > Insert Table of Authorities. The Table of Authorities dialog box appears, as shown in Figure 7-21.

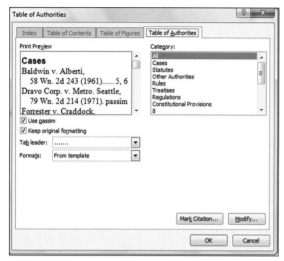

Figure 7-21
Choosing table of authority contents.

10. If you need to limit the table to a particular type of citation, click it in the Category list. (The All option includes all citations in the table.) Also change other formatting settings as desired until the Print Preview area appears as you'd like.

11. Click OK to insert the table of authorities.

12. Choose Home > Paragraph > Show/Hide to turn off the nonprinting characters.

Generating Cross References

A *CROSS-REFERENCE* points to another item or location in the document, such as a particular heading, item in an automatically numbered list, a bookmarked location, footnote or endnote, numbered figure, or a table or equation. (Chapter 15 provides more information about creating bookmarks.) Inserting items as an automated cross-reference provides two advantages. First, the cross-reference is created as a hyperlink by default, so the reader can use it to navigate in the document when viewing it in Word. Additionally, if you move content around in the document, the cross-references update automatically to reflect the changed locations of the cross-references.

Use these steps to insert any type of cross-reference:

1. If you want to enclose the cross references in quotation marks (as when referencing a heading) or parentheses, position the insertion point at the desired location and type the opening quotation mark or left parenthesis.

2. Choose References > Captions > Cross Reference. The Cross-Reference dialog box opens.

3. Make a choice from the Reference Type drop-down list. As shown in Figure 7-22, the list of items matching that reference type appears in the For Which <type> list at the bottom of the dialog box.

4. Click the desired item to cross-reference in the For Which <type> list.

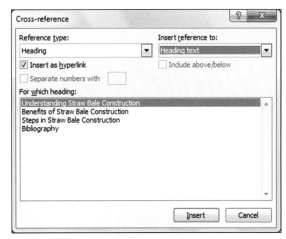

Figure 7-22
Creating a cross-reference.

5. If you would like the cross-reference to display as something other than the text being referenced, such as the page number where the referenced material is located, make the appropriate choice from the Insert Reference To list.

6. Click Insert to create the cross-reference.

Indexing Content

A N INDEX LISTS THE PAGE NUMBERS where important terms appear in a document. While indexes are most common for lengthy publications, such as books, you may need to include an index for a shorter work if it contains a lot of jargon and technical explanations. An index generally appears at the very end of a document, starting at the top of a new page.

As for the other reference features you've already learned about, creating an index is a two-step process. First mark the entries to index throughout the document, and then insert the index.

If an index entry is about a general topic that spans multiple pages, such as the "Creating a Bibliography" section earlier in this chapter, you would first need to select the entire section, and then create a bookmark for it as described in Chapter 15. For standard entries, select the text to mark for the index, and then choose References > Index > Mark Entry. In the Mark Index Entry dialog box that appears (see Figure 7-23), type any subentry that you want to create for the entry in the Subentry text box. If you are creating only a cross-reference, click the Cross-Reference option button and type the term to cross-reference to the right of See in the accompanying text box. Or, if you previously created a bookmark that will serve as the cross-reference, click the Page Range option and select the bookmarked location from the Bookmark drop-down list. Enable options under Page Number Format as desired, and then click Mark to mark only the current selection or bookmark, or click Mark All to have Word find and mark all matching instances of the term for the index. Then click Close.

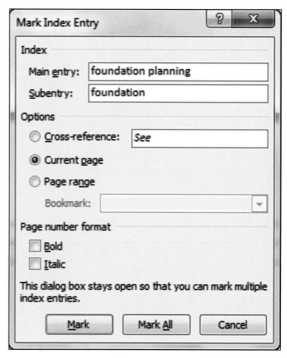

Figure 7-23
Marking an index item.

After you have marked all the items to index, press Ctrl+End to go to the end of the document, and then press Ctrl+Enter to start a new page. Choose References > Index > Insert Index. The Index dialog box appears, as shown in Figure 7-24. In the case of an index, the From Template choice in the Formats list results in a very bland index. If your index is lengthy, consider choosing one of the other Format choices, all of which add a divider to start each new letter of entries. For a brief index,

consider reducing the columns setting from 2 to 1. When you have made those and other choices, click OK. Note that Word does not include a heading for the index, so you should probably insert a top-level (Heading 1 style) heading that reads Index, and update the table of contents to reflect the index location. If you need to update the index itself after marking or deleting terms, choose References > Index > Update Index or press F9.

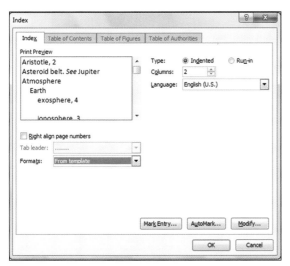

Figure 7-24
Index settings.

Tip

To delete an index entry, choose Home >
Paragraph > Show/Hide. Then select the
entry field and its braces, and press Delete.
Finally, click in the index and choose
References > Index > Update Index.

Working with
Outlines

PICTURE YOURSELF PLAYING FRISBEE with your dog. Your yard has a fence around it so your dog doesn't go outside of its confined area. The protective border also keeps the dog focused on the Frisbee and not the bicyclist riding down the street. In this chapter, you'll work with outlines. By working within the confines of an outline, you stay on track. Outlines contain major topics and subtopics and possible detail information about each.

Also in this chapter, you'll discover master documents and its subdocuments. A master document is the container that includes links to any number of smaller documents, such as a book and all its individual chapters. Think of a master document as the glue that holds a longer document together.

Finally, you'll discover outline numbering, which is far different from an outline. In Chapter 3, you worked with bulleted lists and numbered lists. Outline numbering is similar to a numbered list, but with greater detail. Outline numbering is frequently used in legal documents.

Creating a Standard Outline

A GREAT ORGANIZATIONAL TOOL, Word outlines assist you by using major topics (called *headings*) and subtopics to categorize a task and its subtasks. Most of us work with mental outlines every day. If you were to plan your basic day, you might plan it like this: The major topics would be the places you go that day (work, grocery, dinner), and the subtopics might be what you plan to do at each place. For example, while at work you might write a report that is due, make a few phone calls, or attend a meeting. Those would be subtopics of the Work major topic.

The easiest way to create an outline is by beginning in Outline view. Choose View > Document Views > Outline or just click the Outline view icon located on the status bar. While in Outline view, you see a new tab at the beginning of the Ribbon. The Outlining tab is designed to assist you in creating your outline (see Figure 8-1). The Outlining tab also allows you to display different outline detail levels and reorganize your outline. More about those topics later in this chapter.

Printing an Outline

When you print an outline, Word prints the outline in its entirety as it displays in Print Layout view. The indentation and levels made in Outline view do not appear.

Generating Headings

On a blank document screen in Outline view, you see a small circle with a minus sign. Next to the circle is your blinking insertion point where you begin entering your headings.

Word considers the first line of text you type in an outline to be a Level 1 heading, the top-most level. Word uses styles to track outline headings and sub-headings, and a Level 1 heading is a style. Type the first line of your outline and then press the Enter key, which moves the insertion point to the next line. Type the second line of your outline. Notice from the Outlining tab that the text still appears as

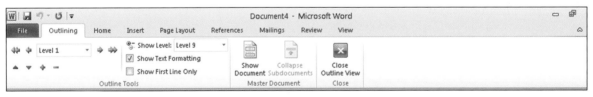

Figure 8-1
The Outlining tab on the Ribbon.

a Level 1 heading. Continue entering your main topic headings as needed. Level 1 headings are formatted with the Heading 1 Quick Style. (Refer to Chapter 3 for a refresher on Quick Styles.)

When you want to create subheadings, use the Tab key to indent the text. Word automatically assigns a Level 2 heading. Each time you press the Tab key, Word creates a lower level subheading. A Word

outline can contain up to nine different heading levels. Again, Word automatically assigns a Quick Style to your subheadings. Word uses Heading 2 styles for a Level 2 heading, Heading 3 for a Level 3 heading, and so forth.

When you need to return to a higher level, press the Shift+Tab keys. Figure 8-2 illustrates a sample document outline with two different heading levels.

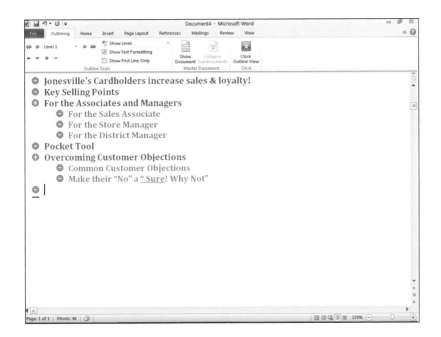

Figure 8-2
A sample outline.

Creating Body Text

If you want to add text to your outline that isn't really an outline heading, you create body text. Typically, body text elaborates more on the outline level heading directly above it. You create body text by using the Outlining tab.

Type the text you want as body text and click the Demote to Body Text button. See Figure 8-3 for an example of body text.

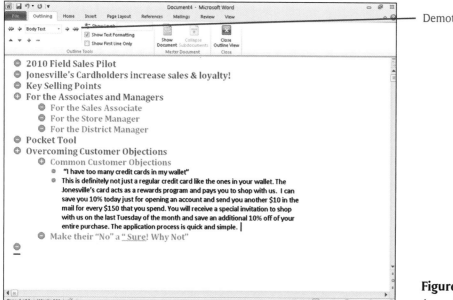

Demote to Body Text

Figure 8-3
An outline with body text.

If you enter your text in Outline view and switch to Draft or Print Layout view, the text retains its Heading styles unless you switch it to body text which uses a Normal style. If you type text in Draft or Print Layout view, and then switch to Outline view, Word assigns a Body Text level to the text you typed in the other views.

Viewing the Outline

While in Outline view, you can expand or collapse the various levels to view only the portions you want to see. For example, you can view upper-level headings only to get an overview of the entire document, thereby helping you further organize your thoughts. Additionally, you can turn the formatting display on or off. Word includes several areas on the Outlining tab to assist you with viewing your outline.

▶ On the outline body, double-click a Heading button that looks like a circle with a plus sign in it (called an Expand and Collapse icon). If the Heading button has a minus sign, there are no subheadings or body text under that heading; however, a plus sign indicates additional items. Word collapses the body text and subheadings of the first level below the currently selected heading, or, if the heading is already collapsed, Word expands the first heading level below the currently selected heading. Each double-click will collapse or expand additional headings.

Tip

Optionally, double-click an Expand and Collapse icon to fully open the selected heading.

▶ From the Outline Tools group on the Outlining tab, click the Show Level down arrow, which displays a drop-down list of heading options. Select a level, and Word displays only the headings at the level you chose and those that are higher. For example, as shown in Figure 8-4, if you select Show Level 2, both Level 1 and Level 2 headings appear but not body text or any Level 3 headings.

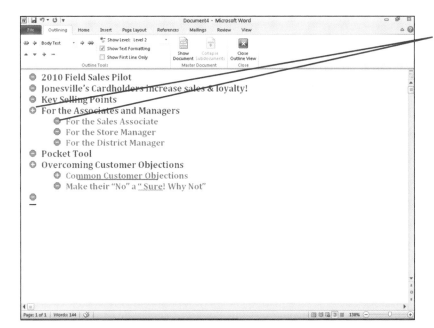

Expand and Collapse icons

Figure 8-4
Displaying only the levels you want to view.

Tip

Click Show All Levels to view the entire outline.

▶ Choose Outlining > Outline Tools > Show First Line Only. The outline display toggles between displaying all the body text or only the first line of each body text paragraph. (See Figure 8-5.) In lengthier documents, you don't have to scroll through pages of text to keep your overall perspective. Show First Line Only applies only to body text. If your headings have multiple lines, Word still displays them in their entirety.

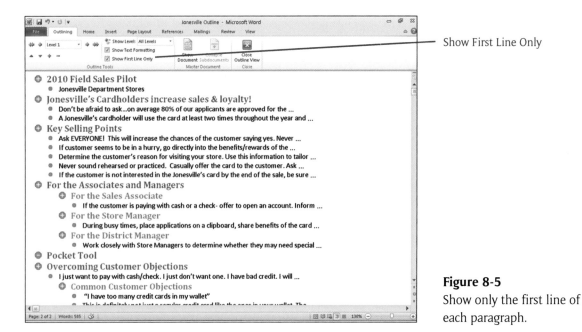

Figure 8-5
Show only the first line of each paragraph.

▶ Choose Outlining > Outline Tools > Show Text Formatting. The Outline view toggles between displaying the outline with or without character formatting. When viewed without character formatting, you can see more of your document on a page. Figure 8-6 illustrates the outline without text formatting.

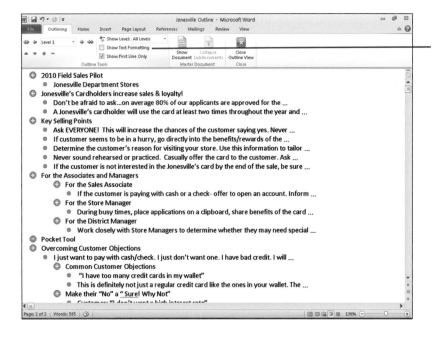

Figure 8-6
Viewing an unformatted outline.

Tip

Choose Outlining > Close > Close Outline View to close the outline and return to Print Layout view.

Reorganizing the Outline

Most of us, when typing the main points we want to relay in a document, will change our minds several times. You determine you should point out Topic B before you mention Topic A. That's okay because it's very quick and easy to reorganize your outline.

Promoting or Demoting Headings

A Level 1 heading is the highest level in an outline, and a Level 9 heading is the lowest. You have a

choice of using the click-and-drag method of moving headings (and body text) or using the buttons on the Outlining tab. Use any of the following methods to promote or demote your headings:

▶ Place the insertion point anywhere in the line you want to promote and click the Promote button or press Shift+Tab. You either click the Promote button or press Shift+Tab for each level you want to promote the text. If you want to demote the heading to a lower level, place the insertion point anywhere in the line and click the Demote button or press the Tab key.

▶ Click anywhere in the line you want to change and click the Current Outline Level drop-down list and choose from the resulting list shown in Figure 8-7.

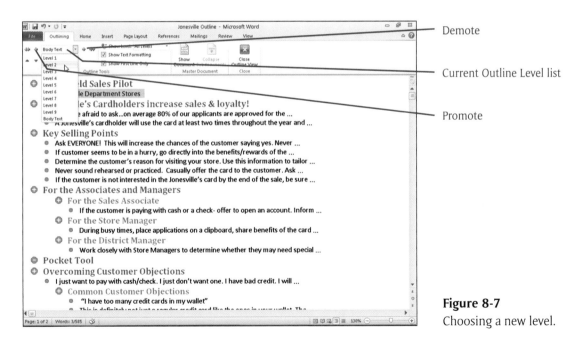

Demote

Current Outline Level list

Promote

Figure 8-7
Choosing a new level.

▶ Click the Expand and Collapse icon for the level you want to move. Word highlights the text. Drag the Expand and Collapse icon left or right in the outline. As you drag the mouse, a gray line appears, as shown in Figure 8-8. Release the mouse when the line indicates the level to which you want the text moved.

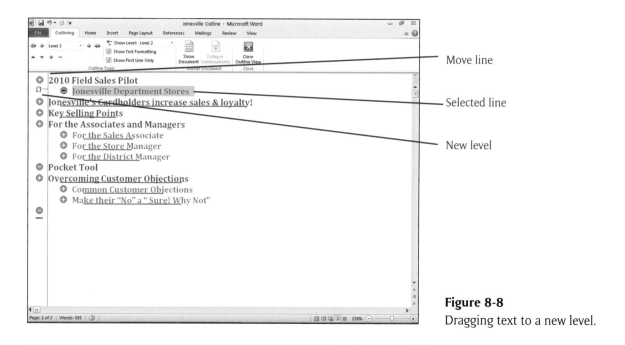

Figure 8-8
Dragging text to a new level.

Promote to Heading 1

The Outlining tab on the Ribbon also contains a button with double arrowheads pointing right. Click that button to quickly promote the current line to a Heading 1, the highest level.

Moving Levels Up or Down

As you organize your thoughts and ideas in an outline, you might change your mind and want to cover a topic earlier than originally planned. You can move selected headings along with any associated subheadings and body text up or down to any location in your outline. Click the Heading icon of the section you want to move and either click the Move Up button or click the Move Down button.

The selected section moves up or down one line with each click of the button.

Optionally, click the Expand and Collapse icon for the level you want to move. Word highlights the text. Drag the Expand and Collapse icon up or down the outline. As you drag the mouse, a gray line appears, as shown in Figure 8-9. Release the mouse when the line indicates where you want the text moved.

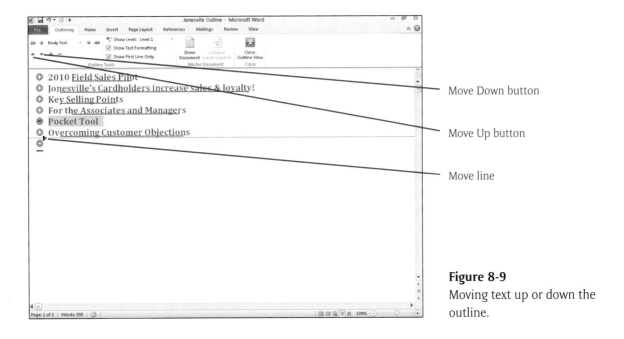

Move Down button

Move Up button

Move line

Figure 8-9
Moving text up or down the outline.

Working with Master Documents

THE OLD PHRASE "too many cooks in the kitchen spoil the soup" can also apply when you have too many people trying to put together a single document. You may have some people doing the same job, making ineffective use of time. Perhaps some of the related documents become lost and you have to start over, or maybe while delegating areas, an important topic gets lost in the diversion.

It doesn't have to work that way. Word's Master Document feature offers a system of organization for larger documents. A master document works as a container for smaller subdocuments. A book is a good example for using a master document. Think of the book title as the master document, and each book chapter is a subdocument. Working with the Master Document feature makes the longer document much more manageable.

Creating a Master Document

The basic principal behind a master document begins with a master document outline. The major headings become the subdocuments, which Word creates and saves into its own document and places hyperlinks in the master document. You, or someone else, then enters the chapter content into each individual subdocument.

1. Choose View > Document Views > Outline, which switches you to Outline view and displays the Outlining tab.

2. Choose Outlining > Master Document > Show Document. The Outlining tab expands with additional choices, as shown in Figure 8-10.

Figure 8-10
Master Document options on the Outlining tab.

Create Auxiliary Items

You can create a table of contents, index, and cross-references for all of the subdocuments in a master document. See Chapter 7 for more information on tables of contents, indexes, and cross-references.

3. At the document beginning, type the first heading or the document title and then press Enter. Word creates the first heading and applies a Heading 1 style.

Tip

For best results, use the Level 1 heading for the document title and Level 2 headings for subdocuments.

4. Press the Tab key, which shifts the second line to a Level 2 heading, and type the first document major topic.

5. Press Enter and continue typing document topics. If desired, you can use the Demote and Promote buttons to organize your topics into major topics and minor topics. See Figure 8-11 for an example.

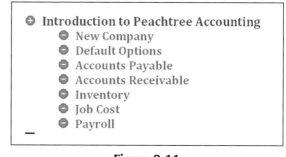

Figure 8-11
Creating the Master Document outline.

Working with Subdocuments

Now that you have the basic structure defined, it's time to assign which headings are subdocuments. You can create the subdocuments from the headings in your outline, or you can indicate existing documents.

Creating Subdocuments

By creating the outline and specifying it's a Master Document, you're only a mouse click away from creating the subdocument. Click anywhere in the first topic you want as a subdocument, and then click Outlining > Master Document > Create. Word puts a border around the topic and places a sub-document icon to the left. (See Figure 8-12.)

Click the Save icon on the Quick Access Toolbar or press Ctrl+S to save the master document. Word also then saves the subtopic as its own Word document. This step is very important, as it creates the connections between the master and any subdocuments.

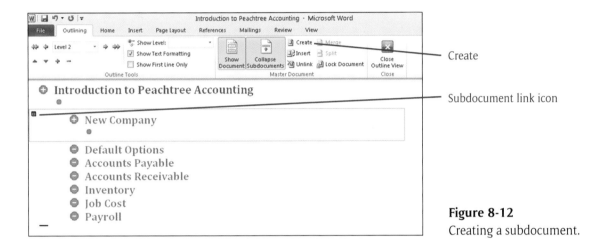

Create

Subdocument link icon

Figure 8-12
Creating a subdocument.

File Locations

Word stores all subdocuments in the same folder as the master document. When you first save the master document, it's a good idea to save it in its own folder so all related documents are kept together.

The subdocument icon, which looks like a small piece of paper, represents the link to the subdocument. Double-click the icon, and Word opens the subdocument shown in Figure 8-13. Notice the document title is the same as the text in the document, which is also the heading you used in the master document.

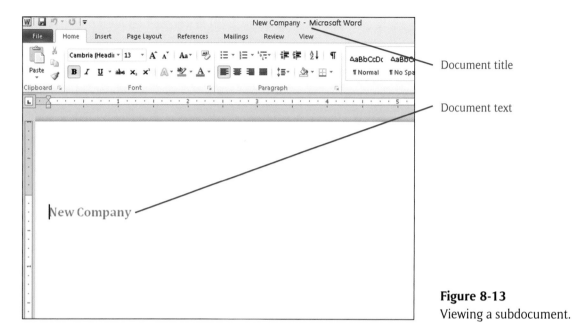

Figure 8-13
Viewing a subdocument.

Any detail or text that needs to be entered should be entered and saved in the subdocument. See Figure 8-14 for an example.

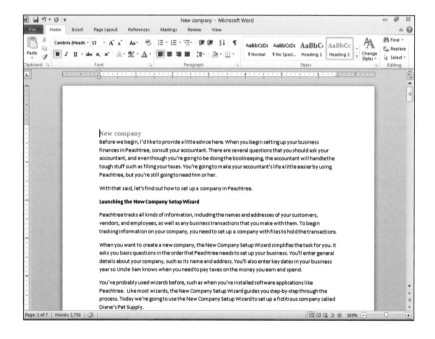

Figure 8-14
Text in the subdocument.

Text that you entered in the subdocument shows up as body text in the master document, as shown in Figure 8-15. You can hide the body text by clicking the plus sign (+) next to the heading. Continue creating subdocuments as needed. Be sure to frequently save the master document.

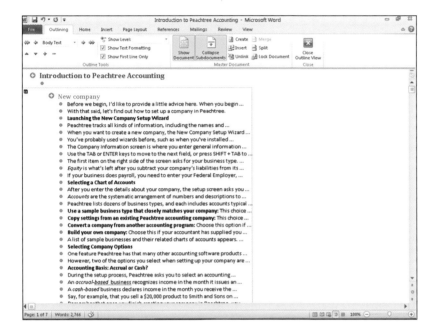

Figure 8-15
Subdocument text in the master document.

Tip

When you create subdocuments, Word automatically creates a section break between the subdocuments. (See Chapter 4 for more information on section breaks.)

Inserting Subdocuments

If you have already created some or all of the documents you want as subdocuments, you can easily insert them into the master document. For example, perhaps you're writing a book and your biography information is already saved. You don't need to recreate and retype the biographical information. You simply tell the master document where you've saved the biography. You don't actually insert the document; you insert a link to the subdocument. Follow these steps:

Subdocument Heading

For best and easiest results, make sure the already created subdocument has a level heading at the beginning. So if you are working with Level 1 headings, the first line in the subdocument should be a Level 1 heading.

1. From the Outline view, click the insertion point in a blank line where you want the already created subdocument.

2. Click Outlining > Master Document > Insert. The Insert Subdocument dialog box shown in Figure 8-16 appears.

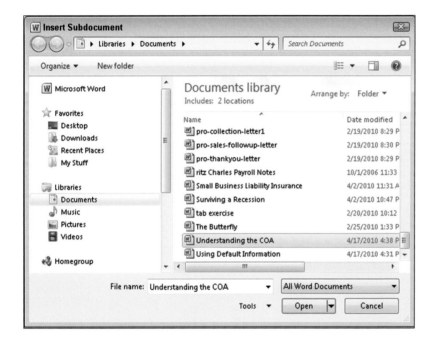

Figure 8-16
Inserting existing documents.

3. Locate and select the document you want and click the Open button. You may see a message about style formatting. Click Yes to All.

4. Save the master document. Word saves the link between the master and subdocument.

5. Continue inserting additional subdocuments if needed. Be sure to frequently save the master document.

Expanding and Collapsing Subdocuments

In the master document, when subdocuments display in expanded mode, you see the text expanded from the subdocuments. If you double-click the plus sign next to the subdocument heading, you can collapse the subheading. From there, you see the subdocument link icon and the heading itself, but no body text.

However, if you choose Outlining > Master Document > Collapse Subheadings, you see the actual links to the subdocuments. When you click the Collapse Subheadings button, Word may prompt you to save the master document. Click Yes.

Your document then looks similar to the one shown in Figure 8-17, in that the Collapse Subdocuments button turns into the Expand Subdocuments button. Instead of the headings, you see the link to the subdocuments including the drive and folder location. You also have the subdocument icon on the left side. You can still access the subdocuments by double-clicking the subdocument icon or by holding down the Ctrl key and clicking on the actual file link.

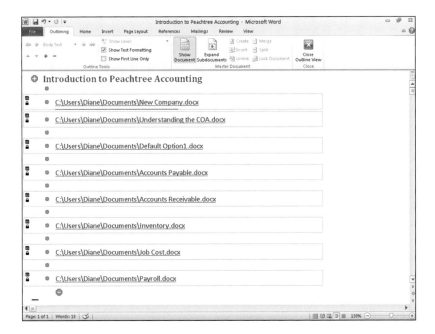

Figure 8-17
Collapsing the subdocuments.

To expand the master document back to where you see the headings, choose Outlining > Master Document > Expand Subdocuments.

Rearranging Subdocuments

Earlier in this chapter, you learned how you can move outline heading levels up or down. You use a very similar method if you need to rearrange your subdocuments. For example, perhaps you want the heading "Company History" before "Company Future."

You select the subdocument you want to move by clicking its subdocument icon. If you want to move multiple adjacent subdocuments, click the first icon, and then hold down the Shift key as you click the last icon in the group you want to move.

Drag the subdocument icon up or down the master document outline. As you drag the mouse, a gray line appears as shown in Figure 8-18. Release the mouse when the line indicates where you want the subdocument moved.

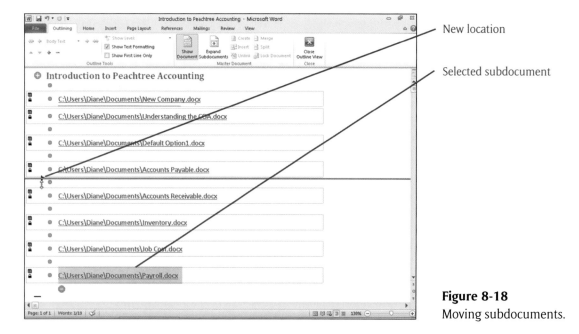

Figure 8-18
Moving subdocuments.

Merging Subdocuments

As you work on a larger document, you may discover two or more topics you want to combine into a single topic. For this, you need to use the Master Document Merge feature.

First of all, the two topics you want to combine must be located together. If the subdocuments are not listed together, you must rearrange one of them. (See the previous section for rearranging topics.)

Select the first topic's subdocument icon, which highlights the entire topic, then hold down the Shift key and click the second topic. Both topics are now highlighted. (See Figure 8-19.)

Figure 8-19
Selecting multiple subdocuments.

Finally, click Outlining > Master Document > Merge. The two topics combine into one, as shown in Figure 8-20. When you combine subdocuments, the first one that you selected before merging them is the file into which Word inserts the contents of the second document. The second subdocument file is still stored on your disk drive, but you can safely delete it if you want to. (See Chapter 1 for information on deleting a file.)

Figure 8-20
Merging subdocuments.

Splitting Subdocuments

On the reverse side of merging subdocuments, you may find you need to split the subdocuments up even more. Perhaps you decided that a particular topic was just too long. As easily as you can merge subdocuments, you can split them.

Open the subtopic document you want to split by double-clicking the subdocument icon. In the document, place a comparable heading level (usually a Level 2) as the other subtopic headings and then save and close the subdocument.

In the master document, select the new heading. The heading and all text below it is highlighted.

Choose Outlining > Master Document > Split. Word moves the selected text into its own section. In Figure 8-21, I want to split the subdocument Payroll into "Payroll" and "Tax Setup." In the subdocument, the newly created heading and any text below it are moved and saved into a separate file, just like all the other subdocuments.

Figure 8-21
Splitting subdocuments.

Deleting Subdocuments

If you decide you don't want to include a subdocument in the master document, you can easily delete it. When you delete a subdocument, you're not deleting the original document, only the connection between the documents is deleted. The original file remains on your disk drive.

To delete a subdocument, from the master document, click anywhere in the subdocument heading and choose Outlining > Master Document > Unlink. The heading remains in the document, but the connection to the saved file is eliminated. Since the deleted file is still stored on your disk drive, you can safely delete it if you want to. (See Chapter 1 for information on deleting a file.)

Creating a Multilevel List

I N CHAPTER 3, you worked with a single-level numbered list, such as Item 1, Item 2, and Item 3. A multilevel list shows the list items at different levels rather than at one level.

By default, Word provides you with seven unique multilevel lists styles. Choose the one you want by following these steps:

1. Click your mouse where you want to begin your list.

2. Choose Home > Paragraph and click the arrow next to Multilevel List. A gallery of styles appears. (See Figure 8-22.)

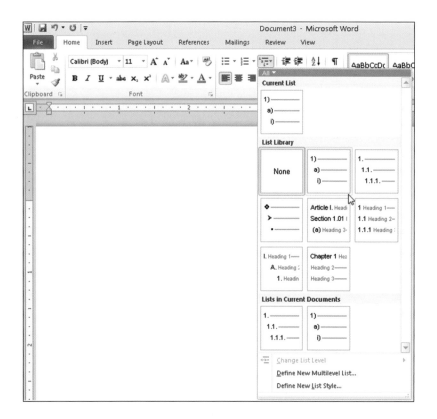

Figure 8-22
Multilevel List options.

3. Click the style you want. Word assigns the first level.

4. Type the text you want and press Enter. Word drops to the next line down, and the next number in the same level appears. Figure 8-23 illustrates a multilevel list.

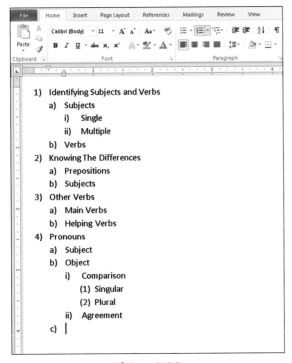

Figure 8-23
A multilevel list.

Creating Form Letters with
Mail Merge

PICTURE YOURSELF OPENING THE MAIL. On the front of the envelope it says in big bold letters that "You have won TEN MILLION DOLLARS." Then, of course, in teeny tiny print it says "*if* you are the lucky winner." It has your name printed in big letters right there on the certificate! The funny thing is that each of your neighbors got exactly the same letter with their name on the envelope and certificate. Probably millions of exactly the same letter arrived in mailboxes all around the country.

Although our society has become a little more paperless than just a few years ago, realistically we still use snail mail for lots of things. We still rely on the postal service for delivery of our bills, catalogs, Christmas cards, and lots of other types of correspondence. And let's not forget the hard-working trash collectors. They might be out of work if it weren't for all the junk mail we receive!

When you plan on sending a group of recipients the same basic letter, that letter is called a *form letter*. A form letter results from merging together a standard generic letter and personalized information. To create form letters in Word, you use the Mail Merge function. This chapter is all about mail.

Creating the Main Document

YOU NEED TWO THINGS to create a personalized mailing with a mail merge: a letter, which is called the main document and contains the information that doesn't change, and codes, called *merge fields*, that act as placeholders for the variable information. This variable information is usually a list of names and addresses, called the *data source*, and contains the information that does change for each letter. When you merge the two, the result is an individualized form letter, called the *merge document*.

For the main document, you can use a letter that you've previously created, or you can create a letter from scratch. Type your letter without filling in any of the information that will vary from recipient to recipient, such as addresses, meeting dates, and such.

The following steps show you how to begin the mail merge process:

1. Open or type the letter you want as the main document.

2. Choose Mailings > Start Mail Merge > Start Mail Merge > Letters. If you were not already in Print Layout view, Word switches to Print Layout view (see Figure 9-1).

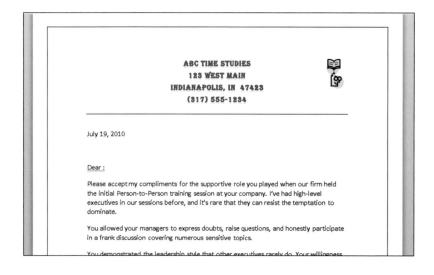

Figure 9-1
A mail merge main document.

Specifying Data for Your Mail Merge

ONCE YOU CREATE your main document, you need to link the document to a file that contains your data. The data source could be in the form of a comma-separated value Word document, or it could be in an Excel worksheet or an Access database. See Figure 9-2 for an example of each document type—Excel, Access, and Word.

Two terms commonly used with merge data files are fields and records. A field is an individual piece of information about someone or something, such as a zip code, first name, or product description. A record is the complete picture of information with all the fields put together.

Selecting a Data Source

For the data source, you can select from a preexisting list or you can create a new one using Word. If you want to choose from an existing file, choose Mailings > Start Mail Merge > Select Recipients > Use Existing List (see Figure 9-3). The Select Data Source dialog box opens. Locate your data file and choose Open.

Figure 9-2

Possible data sources.

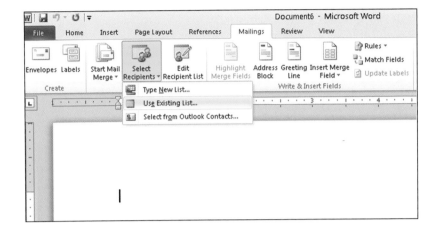

Figure 9-3
Selecting an existing data source.

If you have not already created a data source, you can create it with Word. Following are the steps for creating a data source in Word:

1. Choose Mailings > Start Mail Merge > Select Recipients > Type New List. The New Address List dialog box appears. Word tries to anticipate your needs by providing the most commonly used data fields. (You'll soon see how you can add extra fields.)

2. Enter the data for the first recipient. You do not need to enter data into every field, as you see in Figure 9-4.

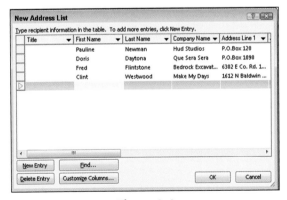

Figure 9-4
Adding records.

Tip

Use the Tab key to move from one field to the next, or press Shift+Tab to return to a previous field.

3. Click the New Entry button, which creates a blank line for the next recipient. Optionally, as you press Tab after the last field, Word automatically adds a line for the next recipient.

4. Repeat steps 2 and 3 for each additional recipient.

Although Word includes commonly used data fields, you may need to add your own fields or remove the predefined fields you don't want. Click the Customize Columns button in the New Address List dialog box. The Customize Address List dialog box appears, like the one shown in Figure 9-5. Make any desired changes and then click OK.

Figure 9-5
Customizing data fields.

Here are the options available in the Customize Address List dialog box:

▶ **Add:** To add additional fields, click the Add button. As shown in Figure 9-6, Word prompts you for a name for the new field. Type the name and click OK.

Figure 9-6
Adding an additional data field.

▶ **Delete:** To delete an unwanted field, click a field name and then click the Delete button. A confirmation message appears. Click Yes to confirm the deletion.

▶ **Rename:** To rename a field, click the field name and then click the Rename button. Enter the new name in the resulting dialog box and click OK.

▶ **Move up:** To move a field farther up in the list, click the field name and click the Move Up button until the field is located where you want it.

▶ **Move down:** To move a field farther down in the list, click the field name and click the Move Down button until the field is located where you want it.

Tip

If you want to delete a record, click anywhere in the record and click the Delete Entry button. Click Yes to the resulting confirmation message.

When you have all your entries in the New Address List dialog box, click the OK button. Word prompts you to save your address list. By default, Word attempts to save the file in the Documents > My Data Sources folder. Select a different folder if desired. Enter a file name and then click Save.

Tip

Word saves the data file as an MDB file, which is an Access database file.

Selecting Recipients

You may have a number of names in your data file, but perhaps you don't want to send the merged letter to everyone in the file. By default, Word assumes you want everyone in the data file, but you can pick and choose which recipients you want to use. Just follow these steps:

1. Choose Mailings > Start Mail Merge > Edit Recipient List. You see a Mail Merge Recipients list similar to the one displayed in Figure 9-7.

Tip

Click any column heading to sort the records by the selected column.

2. Click the check box to the left of the name for any recipient to whom you don't want to send the form letter. The checkmark will be removed.

Tip

To edit recipient information, click the data source name, then click the Edit button. The Edit Data Source dialog box appears, from which you can make any desired changes.

3. After determining that the desired recipients are checked, click the OK button.

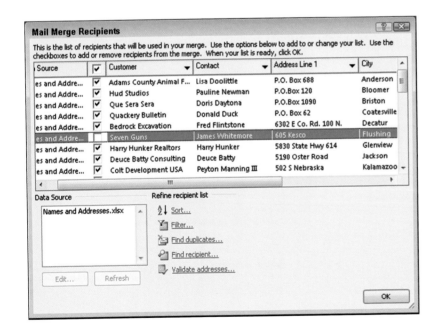

Figure 9-7
Deselect any recipient you don't want to include.

Inserting Merge Fields

NOW THAT YOU'VE CREATED the main document and have selected a data source, the next step is to enter the merge fields (also called *merge codes*) into the main document, thereby instructing Word exactly where you want those data fields placed.

You have the option of placing a group of fields together or choosing the individual fields you want to enter. The field groups come in the two different forms. The first group is for an Address Block, which consists of the following fields: Title, First Name, Last Name, Company Name, Address Line 1, Address Line 2, City, State, and ZIP Code. The second group is for the Greeting Line, which includes a greeting such as "Dear" or "To," followed by the First Name and Last Name, and then a punctuation choice, such as a comma.

Adding an Address Block

Begin by adding an Address Block. In the main document, click the insertion point where you want the recipient name and address. Choose Mailings > Write & Insert Fields > Address Block. The Insert Address Block dialog box appears, as shown in Figure 9-8.

Since Word recognizes the individual fields—including name, address, city, state, and ZIP—as part of the Address Block, using the Address Block saves you the steps of inserting each of those fields individually. You can, however, choose the style of Address Block you prefer. Click on the various address formats and review in the Preview panel just how your data looks with each format.

Match Fields button

Figure 9-8
Setting options for an Address Block.

Click OK when you've decided on the format you want. Word returns to the main document and inserts a field <<AddressBlock>> at the insertion point. This is a hidden code to Microsoft Word. Don't try to just type <<AddressBlock>>.

Selecting a Greeting Line

Most form letters also include a personalized greeting. Use the Greeting Line field box to assist you. Begin by positioning the insertion point where you want the Greeting Line, usually two lines under the Address Block. Choose Mailings > Write & Insert Fields > Greeting Line. The Insert Greeting Line dialog box appears (see Figure 9-9).

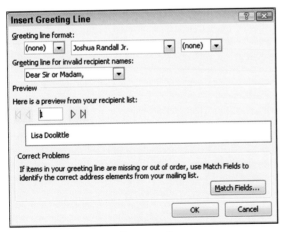

Figure 9-9
Choosing a Greeting Line format.

Select a greeting from the first drop-down list. Choices include Dear, To, or nothing at all. From the second drop-down list, select the name format you like best, and then from the third drop-down list, choose a punctuation mark of comma or a colon, or choose no punctuation.

In the event that one or more of your recipients doesn't have data in the first and last name fields, the Greeting Line for Invalid Recipient Names drop-down list provides a couple of alternatives. Select the one you prefer for your document. Or you might have to click the Match Fields button and select the proper field.

Click the OK button, which returns you to the Word main document where you now see the <<GreetingLine>> field code.

Adding Individual Fields

If the field information you want to insert into your document doesn't fall into the Address Block or Greeting Line groups, you can manually insert fields into desired document areas. Just click the mouse pointer where you want the field to appear. Choose Mailings > Write & Insert Fields > Insert Merge Field and select the field you want in the letter.

Figure 9-10 illustrates a sample form letter with an Address Block, Greeting Line, and an individual data field entered into the letter. To make it easier for you to see, I highlighted the fields in yellow.

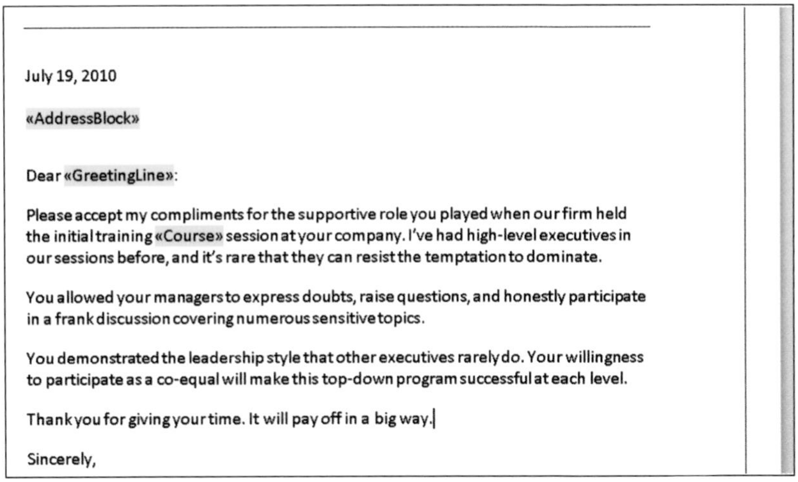

July 19, 2010

«AddressBlock»

Dear «GreetingLine»:

Please accept my compliments for the supportive role you played when our firm held the initial training «Course» session at your company. I've had high-level executives in our sessions before, and it's rare that they can resist the temptation to dominate.

You allowed your managers to express doubts, raise questions, and honestly participate in a frank discussion covering numerous sensitive topics.

You demonstrated the leadership style that other executives rarely do. Your willingness to participate as a co-equal will make this top-down program successful at each level.

Thank you for giving your time. It will pay off in a big way.

Sincerely,

Figure 9-10
A sample form letter.

Finishing the Merge

BEFORE YOU ACTUALLY PRINT all the records, you should preview them. Choose Mailings > Preview Results > Preview Results. You see your letter with data filled in from one of the records (see Figure 9-11). In the Preview mode, you can manually make any formatting or text changes, and the changes will appear for all recipients.

Use the Preview Results scroll buttons to browse between the previous and next records or the first and last records. Again, in Figure 9-11, I left the fields highlighted in yellow to make it easier for you to see.

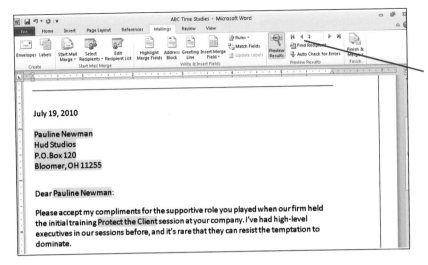

Figure 9-11
Previewing the merged letter.

When you are satisfied with the results, you're ready to finish the merge. Choose Mailings > Finish > Finish & Merge. A menu of options appears where you can edit the individual documents, print the documents, or send the documents via e-mail.

▶ **Edit the Individual Documents:** Choose this option if you want to personalize your

letters. This option creates a new Word document where each letter is on its own page, and any changes you make affect the individual current record only—not the other recipients. You have the option to merge all records, the current record, or a range of record numbers (see Figure 9-12).

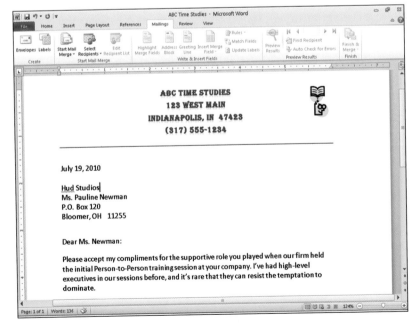

Figure 9-12
Displaying the merged letters in a new Word document.

▶ **Print Documents:** Choose this option if you don't need to make any individual changes and just want to print the merged documents. When you choose this option, you can choose to merge all records, the current record, or a range of record numbers.

▶ **Send E-Mail Messages:** This option sends the document to the recipient via e-mail. The e-mail option only works if the individual record data includes e-mail addresses. When you choose this option, like the others, you can merge all records, the current record, or a range of record numbers. Additionally, as shown in Figure 9-13, you determine which field in your data source contains the e-mail address as well as enter a subject line. Also, you determine if you want the letter sent as an attachment to the e-mail, in HTML format, in the e-mail, or in just a plain text with no formatting in the e-mail.

Tip

Don't leave the subject line blank. Many e-mail filters will not display an e-mail without a subject.

Figure 9-13
Sending the merged letters via e-mail.

Printing Envelopes and
Labels

PICTURE YOURSELF DRIVING TO THE POST OFFICE. There's a sign ahead: a stop sign. Just past the stop sign, you see another sign. This one tells you how fast you can drive. When you arrive at the post office, you see another sign; this one tells you you've reached your destination. Everywhere you go, you see signs providing directional information.

Envelopes are signs, too. Of course, they are smaller than most signs, but they are directing the mailman where to deliver your important message.

Now think about labels. They are signs, too. You place labels on a gift to make sure the gift is given to the right person. You probably don't want your mom to open the gift containing a tie and your dad to get the one with the perfume! You label your inventory so you don't send the wrong item to your customer. We all use labels for many different things pertaining to daily life.

By using Word's Mail Merge feature in the previous chapter, you discovered how you can create a single letter and easily personalize it to send to many different people. You can also use the Mail Merge feature with envelopes—creating a single envelope and sending it to many different addresses. Or perhaps you only need a single envelope for a letter you just created in Word. If your Word document contains the recipient address, you're only a few mouse clicks from printing the envelope.

And just as easily, you can create labels—either a full sheet of labels with the same information, or a full sheet of labels, each with a different address. Are you ready to get started?

Generating a Single Envelope

BECAUSE OF THE AUTOMATION used by the post office when sorting mail, it's important to make sure the envelope address is clear and concise. Hand-addressed envelopes can easily be misread by both man and machine and, frankly, they often look very unprofessional.

By using Word to address your envelopes, you can create neat, accurate addresses for both the mailing address and the return address. You can even add a bar code that can often speed up delivery time or a graphic image to make your envelope personalized.

Creating the Envelope

When you generate an envelope, Word displays an Envelopes and Labels dialog box. Obviously, for the envelope, you'll need a delivery address. First take a look at several methods Word uses to obtain a delivery address:

▶ If you have a letter or other document already open on your screen, you can let Word automatically find the recipient address and fill it directly into the Delivery Address box. By far, this is the fastest and easiest method! Refer to Figure 10-1 for a sample letter that contains a recipient address.

▶ You can type the address directly into the Delivery Address box in the Envelopes and Labels dialog box.

▶ From the Envelopes and Labels dialog box, you can choose an address from your Outlook contact list.

▶ You can copy the address (Ctrl+C) from another source and then paste it into the Delivery Address box. Use the Ctrl+V keyboard shortcut to paste the address.

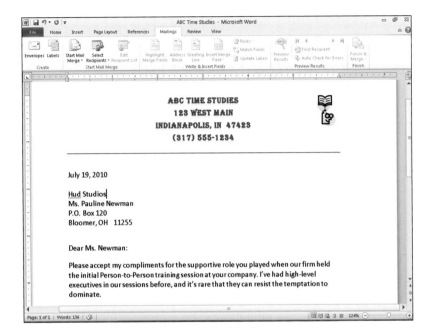

Figure 10-1
Word can pick up the mailing address from the current document.

Choose Mailings > Create > Envelopes. The Envelopes and Labels dialog box seen in Figure 10-2 appears. If your document contained the mailing address, the address already appears in the Delivery Address area. If you don't see the delivery address in the dialog box, you need to enter the address using one of the previously listed methods.

Figure 10-2
Envelope settings.

Following are the other choices on the Envelopes tab:

- ▶ If you subscribe to an electronic postage service, such as Stamps.com, check the Add Electronic Postage box. You also should then click the E-Postage Properties button to set any desired options for your e-postage subscription.

- ▶ Enter your return address in the Return Address box, or click the address book icon above it to extract your address from your Outlook contact list. When you exit the Envelopes and Labels dialog box, Word asks whether you want to save the return address as the default return address. If you choose Yes, the next time you open the Envelopes and Labels dialog box, your address will already be listed in the Return Address section. You can change the default return address at any time.

- ▶ Click the Omit check box if you don't want Word to add a return address to the envelope.

- ▶ Click the Options button to display the Envelopes Options dialog box. From this dialog box, you select the envelope size as well as a default font you want for the addresses.

- ▶ The Printing Options tab (in the Envelopes Options dialog box) displays options for feeding envelopes, but I recommend you leave it at Automatically Select, since Windows already knows how your current printer accepts envelope feeds.

Printing Envelopes

Each printer model handles envelopes a little differently. Review your printer manual for envelope feed information.

Once you select the envelopes options, you now can either create or print the envelope. If you click the Print button, Word sends the printing information directly to your default printer. Make sure you have the printer on and the envelope inserted into the appropriate location. If you click the Add to Document button, Word adds a new page to the top of the document and displays the envelope (see Figure 10-3).

Figure 10-3
Adding an envelope to your document.

If you add the envelope to the document, you can, by using the Word tools you already know, edit the envelope addresses, change fonts, or even add a graphic to the envelope. If you want to change the envelope options, click anywhere inside the envelope area and choose Mailings > Create > Envelopes again, which redisplays the Envelopes and Labels dialog box. Make any desired changes and then click Change Document.

Adding a U.S. Bar Code

The computerized sorting equipment used by the United States Post Office relies on delivery point bar codes, which are also known as POSTNET bar codes. You can easily add a bar code to your envelope. Follow these steps:

1. Add the envelope to your document. (See the previous section.)

2. Click the insertion point where you want the POSTNET bar code located, which is typically directly above or below the delivery address.

3. Choose Insert > Text > Quick Parts > Field. The Field dialog box appears.

4. In the Field Names list, click once on BarCode. Bar code options appear on the right side of the dialog box, as shown in Figure 10-4.

Tip

If you are processing a bulk mailing, you can save money by presorting the envelopes and including the POSTNET barcodes. Contact your post office for more information on bulk mail postal rates and requirements.

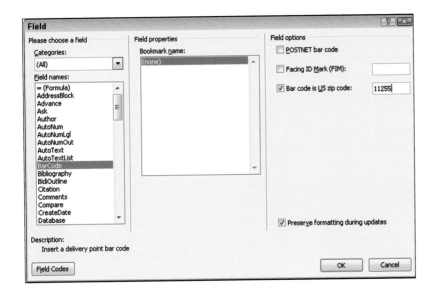

Figure 10-4
Generating a bar code.

5. In the Field Options section, click the Bar Code Is US Zip Code option.

6. Next to the Bar Code Is US Zip Code option, type the recipient zip code and then click the OK button.

As you see in Figure 10-5, Word inserts the bar code at the insertion point.

Figure 10-5
A POSTNET bar code.

Creating Labels

YOU CAN PURCHASE SHEETS of labels that feed easily into both inkjet and laser printers, making mailing labels easy to produce using Word's Label function. Labels are especially useful if you have large quantities of letters to mail, and, of course, some envelopes are simply too big or bulky to fit into your printer. You can also use labels to create hundreds of different items, such as name tags, product information, file folder labels, or return address labels.

Like an envelope, if you want Word to pick up the address automatically, create it in the form of a letter or document before you begin label creation. Otherwise, start with a blank document, and then follow these steps:

1. Choose Mailings > Create > Labels. The Envelopes and Labels dialog box appears with the Labels tab on top.

2. Click the Options button. The Label Options dialog box shown in Figure 10-6 appears.

3. Click the Tray drop-down list and select the printer tray you plan on using for labels.

4. Click the Label Vendor's drop-down list and select the manufacturer of the labels you plan on using.

5. Click the label Product Number you want to use. A description of the selected label appears on the right side in the Label Information area.

6. Click the OK button. You return to the Envelopes and Labels dialog box.

7. Choose the Full Page of the Same Label option. Select this option even if you want to enter different information on each label.

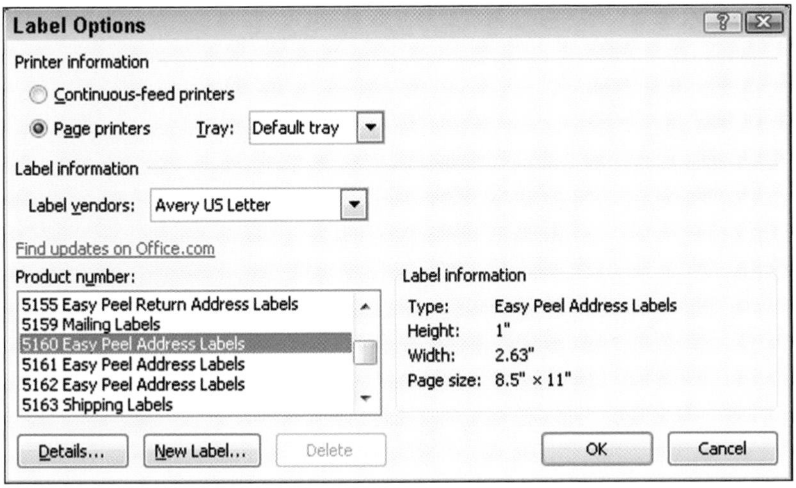

Figure 10-6
Choosing a label size.

8. If you want a full page of the same label, enter or edit the label information in the Address section (see Figure 10-7) or click the Insert Address icon to choose from an Outlook contact.

Tip

If you want to type individual information on each label, leave the Address box blank.

Figure 10-7
Enter address label information.

9. Click New Document. A screen full of labels or a label grid appears.

10. You can now optionally edit the individual labels and print them whenever you're ready (see Figure 10-8).

Show Me the Gridlines

Word uses tables when creating labels. If you don't see the gridlines indicating labels, click Table Tools Layout > Table > View Gridlines.

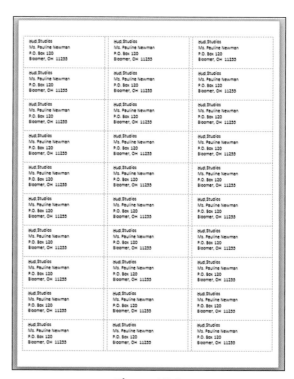

Figure 10-8
A full page of labels.

Tip

If you find that your labels are printing too close to the left edge of the label, press Ctrl+A to select all of the labels, and then drag the left indent mark a little to the right on the ruler.

Part 3
Word Columns, Tables, and Graphics

Newspapers, newsletters, magazines, and many Web sites format information in columns. Doing so allows for more flexibility in arranging topics within a larger document. In Word, using columns makes your information easy to find and read when creating newsletters and other documents.

You also have tables, which are a grid of columns and rows and great for comparing or following information across several columns. If you have used Microsoft Excel or another spreadsheet program, you will find working with tables in Word very similar. In fact, on a very small scale, Word tables are small spreadsheets.

And finally, in this part of the book, you'll work with graphics, such as pictures, shapes, or diagrams. Using a few carefully placed graphics in your document can be just the enhancement the document needs to keep your reading audience interested. You'll learn how to place them into your document and manipulate their size, color, arrangement, and more. Working with Word graphics is fun and easy.

Working with
Columns

PICTURE YOURSELF WORKING in your vegetable garden on a bright, sunny day. You have several packets of seeds that you want to plant, so you consult the directions on the back of each packet. Most of the packets recommend planting the seeds in rows, with a certain amount of space between rows to allow the plants room to reach their mature size without crowding one another. Better pick up the hoe and start making rows!

Columns in a document help you organize text in vertical "rows" for easier reading. Newspapers, newsletters, magazines, and many Web sites all format information in columns to allow for more flexibility in arranging shorter topics within the context of the larger document. Whether you're creating a meeting summary for colleagues or a newsletter to send to family and friends, using columns will enable you to create an attractive look that makes stories easy to find and read.

Adding Columns

NEWSPAPERS AND MAGAZINES are just a few of the documents that use *columns* to break up stories, with the text flowing from the bottom of one column to the top of the next. Of course, columns can be used for many other items, such as creating attractive newsletters, forms, or marketing materials.

When you format text in columns, you should do so with the reader in mind. Columns provide a means of not only arranging information on the page, but also for making a document more readable. The rule of thumb is that the smaller font size applied to text, the narrower the size of the overall line (also called line length) should be. The default 11-point font in Word works fine for a margin-to-margin line, but at 8 points, a line like that might be hard to read. When you need to use a smaller font to pack more information onto a page, using columns will maintain the text's readability.

Newspaper-Style Columns

The type of columns that Word creates by default, where the text fills one column and then starts down the next, are called *newspaper-style columns*. To create columns that flow in another way, use text boxes.

Word applies columns to the entire document unless you first select the portion you want changed into columns, or you can create section breaks and apply the column settings to the current section. (You first discovered section breaks in Chapter 4.)

Choose Page Layout > Page Setup > Columns. As shown in Figure 11-1, you see a drop-down list of preset column options. Click one of them to apply the columns that you want. Take a look at what each choice represents:

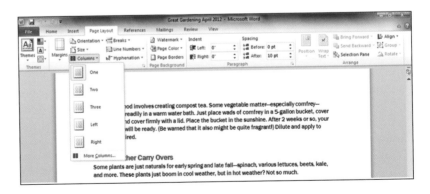

Figure 11-1
Choosing column settings.

▶ **One:** Use this choice to transform the document (or section) from multiple columns back to a single column.

▶ **Two:** Select this to divide the page into two equally spaced columns.

▶ **Three:** If you want three equally spaced columns on the page, choose this option.

▶ **Left:** The Left option divides the page into two columns, but the left column is smaller than the right (see Figure 11-2).

▶ **Right:** The Right option divides the page into two columns, but the right column is smaller than the left.

▶ **More Columns:** This option displays the Columns dialog box where you can customize your column settings.

Use Section Breaks

Remember that if you want to make column changes to only a portion of the document, you must select that portion or click in the section before choosing options from the Columns dialog box.

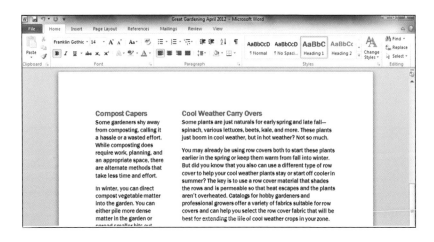

Figure 11-2
The left column is smaller than the right.

Figure 11-3 illustrates a newsletter created in Word using columns, a section break, shading, and a few graphics.

Figure 11-3
A finished newsletter.

Tip

To create the large first letter shown in the main story in Figure 11-3, called a *drop cap*, select the first letter and choose Insert > Text > Drop Cap > Dropped.

Typing in Columns

A S WITH A LOT of other formatting in Word, you can apply column formatting either before or after you create the text for a document. There are advantages to both methods. If you've already typed your text, applying the columns after the fact will give you the opportunity to work with column widths and edit the text to fit the columns. Applying the columns first gives the advantage of enabling you to see how much text will fit on the page using the number of columns and font size that you want to use. This shows you if you have room for more information or need to be more concise.

Follow these steps to apply columns and then type text in a document:

1. Position the insertion point where you'd like to start typing in columns. You can start columns at the top of a new page or at some point on an existing page, such as after the title for a newsletter, although it's usually not good design to format most of the page in a single column and the end of the page in multiple columns.

2. Choose Page Layout > Page Setup > Columns, and then click one of the preset column options. (You also can use the More Columns choice, which you'll learn about in the next section, to set up the columns.)

3. Type your text. When you reach the bottom of the first column, simply keep typing. As shown in Figure 11-4, the insertion point automatically moves to the top of the next column, flowing the text to that column, just as word wrap flows text from one line to the next.

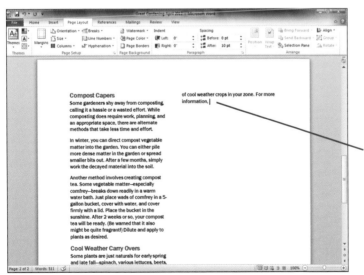

Text typed at top of second column

Figure 11-4
Typing with columns.

Creating Custom Columns

YOU AREN'T LIMITED to creating three columns of equal size or two-column documents with narrow left or right columns. You can create up to 45 columns, and you can specify a precise width for each of the columns. For example, if you are creating your own brochures using legal-sized paper, you could format the document in the landscape orientation and set it up to have four columns of information. Each of the columns would then appear as a "panel" once you folded the brochure to its finished size. Or, you might need two narrower columns at the left side of the document and one larger column at the right.

The Columns dialog box enables you to create more than three columns as well as make columns that are precise in width. Select the text to which you'd like to apply the columns or position the insertion point where you'd like to start typing in columns. Choose Page Layout > Page Setup > Columns > More Columns. The Columns dialog box shown in Figure 11-5 appears. Make sure the Apply To drop-down list has the correct setting selected. The available choices will depend on whether you selected text in advance or simply positioned the insertion point at the location where you want the columns to start.

Apply To list   Choose number of columns

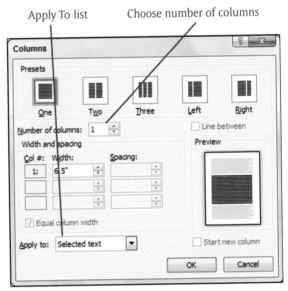

Figure 11-5
Creating multiple columns.

If you selected text first, here are the choices:

▶ **Selected Text:** Choose this option to apply the column changes to the selection only.

▶ **Selected Sections:** Use this choice to apply the column changes to the entire section(s) that contains the text you selected.

▶ **Whole Document:** Choose this option if you realize that you want to format the whole document in columns.

If you instead positioned the insertion point at the location where you want the columns to start, the Apply To choices are as follows:

▶ **This Section:** Applies the column changes to the section holding the insertion point only.

▶ **This Point Forward:** Applies the column settings to the section holding the insertion point and any subsequent sections in the document.

▶ **Whole Document:** Applies the column settings to the entire document.

Once you've determined where to apply the columns, move on to indicating the number of columns to create. You can click one of the choices in the Presets section and modify settings from there, or you type an entry in the Number of Columns text box or use its spinner arrows to indicate how many columns you need. For example, Figure 11-6 shows 4 columns specified.

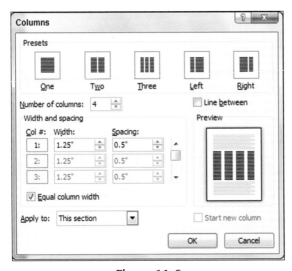

Figure 11-6
Adding columns.

Click OK. The document displays with the columns in place. Figure 11-7 shows a document with four columns, as specified in Figure 11-6.

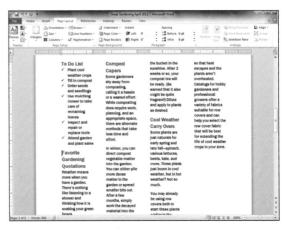

Figure 11-7
A four-column section.

Tip

Some pros at document design recommend decreasing margin widths if you add more than two or three columns in a document to provide more room for text and column spacing. Refer back to Chapter 4 to refresh your memory about setting margins.

Changing Column Size

OFTEN, YOU DON'T WANT all the columns in a document to have the same width. For example, if a newsletter you're creating includes a list of articles, you may want that list to appear in a very narrow column at the left or right while having two other larger columns for the articles themselves. Or if you want a lot of space between columns in a document, you might reduce column width to allow for more space.

The Width and Spacing section of Word's Columns dialog box displays a row of settings for each column you created. Choose Page Layout > Page Setup > Columns > More Columns to open the dialog box. To be able to customize the columns individually, click the Equal Column Width option at the bottom of the section to clear the check box. The controls on each row then become active.

You can use the Width controls to specify the corresponding column's width. For example, Figure 11-8 shows the settings for a three-column layout where the first two columns are 1.2 inches wide. After you click OK, Word adjusts the column sizes accordingly. Figure 11-9 shows how the column width settings applied in Figure 11-8 look in a newsletter document.

Width for leftmost columns

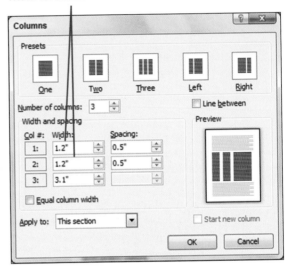

Figure 11-8
Custom column width.

Figure 11-9

Two narrow left columns.

Smaller Columns, Smaller Font Size

Don't forget that when you make a column narrower, as a result you have more leeway to reduce the size of the text in the column. This means you can add more information into a small column holding a list of contents or tips.

Changing Space Between Columns

CONTROLLING THE SPACING between columns also impacts the look of the document and the readability of text. Compare the examples in Figure 11-10. The top example has 0.5 inches of space between columns, while the bottom example has only 0.2 inches. This subtle change reduces some of the excess space in this example and also better aligns the larger main column at right with the newsletter title above.

Reduced spacing   Improved alignment with title

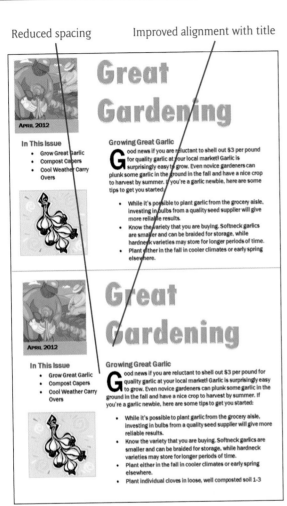

Figure 11-10
Changing column spacing.

The row for each column in the Width and Spacing section of the Columns dialog box includes a Spacing control that you can use to adjust column spacing. To be able to customize the columns individually, click the Equal Column Width option at the bottom of the section to clear the check box. Then, you can adjust not only the width for each column, but also change the spacing that appears to the right of the column by changing the value in the Spacing field on the same row (see Figure 11-11). You can change column spacing either when you create custom columns or after you've created columns.

Follow these steps to change the width between columns in text already formatted in columns:

1. Click anywhere in the section formatted in columns.

2. Choose Page Layout > Page Setup > Columns > More Columns. The Columns dialog box appears.

3. If it isn't already unchecked, click the Equal Column Width check box to remove the checkmark.

Tip

When you set custom column widths, Word recalculates the widths for other columns but does not recalculate spacing. You have to change spacing manually when needed.

Spacing to the right of columns

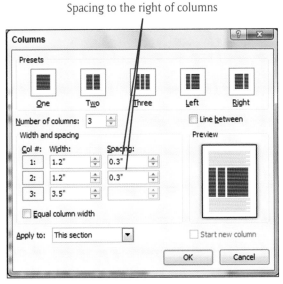

Figure 11-11
Controlling column spacing.

4. For each column for which you'd like to adjust the spacing, use the spinner arrows to increase or decrease the Spacing setting.

5. Click OK to apply the column spacing.

Figure 11-12 shows how a newsletter page looks with the settings shown in Figure 11-11 applied. Each of the left columns is 1.2 inches wide, with 0.3 inches of spacing. Word recalculated the width of the right column to be 3.5 inches based on the reduced spacing.

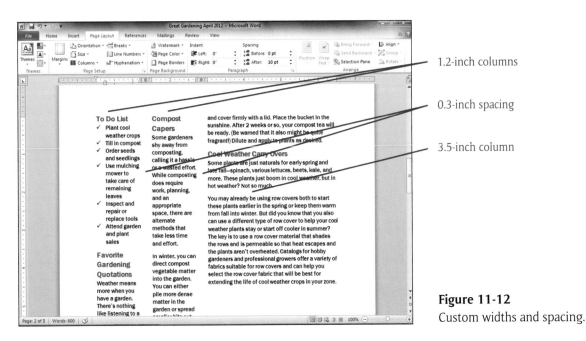

1.2-inch columns

0.3-inch spacing

3.5-inch column

Figure 11-12
Custom widths and spacing.

Inserting Lines Between Columns

IF YOU NEED TO INCLUDE so much text in a document that you really want to squeeze the spacing between columns to the smallest possible size, you can add lines between columns to help your readers. The lines visually separate the columns of text, preventing the reader's eye from wandering right past that narrow space to the next column over. As for the other settings for customizing columns that you've seen so far, you use the Columns dialog box to add or remove lines. You can add or remove the lines while customizing columns, or at a later time.

Follow these steps to add vertical lines between columns in text already formatted in columns:

1. Click anywhere in the section formatted in columns.

2. Choose Page Layout > Page Setup > Columns > More Columns. The Columns dialog box appears.

3. Click the Line Between option to check it, as shown in Figure 11-13. The Preview area in the Columns dialog box shows you where the lines will appear.

4. Click OK to apply the line setting.

Line Between check box

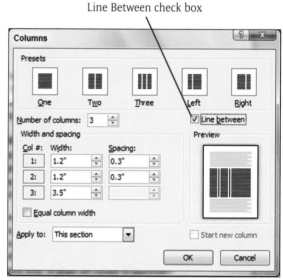

Figure 11-13
Adding lines between columns.

Figure 11-14 shows the example newsletter with lines between columns. You may have noted that the Columns dialog box doesn't present any options for formatting the lines between columns. If you need more flexibility in the appearance of the lines, you can manually insert line shapes and format them individually. (Chapter 13 explains how to add and format shapes.) Another approach would be to create a table rather than columns, and display and format only vertical borders between cells. (Chapter 12 shows how to create and format tables.)

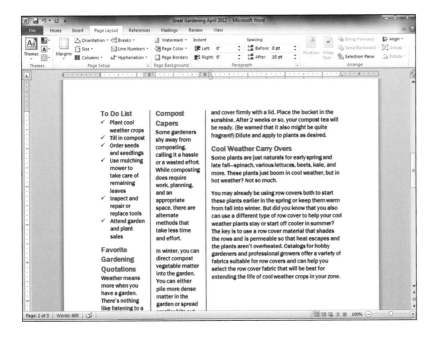

Figure 11-14
Lines separating columns.

Adding and Deleting Column Breaks

BY DEFAULT, TEXT WILL FLOW down one column, then over to the next column. If you want the column to break at a particular point, you can insert a manual column break. Column breaks are similar to page breaks in that you cannot create a manual column break to make the column longer than the page margins, but you can make a column shorter. Here are a few examples of when you might add column breaks in a document:

▶ Insert a column break just before a column heading to force the column heading to the top of the next column.

▶ Similarly, insert a column break before a paragraph to shift the entire paragraph to the next column so that you avoid an awkward split in the paragraph.

▶ Insert a column break to balance columns. For example, if a two-column document has a full left column but little text in the right column, use a column break to shift more text to the right-hand column for a more attractive appearance.

To create a manual column break, position the insertion point where you'd like the break to begin. That is, click immediately to the left of the text that you want to shift to the top of the next column. Choose Page Layout > Page Setup > Breaks > Column.

Removing a column break works just as easily. You can click in the same position that you clicked to create the column break (such as immediately to the left of a heading), and press the Backspace key. Another method is to choose View > Document Views > Draft. The column break appears as a dotted line with the text "Column Break" at the center. Double-click on the Column Break line to select it,

as shown in Figure 11-15, and then press the Delete key to remove the break. Choose View > Document Views > Print Layout to leave Draft view.

Headings and Columns

If a column heading lines up at the top of a column, check its position. Most heading styles include extra space before the heading, preventing the heading from aligning properly. See "Adjusting Spacing Between Paragraphs" in Chapter 3 to learn how to remove the space.

Figure 11-15
Removing a column break in Draft view.

Deleting Columns

YOU MAY WANT TO REMOVE columns if you apply multiple columns and don't like the result you get, or if you're working with a copy of a document file and need to remove the columns to reformat the text for another audience

or document type. The simplest way to remove the columns is to click in the section formatted in columns, and then choose Page Layout > Page Setup > Columns > One, as shown in Figure 11-16.

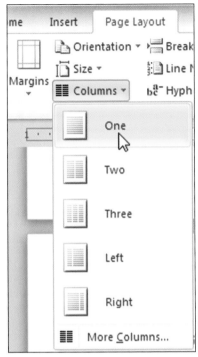

Figure 11-16
Removing columns in a section.

If you inserted column breaks, they will function as page breaks when you return the document to one column. Delete the column breaks as described in the previous section.

If you want to delete the columns in a section as well as all other section formatting, delete the section break that follows the column. Choose View > Document Views > Draft. The column break appears as a double dotted line with the text "Section Break" and the name of the break type at the center. Click on the Section Break line to select it, and then press the Delete key to remove the break. Choose View > Document Views > Print Layout to leave Draft view.

Working with
Tables

PICTURE YOURSELF CRAWLING out of your warm bed after a good night's sleep. A luxurious aroma wafts through the house and you anticipate your first cup of hot coffee. You sit at the table and begin reading the morning paper, scanning the headlines and reading some articles in their entirety. You look at the financial section to check your stocks, and you review the weather forecast for the next few days.

When you look at the financial page or the weather forecast, you're usually looking at a table. Tables are great for organizing information. A table is a grid of columns and rows, and the intersection of a column and row is called a cell. When you need to compare data or follow information across several columns, it's easier if the information is displayed in a table. You can use tables to place pieces of data side by side in a document—for example, in the various sections of an invoice or address list.

If you have used Microsoft Excel or another spreadsheet program, you will find working with tables in Word very similar. In fact, on a very small scale, Word tables are small spreadsheets.

That's what this chapter is all about—creating the type of document designed for reading large amounts of information quickly and easily.

Creating a Simple Table

WHEN YOU CREATE A TABLE, all you need to do is estimate the number of rows and columns you need. Notice I said *estimate*. You'll find it easy to add or delete rows or columns after you create the table. Use the following steps to create a table:

1. Position the insertion point where you would like the table to begin.

2. Choose Insert > Tables > Table, which displays a table grid like the one you see in Figure 12-1.

3. Drag the mouse across the squares that represent the number of rows and columns you want in your table. Word's Live Preview feature draws a sample of the table in your document.

Tip

If you don't want to drag across the table grid to set the table size, choose Insert > Table > Insert Table. The Insert Table dialog box appears, in which you can type how many rows and columns you want in your table.

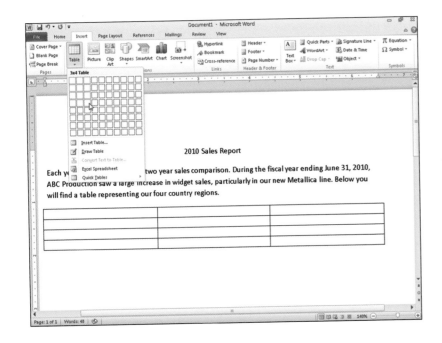

Figure 12-1
The table grid.

4. Click the square that represents the lower right corner of your table. Word places the table into your document.

Notice in Figure 12-2 that the blinking insertion point is in the first table cell and that the Ribbon now contains two Table Tools tabs: Design and Layout.

Figure 12-2
Creating a table.

Tip

A table cell is a box that appears at the intersection of a row and column. Although the names don't display, each column takes an alphabetic letter, A, B, C, and so forth. Each row is indicated by number. A cell, then, is referred to by both the column and row, such as A2 or B5. This is especially important if you create a formula in your table. (See "Creating Table Formulas" later in this chapter.)

Entering Text

ONCE YOU HAVE YOUR TABLE in the document, you can start adding text to it. Click in the cell where you want to enter information and begin typing, as shown in Figure 12-3. If needed, Word automatically wraps the text and expands the row height to accommodate the text. You can press the Tab key to move to the next cell or press Shift+Tab to move to the previous cell. You can also use the up and down arrow keys to move up or down a row at a time, and of course you can click your mouse in any cell.

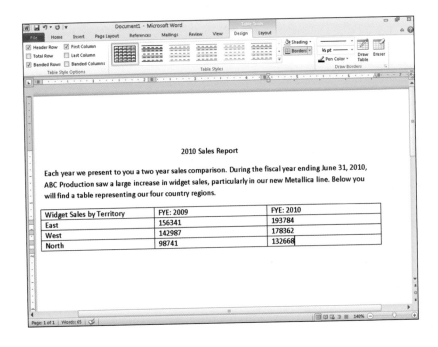

Figure 12-3
Entering text into table cells.

Converting Tables

ANOTHER METHOD YOU CAN USE to insert a Word table is by using existing text. If you already have a list where each column is separated by a tab, a comma, or other consistent character, you can easily convert that list to a table so you won't have to create the table and retype all the text. (See Figure 12-4). Conversely, if you put text into a table and then decide you would prefer it in tabular columns, you can convert the table into a list.

Be Consistent

In order for the conversion feature to work correctly, you must be consistent with the character you use to separate the items.

To convert a text list into a Word table, select the list and choose Insert > Tables > Table > Convert Text to Table. The Convert Text to Table dialog box shown in Figure 12-5 appears.

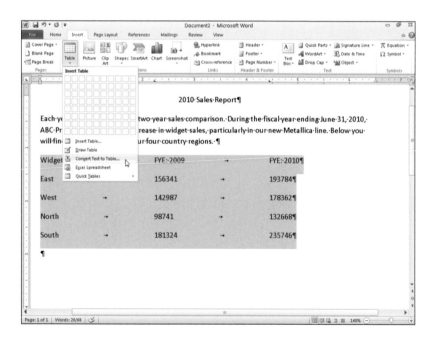

Figure 12-4
Converting an existing list into a Word table.

Other separation character

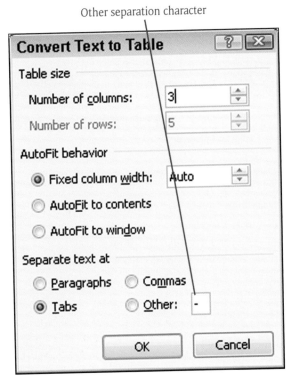

Figure 12-5
The Convert Text to Table dialog box.

Based on the data you selected, Word guesses the number of columns you want. If you did not separate your columns with commas or tabs, in the Separate Text At section, choose Other and type the character you used, such as an asterisk or dash. Click OK, and Word converts the list into a table.

If your text is already in a table, but you would prefer it in a list, click anywhere in the table and choose Table Tools > Layout > Data > Convert to Text. You see the Convert Table to Text dialog box, as shown in Figure 12-6. Choose the printing or non-printing character you want the text separated with and then click OK. The table disappears and the text remains.

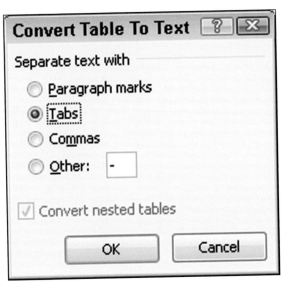

Figure 12-6
Converting a table to standard text.

Creating a Quick Table

A THIRD METHOD for creating a table is using one of Word's Quick Tables. Quick Tables are nine predefined tables that include sample data and formatting. If you find a Quick Table close to what you actually need, you can save time by choosing the Quick Table and then changing the elements you want changed. Choose Insert > Tables > Table > Quick Tables and choose from one of the preformatted templates as shown in Figure 12-7.

Save Table Styles

If you create and format a table style you like and frequently use, select the table and choose Insert > Tables > Table > Quick Tables > Save Selection to Quick Tables Gallery. The next time you need that table, you can select it from the Quick Tables gallery.

Okay—one more rather fun way to create a Word table is by simply typing out a string of plus signs (+) and minus signs (–). Word uses its AutoCorrect feature to interpret your typing and convert it to a table. Type a plus sign and then type a series of minus signs until you have the first column width you want for your table. Type another plus sign, followed by more minus signs. Repeat these steps, placing a plus sign at the end of the series of minus signs (see Figure 12-8). When you press Enter, Word automatically converts it to a table.

Figure 12-7
Choosing a Quick Table style.

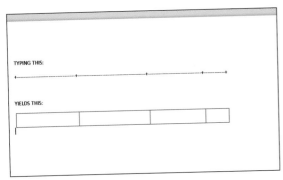

Figure 12-8
Manually typing table boundaries.

No matter which method you used to create your table, you enter the data as well as format or modify the table in the following ways.

Working with Table Layout

WHEN YOU CREATED your table, Word displayed two additional Ribbon tabs. The Layout tab, shown in Figure 12-9, provides the tools you need to modify the table properties such as how many rows and columns or how the data lines up in the individual table cells.

Changing Table Size

Okay, now you have your table created, but it doesn't contain the right number of rows or columns. You can easily change the table size by adding or deleting rows or columns from your table. Table 12-1 illustrates some of the different ways you can change the table size.

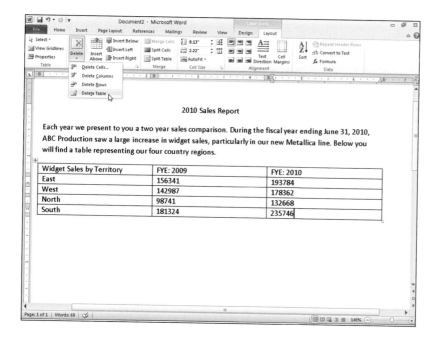

Figure 12-9
Deleting unwanted table areas.

Table 12-1 Changing Table Size

To. . .	Do This
Add rows to the table end	Click in the last table cell and press the Tab key, or click in the last row and choose Table Tools > Layout > Rows & Columns > Insert Below.
Add rows in the table middle	Click in a cell and choose Table Tools > Layout > Rows & Columns > Insert Below (or Insert Above).
Add columns	Click in a cell and choose Table Tools > Layout > Rows & Columns > Insert Left (or Insert Right).
Delete a column	Click in the column you want to delete and choose Table Tools > Layout > Rows & Columns > Delete > Delete Columns.
Delete a row	Click in the row you want to delete and choose Table Tools > Layout > Rows & Columns > Delete > Delete Rows.
Delete an entire table	Click anywhere in the table and choose Table Tools > Layout > Rows & Columns > Delete > Delete Table (refer to Figure 12-9).

Adjusting Column Width

When you begin typing in a cell, as you type, the text wraps to the next line in the same cell. You may find that you don't want the data to wrap around, but the column is not wide enough to hold your data. You can easily change the width of columns or the height of rows. You can manage the task with the mouse or you can choose options in the ribbon. First, look at the methods you can use to change column width:

▶ Position the mouse over the edge of any cell in the column you want to adjust. Notice the mouse pointer changes to a bar with both left and right pointing arrows. Drag the edge of the cell until the column is the width you want (see Figure 12-10).

▶ Drag the column boundary marker on the ruler.

▶ Click in any cell of the column you want to adjust and choose Table Tools > Layout > Cell Size > Table Column Width. Use the up/down arrows to set the desired column width.

▶ To force the column width so it's wide enough to fit the widest entry in the column, position the mouse pointer over the left edge of any cell in the column. When the mouse pointer changes to a bar with the left and right pointing arrows, double-click the mouse. Word automatically expands the column to fit the widest entry.

▶ To force all columns to the same width, choose Table Tools > Layout > Cell Size > Distribute Columns

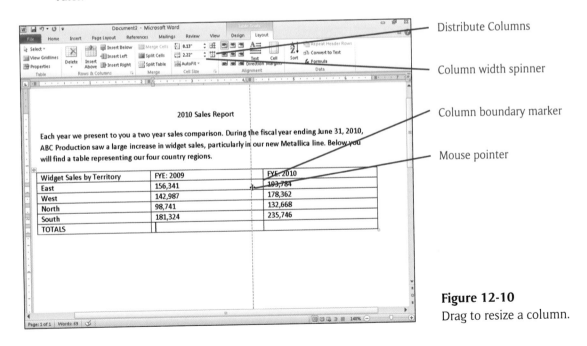

Figure 12-10
Drag to resize a column.

▶ To adjust the width of *all* of the table columns to fit their widest entry, choose Table Tools > Layout > Cell Size > AutoFit > AutoFit Contents.

Manipulating Row Height

Sometimes you want a little clearance above and below the cell contents. You can do that by increasing the row height. The methods for modifying row height are very similar to those you use to change column width:

▶ Position the mouse over the bottom edge of any cell in the column you want to adjust. Notice the mouse pointer changes to a bar with both up and down arrows. Drag the bottom edge of the cell until the row is the height you want. (See Figure 12-11.)

▶ Click in any cell of the row you want to adjust and choose Table Tools > Layout > Cell Size > Table Row Height. Use the up/down arrows to set the desired row height.

▶ To adjust the height so it's tall enough to fit the tallest data entry, position the mouse pointer over the bottom edge of any cell in the row and double-click the mouse.

▶ To force each row to the same height, choose Table Tools > Layout > Cell Size > Distribute Rows.

Changing Table Dimensions

If you find that your table dimensions don't quite provide the look you want, besides changing column widths and row heights, you can easily change the size of the entire table. Just follow these steps:

1. While in Print Layout view (View > Document Views > Print Layout) or Web Layout view (View > Document Views > Web Layout), position your mouse anywhere over the table until you see a sizing handle appear in the lower right table corner. The sizing handle is a small white square.

2. Move the mouse pointer over the handle until the pointer changes to a diagonal double-headed arrow. (See Figure 12-12.)

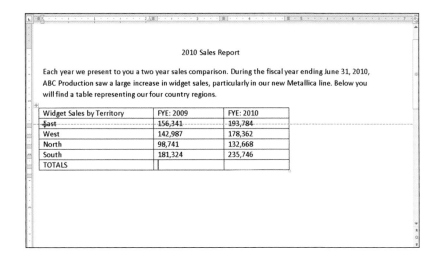

2010 Sales Report

Each year we present to you a two year sales comparison. During the fiscal year ending June 31, 2010, ABC Production saw a large increase in widget sales, particularly in our new Metallica line. Below you will find a table representing our four country regions.

Widget Sales by Territory	FYE: 2009	FYE: 2010
East	156,341	193,784
West	142,987	178,362
North	98,741	132,668
South	181,324	235,746
TOTALS		

Figure 12-11
Modifying row height.

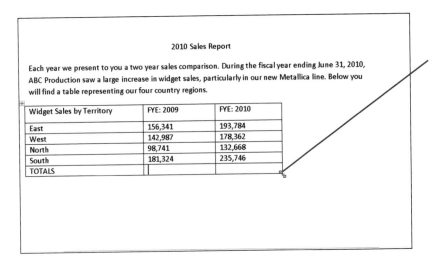

Mouse pointer over sizing handle

Figure 12-12
Resizing a table.

3. Drag the sizing handle, which resizes the table. As you drag the handle, you see a dashed line that represents the new table size.

4. Release the mouse button to accept the new table size.

Moving a Table

The first step when creating a new table was to position the insertion point where you want the table. If you didn't have your insertion point in the right location, or you just decide you want to move the table, you can easily drag it to a different document area.

From Print Layout view or Web Layout view, as you move your mouse over the table, notice the upper-left table corner has a small box with a four-headed arrow in it. This is the Table Move handle. Position your mouse pointer over the Table Move handle until the mouse pointer also changes to a four-headed arrow, and then drag the table to a new location. As you move the table, you see a dashed line which represents the new table position. See Figure 12-13 for an example.

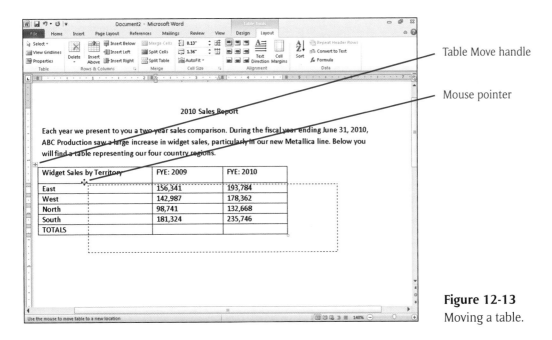

Table Move handle

Mouse pointer

Figure 12-13
Moving a table.

Tip

If you want to copy the table instead of moving it, hold down the Ctrl key as you drag the table.

Selecting Table Areas

Often you want to make changes to an entire column or an entire row. Or perhaps you want to apply a certain formatting option to the entire table. While you could make any desired changes one cell at a time, Word includes several methods you can use to select portions of the table so you

can quickly apply any changes to the entire selection. The following list shows you several ways to select table cells:

▶ To select sequential cells, click in the first cell, then hold down the Shift key and select the last cell you want. Optionally, drag the mouse over a group of cells to select a sequential area. All cells in the selected area are highlighted.

▶ To select non-sequential cells, hold down the Ctrl key and click each additional cell you want to select. Figure 12-14 shows non-sequential cells selected and highlighted in blue.

2010 Sales Report

Each year we present to you a two year sales comparison. During the fiscal year ending June 31, 2010, ABC Production saw a large increase in widget sales, particularly in our new Metallica line. Below you will find a table representing our four country regions.

Widget Sales by Territory	FYE: 2009	FYE: 2010
East	156,341	193,784
West	142,987	178,362
North	98,741	132,668
South	181,324	235,746
TOTALS		

Figure 12-14
Selecting cells.

▶ To select a single entire column, position the mouse pointer at the top of a column until the mouse turns into a down-pointing arrow, and then click.

▶ To select multiple columns, make sure the mouse pointer is the down-pointing arrow, and then drag across multiple columns.

▶ To select a single entire row, position the mouse pointer at the left of the row column until the mouse pointer turns into a white, right-pointing arrow, and then click.

▶ To select multiple rows, make sure the mouse is the right-pointing white arrow and then drag across multiple rows.

Select Non-Sequential Cells

When making non-sequential cell selections, you can include entire rows and entire columns along with individual cells or groups of cells.

▶ To select the entire table, click the small box in the upper left table corner.

▶ To clear any selection, click any non-selected cell or click outside of the table.

Merging Table Cells

By default, Word creates tables with each cell in a column the same width as the cell below it. Sometimes, especially if you are creating a form with your table, you may find some cells too small. Fortunately, you can combine adjacent cells to become larger cells. This is especially useful if you want to create a table header row, such as the one shown in Figure 12-15.

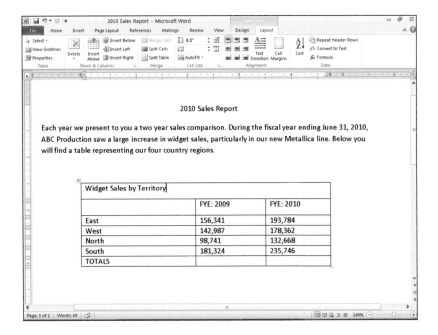

Figure 12-15
Merging multiple cells into one larger cell.

Drag across the two or more cells you want to merge and then choose Table Tools > Layout > Merge > Merge Cells. The highlighted cells combine into one larger cell. You can merge cells horizontally or vertically.

Splitting Table Cells

If you want to split a cell into smaller cells, you need to tell Word how many columns and rows you want in the cell. Click anywhere in the cell you want to split and choose Table Tools > Layout > Merge > Split Cells. The Split Cells dialog box shown in Figure 12-16 appears. Choose how many columns and rows you want, and then click the OK button.

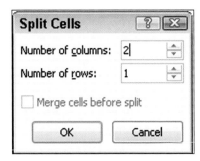

Figure 12-16
Dividing a cell into multiple cells.

Using Table Design

I F YOU WANT TO CHANGE the appearance (formatting) of the table cells, you select the cells you want to modify and apply any of the standard formatting choices such as fonts, shading, and borders.

For example, if you want to set your table headings apart from the table remainder by making them bold, larger and with shading, you select the heading cells and choose options from the Home tab, as shown in Figure 12-17. (See Chapter 3 for more information about formatting options on the Home tab.)

However, Word also supplies a quick and easy way to format your table. By selecting from Word's large gallery of table styles, you can apply attractive formatting with a click of the mouse. If needed, you then can make any additional adjustments to better meet your needs.

Take a look at the Design tab, shown in Figure 12-18. With the insertion point anywhere in your table, the Design tab displays a number of different predefined themed formats. As you hover your mouse over any design option, Live Preview allows you to see the formatting as it would look in your actual document. When you find the style you want, click the mouse to actually accept the style.

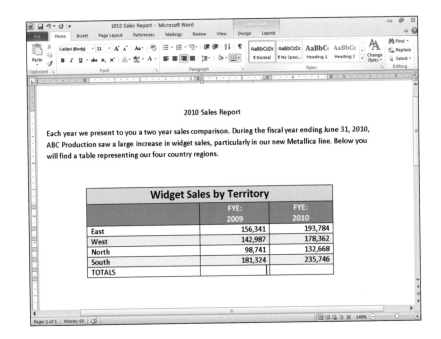

Figure 12-17
Apply formatting to selected cells.

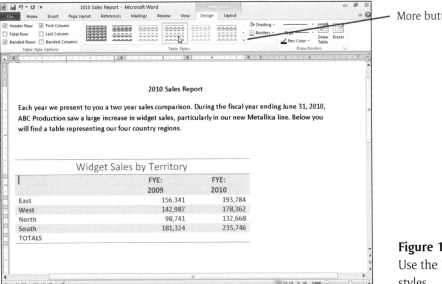

More button

Figure 12-18
Use the Design tab to apply table styles.

▼ Click the More button to display many more choices, as shown in Figure 12-19.

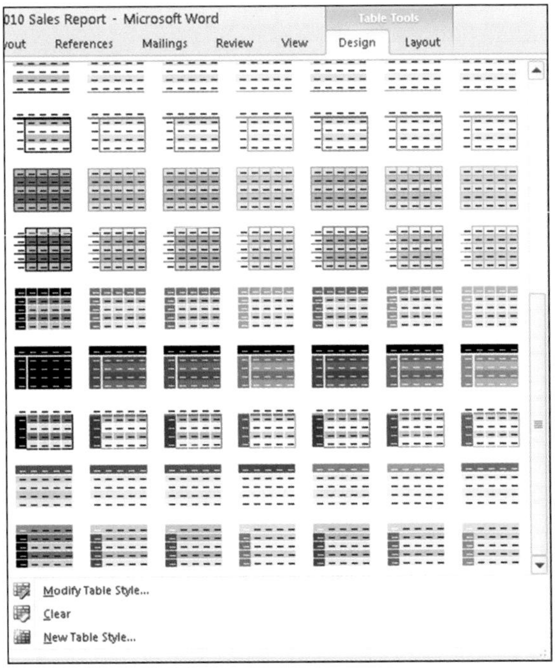

Tip

You can also easily adjust table formatting options by experimenting with the choices in the Table Style Options group.

Figure 12-19
Choose from any of the many themed table styles.

Creating Table Formulas

I F YOU HAVE A COMPLEX TABLE with lots of calculations, consider using Excel to perform the calculations and then insert the spreadsheet into Word. The next section shows you how to accomplish that. But if you want a simple calculation, such as adding a column of values, go ahead and let Word do the work for you.

There are two rules you must follow when creating Word calculations. One is that the entire calculation must be enclosed in a Word field. Word fields, which you'll see how to create shortly, are displayed with opening and closing braces, { and }. The second rule is that all calculations must begin with an equals sign (=).

You create Word arithmetic formulas using operators to perform the calculation you want. Table 12-2 shows the mathematic operators used in Word tables along with an example of each.

Table 12-2
Mathematical Operators Used in Word

Name	Operator	Example	Result
Addition	+	{=6+3}	9
Subtraction	-	{=6-3}	3
Multiplication	*	{=6*3}	18
Division	/	{=6/3}	2
Percentage	%	{=6%}	.06
Exponentiation	^	{=6^3}	216

When creating a calculation, the power comes in to play in that you typically don't use the actual values; instead, you create a reference to them. Suppose cell B2 has a value of 6 and cell B3 has a value of 3. Now, suppose you want, in cell B4, to multiply those two values. In cell B4, you won't enter =6*3; instead, you'll enter =B2*B3. The advantage is that if you later change the value in cell B2 from 6 to 8, you won't have to retype the calculation—you'll simply tell Word to recalculate it. Look at how this is all accomplished:

1. First you must realize that calculations in Word tables are generated from formula fields. Click the cell in which you want a formula field and choose Table Tools > Layout > Data > Formula. You see the Formula dialog box shown in Figure 12-20.

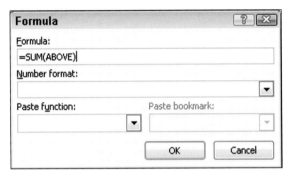

Figure 12-20
The Formula dialog box.

2. Sometimes Word can detect the formula you want and automatically create instructions. In the previous figure, Word assumes we want to add together (SUM) the cells above the current cell. We do, but to illustrate a formula, we're going to manually enter it. Highlight the existing text in the Formula text box and type an equals sign (=).

3. Type the rest of your formula, as shown in Figure 12-21. In this example, I want to add cells B3, B4, B5, and B6, which will give us the total amount.

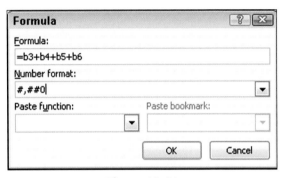

Figure 12-21
Creating a calculation.

4. Next, choose an option from the Number Format drop-down list. This option determines the appearance of your answer, such as whether to include a dollar sign, a percent symbol, or two decimal points.

5. Click OK. Word calculates the formula and displays the results. (See Figure 12-22.)

ABC Production saw a large increase in widget sales, particularly in our new Metallica line. Below you will find a table representing our four country regions.

Widget Sales by Territory	FYE: 2009	FYE: 2010
East	156,341	193,784
West	142,987	178,362
North	98,741	132,668
South	181,324	235,746
TOTALS	579,398	

Figure 12-22
Displaying calculated results.

If you later make a change to any of the table cells referenced in the formula, Word doesn't automatically update the formula answer. Right-click over the current answer and choose Update Field. If you need to modify the formula, right-click over the current answer and choose Edit Field. You'll see the Field dialog box. Click the Formula button to redisplay the Formula dialog box where you can make any desired changes. Click OK when you are finished.

If you want to see the actual formula instead of the result, right-click over the answer and choose Toggle Field Codes. You see the actual formula in the field, as shown in Figure 12-23. To view the answer again, repeat the action.

Word contains a number of predefined calculations, called *functions*, that you can plug into your formula fields. For example, if you simply want to add adjacent cells, use the SUM function, such as =SUM(ABOVE) or =SUM(LEFT). The ABOVE reference tells Word to add all the non-blank cells directly above the answer cell. The LEFT reference tells Word to all add the non-blank cells directly to the left of the answer cell. To use a function choose Table Tools > Layout > Data > Formula. You can either accept the suggestion provided by Word, or click the Paste Function drop-down list and choose a different function (see Figure 12-24).

will find a table representing our four country regions.

Widget Sales by Territory	FYE: 2009	FYE: 2010
East	156,341	193,784
West	142,987	178,362
North	98,741	132,668
South	181,324	235,746
TOTALS	{ =b3+b4+b5+b6 \# "#,##0" }	

Figure 12-23
Viewing the calculation.

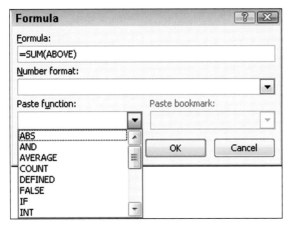

Figure 12-24
Select a function.

Tip

Word cannot use a function to total the entire column or row if your column or row contains blank cells or cells with text instead of values.

Adding an Excel Table to a Word Document

I N THIS CHAPTER, you've seen some of the power behind a Word table. As mentioned at the chapter beginning, a Word table is basically a small spreadsheet. This book doesn't cover creating Excel worksheets, but you should also know that once you create an Excel worksheet, you can insert it into a Word document. Just follow these steps:

1. Position the insertion point where you want the Excel worksheet placed.

2. Choose Insert > Text > Object > Object. You see the Object dialog box shown in Figure 12-25.

3. Click the Create from File tab.

4. Click the Browse button. A Browse window opens.

5. Locate and double-click the file you want to insert. The Object dialog box reappears with the file name you selected (see Figure 12-25).

Figure 12-25
Select the Excel file you want to include.

Word considers the table an object in the document. To make any changes, double-click the inserted Excel worksheet where you will see the Excel worksheet Ribbon and options, as shown in Figure 12-27. Click outside the table to return to Word. Changes you make in the Word table do not affect the saved Excel worksheet.

6. Click OK. The Excel worksheet along with any formulas and formatting appears in your document. See the example in Figure 12-26.

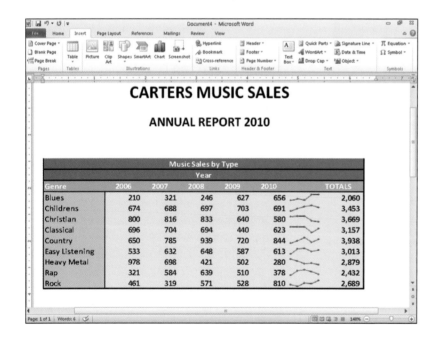

Figure 12-26
An Excel worksheet in a Word document.

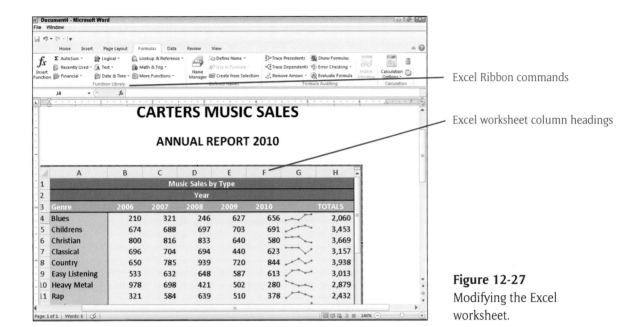

Excel Ribbon commands

Excel worksheet column headings

Figure 12-27
Modifying the Excel worksheet.

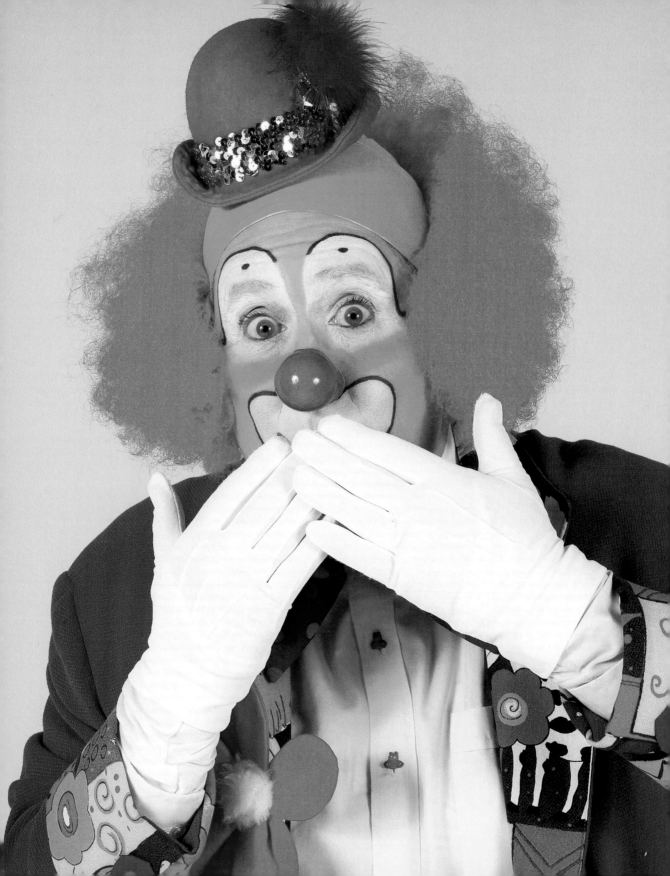

Working with
Graphics

PICTURE YOURSELF APPLYING stage makeup. You're an actor or actress, and if you don't apply some makeup you'll appear lifeless and dull and perhaps go unnoticed by the audience. But if you apply too much makeup or apply it sloppily, you'll look clownish and the audience might not take your role seriously.

Using a few carefully placed graphics in your document can be just the makeup the document needs to keep your reading audience interested.

Graphics can be many different types, such as pictures, shapes, cartoon art, or diagrams. This chapter is about working with graphics. From getting them into your document to manipulating their size, color, or arrangement, you'll find Word graphics can be fun and easy.

One thing to note about working with any graphics image is that you can only see them while in Print Layout, Full Screen Reading, or Web Layout view. Graphics are hidden while in Outline or Draft views.

Working with Pictures

YOU CAN INSERT PICTURES from a variety of places, including those stored on your computer or perhaps a picture from the Web. Once you have the photograph in your document, you can then move it around, resize it, or perform a number of enhancements to the photo.

Placing Pictures

Besides lots of text in your document, if you have a digital photograph or other graphics image, such as a company logo, you can place it in the document as well. To insert an existing graphics file into your document, follow these steps:

1. Click the cursor where you want to place a picture, and choose Insert > Illustrations > Picture. The Insert Picture dialog box opens. (See Figure 13-1.)

2. Locate and select the image you want to insert.

3. Click Insert. Word inserts the image you selected into the document. (See Figure 13-2.) You also see a new Picture Tools > Format tab.

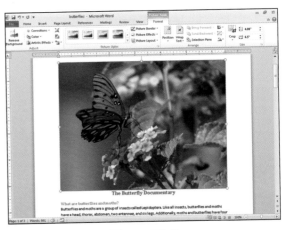

Figure 13-2
Adding a picture to the document.

Tip

To delete a picture, make sure it is selected. You will see eight small handles around it. Press the Delete key.

Figure 13-1
The Insert Picture dialog box.

Using Picture Tools

When you place a picture in the Word file, you get quite a few options to perform some fairly sophisticated tasks. You can adjust the image brightness and contrast, apply a color accent, give it a frame, or rotate it three-dimensionally. You can even crop it to get rid of unwanted areas. You accomplish all of these picture tasks by using the Picture Tools > Format tab that appears on the Ribbon when you select a picture (see Figure 13-3).

Making Picture Adjustments

The Adjust group contains seven different options. The first option, the Remove Background feature, is new to Word 2010 and lets you to remove background detail from an image, allowing only a selected portion to remain visible. Begin by selecting the picture you want to modify, and from the Picture Tools > Format tab in the Adjust group, click the Remove Background button. Your screen changes, similar to the one shown in Figure 13-4.

Word guesses the image background and turns it magenta. The image foreground remains visible.

If you need to adjust the image boundaries so it better fits the area you want, drag any of the selection lines so the selection box contains the image portion you want. If you want to be more specific in the areas you want to keep, click Background Removal > Refine > Mark Areas to Keep and draw around the areas you want. You can also click the Mark Areas to Remove button and draw around areas you don't want. Each time you draw an area, you see a white marker. If you mark an area in error, click the Delete Mark button and click the marker you don't want.

When you are finished, click Background Removal > Close > Keep Changes. Word removes the background. You can then add effects, such as shadows, reflections, or glows, to the remaining image portion. See Figure 13-5, where I added, cropped, and resized the butterfly and added a shadow to it.

Figure 13-3
The Picture Tools > Format tab.

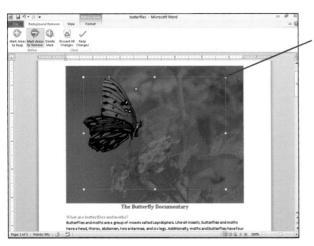

Selection border

Figure 13-4
Removing the background area.

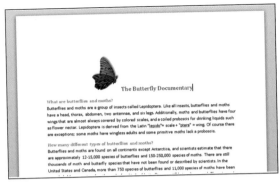

Figure 13-5
After removing the background.

Other picture adjustments include the following:

► The **Corrections** button displays a gallery where you can adjust the image brightness and contrast. The original image begins at 0%, and you can make the image up to 40% brighter or darken it by 40%.

► The **Color** button applies a coloring effect, such sepia, black and white, or other color variations.

► The **Artistic Effects** button displays a gallery (see Figure 13-6) where you can apply cool effects such as texture, water sponge or photocopy. Pause your mouse over any effect to see a preview of the effect on your picture.

► The **Compress Pictures** button applies a compression algorithm to all the document pictures in order to reduce the document size.

► The **Change Picture** button displays the Insert Picture dialog box, where you can replace the current picture.

► The **Reset Picture** button undoes any editing and formatting you performed on the selected picture. Trust me—this button will become your friend!

Figure 13-6
Adding artistic effects.

Working with Picture Styles

The Picture Styles group on the Picture Tools > Format tab offers a gallery of styles with preformatted shapes and three-dimensional effects. Click the More button to see the complete gallery, as shown in Figure 13-7. Pause your mouse over any picture style to see its effect on your picture.

In the same group, you also have options to change the picture border or to add effects. The Picture Border option allows you to assign a color to the frame around your picture. From here you can also choose if you want a thick or thin border.

The Picture Effects option provides options for adding shadows, reflections, glows, soft edges, and other options. (See Figure 13-8.)

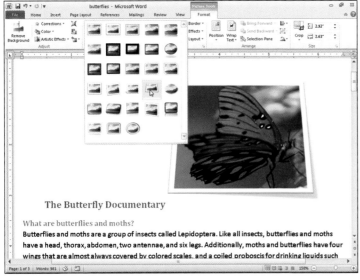

Figure 13-7
Applying a picture style.

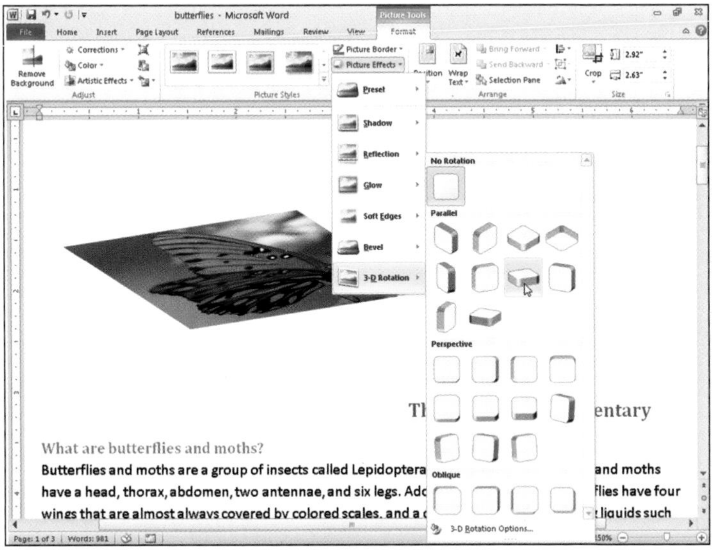

Figure 13-8
Adding picture effects.

The Picture Layout option lets you use your picture in a diagram. See "Symbolizing with SmartArt" later in this chapter.

Cropping the Picture

Sometimes you only want part of what appears in the picture. With the Word tools, it's easy to cut away the portions you don't want. Called *cropping*, the process removes unwanted portions of an image.

1. Select the picture you want to crop and then choose Picture Tools > Format > Size > Crop. (You don't need to click the arrow under the Crop button.) Your mouse pointer turns into a cropping tool, and instead of selection handles the picture has cropping handles, as shown in Figure 13-9.

Cropping handles   Crop button

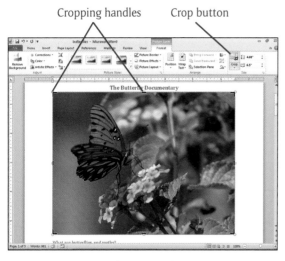

Figure 13-9
Cropping the picture.

2. Drag a cropping handle to begin the cropping process. The mouse pointer changes to a black cross, as shown in Figure 13-10. You may need to crop from several sides of your image. As you drag a cropping handle, a line appears representing the new picture edge.

Mouse pointer

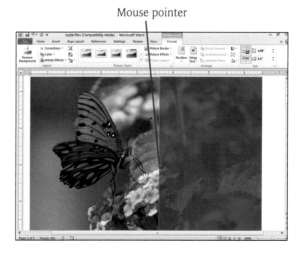

Figure 13-10
Drag from an image edge.

Tip

If you crop too much off the image, drag the cropping handle the opposite way. What you cropped reappears.

3. Click the Crop button again or press the Esc key to turn off the cropping feature.

Wrapping Text Around a Picture

In most situations, the picture doesn't appear on a page by itself. There is related or explanatory text around the picture. You can control how the text appears surrounding the image. By default, Word places the image in-line with the text, which means the image appears where you inserted it; if you move the text on the same line, the image moves as well.

Other choices allow you more flexibility in placing the image. If you choose the Tight text wrapping option, the text wraps around the image and stays pretty close to the image. However, if you move the text, the image doesn't move. It remains in the same position. Square and Tight wrapping are very similar, except that if your picture has an irregular shape, the Tight option wraps around the shape as well.

Other choices include placing the image on top of the text; however, that's not typically a good idea because you can't read the text underneath the image. You can have the image under the text, but if the image is dark, you may not be able to easily read the text on top of the image.

You position text around the graphic by first making sure you have the picture selected, then choosing Picture Tools > Format > Arrange > Wrap Text and making a selection. Figure 13-11 shows you the text wrapped tightly around the picture.

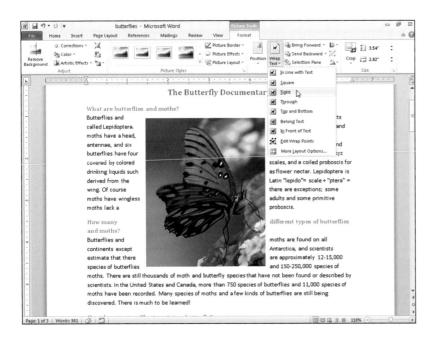

Figure 13-11
Wrapping text around the image.

Inserting Clip Art

WHILE MOST OFFICE applications have the ability to insert clip art into a file, adding clip art to a document brings both interest and distraction to an otherwise dull document. Office ships with hundreds of clip art images and thousands more are available online, free from Microsoft. Office stores clip art in collections with keywords so you can easily locate the image you want. Whatever the topic, you are sure to find a clip art image that compliments it. Here is how you can add clip art to a document:

1. Click the cursor where you want a picture, and choose Insert > Illustrations > Clip Art. The Clip Art pane appears on the right side of the screen.

2. In the Search For box, type a word or short phrase that best describes the kind of image you want. For example, typing *dairy* brings up a collection of artwork ranging from cows to cheese to milk cartons.

3. Click the Go button. Office displays the available clip art that matches your request (see Figure 13-12).

4. Click the image you want. The image appears in the document, as shown in Figure 13-13.

5. Click the Close button to close the Clip Art pane.

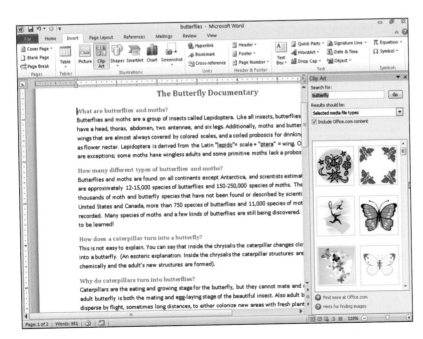

Figure 13-12
Click the clip art graphic you want to use.

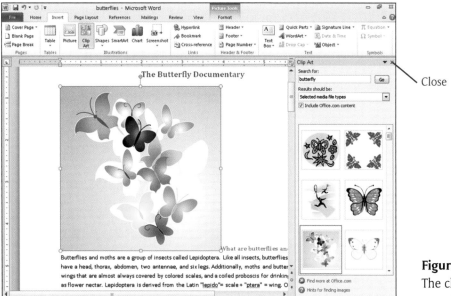

Close

Figure 13-13
The clip art image appears in your document.

Tip

Using the Picture Tools > Format tab, you can perform most of the same modifications to clip art as you can to photographs.

Using Shapes

EVEN IF YOU DO NOT have an artistic bone in your body, you can still draw with the Word drawing features. You can draw arrows, boxes, stars, circles, callouts, and dozens of other objects. The Shapes feature is also available in Excel, PowerPoint, and Publisher.

Follow these steps to draw a shape:

1. Click the cursor where you want a shape to appear and choose Insert > Illustrations > Shapes. A gallery of shapes appears, as shown in Figure 13-14.

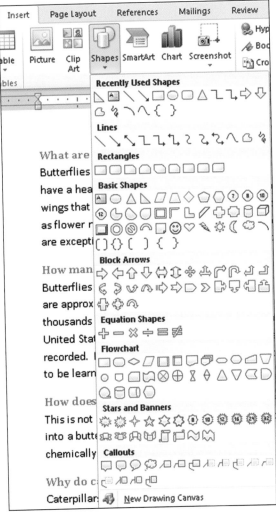

Figure 13-14
Selecting a predefined shape.

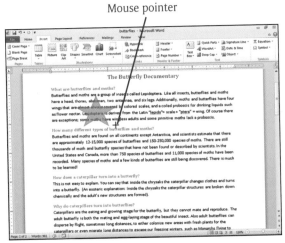

Figure 13-15
Drawing shapes.

Tip

To constrain the shape so it is equally sized, such as a perfect circle or a completely straight line, hold down the Shift key when drawing.

After you draw the shape, you can apply many different style changes to it. After you select the object, choose Drawing Tools > Format > Shape Styles. From there, you can do the following:

▶ Click the Shape Styles More button and select from the available styles. The choices you have depend on any theme you have assigned to your document (see Figure 13-16).

2. Choose the shape you want. The gallery closes, and your mouse pointer turns into a small black plus sign.

3. Click and drag in the document until the shape that appears is about the size you want (see Figure 13-15). When you release the mouse button, the shape object becomes selected.

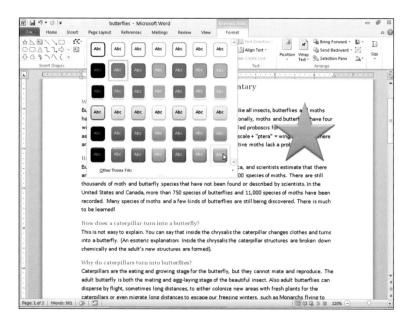

Figure 13-16
Changing a shape style.

► Click the Shape Fill option to change the object fill. Choices include solid fills, gradients, pictures, and textures.

► Click the Shape Outline option to change the border around the object. You can select a border color, size, and style.

► Click the Shape Effects option to add special effects, such as shadows, reflections, borders, or rotation (see Figure 13-17).

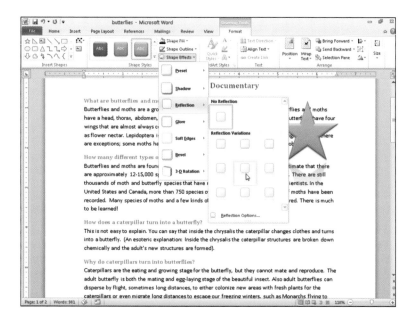

Figure 13-17
Adding shape effects.

Adding Screen Shots

SUPPOSE YOU'RE LOOKING at a Web page, and you want to insert a picture of it into your Word document. You can now easily do so with the new Screenshot function included with Office 2010. You can take a picture of the entire program window or use the Screen Clipping tool to select only a part of a window. Follow these steps:

1. Make sure the window you want to capture is *not* minimized. The Screenshot feature doesn't work with windows that are minimized. Use the Alt+Tab keys to easily switch between your applications.

2. In Word, click the cursor where you want to insert a screenshot and choose Insert > Illustrations > Screenshot. The Available Windows gallery appears, as shown in Figure 13-18.

3. Click the application of which you want a screen shot. The image appears in your Word document. (See Figure 13-19.)

Figure 13-19
A screenshot in a Word document.

If you only want part of the window for the screenshot, first of all, make sure the window you want to capture is right behind your document. If necessary, close other applications.

Choose Insert > Illustrations > Screenshot and click Screen Clipping. When the screen turns translucent and the mouse pointer becomes a cross, press and drag the mouse button (as shown in Figure 13-20) until you've selected the area you want. When you release the mouse button, the portion you clipped appears in your document.

Figure 13-18
Available windows.

Mouse pointer

Figure 13-20
Using screen clipping.

Managing Objects

NOW THAT YOU HAVE all of these objects in your document, you probably need to manipulate them a little. You can move them to different locations, adjust their size, or change their color. If you have multiple objects, you can align them, group them, or even place one object on top of or beneath another. In this section you will discover how to make any of those adjustments to any object, whether a picture, clip art, screenshot, or shape.

Moving Objects

If an object is not where you want it, you can easily move it to another place in the document. Click the image to select it, and then position the mouse pointer over any part of the selected image *except* the selection handles or the green rotation handle. The mouse pointer has four arrow heads. Drag the image to the desired position. As you can see in Figure 13-21, a lightly transparent version of the object indicates the new position. When you release the mouse button, the object moves to the new location.

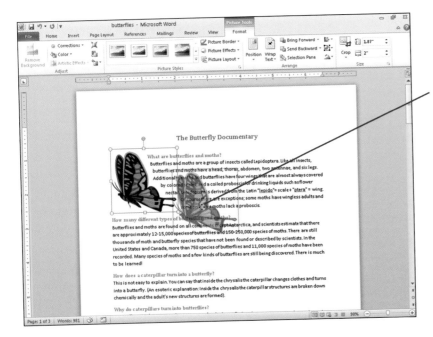

Mouse pointer

Figure 13-21
Dragging the object to a new position.

If you want to move the object just a little bit, you may find it easier to use the keyboard. After selecting the object, use the up, down, left, and right arrow keys to nudge the object into a different position.

Tip

If you want to move the object to a different page, use the cut and paste features.

Deleting Objects

Okay, this process is so simple it really doesn't deserve its own section, but putting it in one makes it easier for you to find. To delete an unwanted object, click the object to select it and press the Delete key. That's it—end of this section.

Resizing Objects

The object may not fit on the page exactly as you envisioned it. You can easily make the object smaller or larger. Just follow these steps:

1. Select the object you want to resize. The selection handles appear around the object.

2. Position the mouse pointer over one of the eight handles. (Do not select the green rotation handle.) Your mouse pointer turns into a white double-headed arrow, as shown in Figure 13-22.

3. Drag a selection handle in one of the following manners (as shown in Figure 13-23).

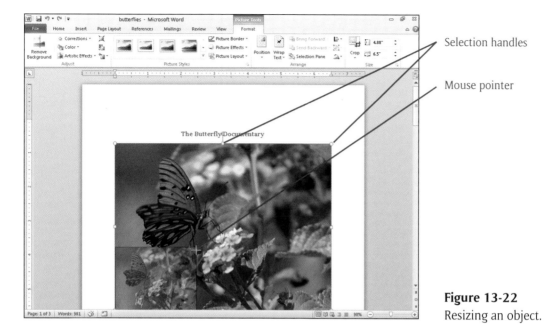

Selection handles

Mouse pointer

Figure 13-22
Resizing an object.

Tip

When you begin dragging a handle, the mouse pointer turns into a plus sign.

▶ Drag a top or bottom handle to change the object height.

▶ Drag a left or right side handle to change the object width.

▶ Drag a corner handle to resize both the height and width at the same time.

4. When the object is the desired size, release the mouse button.

Rotating Objects

Most graphics objects appear in the document in a horizontal or vertical pattern. And most of the time, that's exactly what you want. But in some cases, tilting the object at a fashionable angle provides just the right touch to a document. Word objects come with a rotation handle with which you can rotate an object clockwise or counterclockwise.

Select the object you want to rotate and position the mouse pointer over the green rotation handle. Drag the rotation handle clockwise or counter-clockwise until the graphics object is at the angle you want. Notice in Figure 13-23 that the mouse pointer turns into a circular arrow.

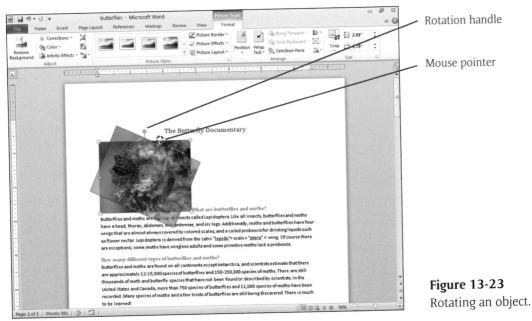

Rotation handle

Mouse pointer

Figure 13-23
Rotating an object.

Flipping Objects

If you want to reverse the direction of a picture or other object, you can flip it either vertically or horizontally. Take a look at the butterflies in Figure 13-24. In the picture on the left, the butterfly is facing right, but on the right side image, which is the same photograph, the butterfly is facing left. To flip an object, select the object and choose Picture Tools > Format (or Drawing Tools > Format) > Arrange > Rotate and choose Flip Horizontal or Flip Vertical.

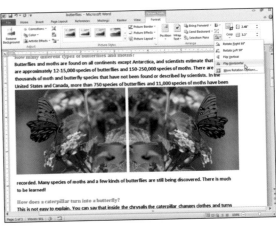

Figure 13-24
Flipping an image.

Aligning Objects

If your document contains multiple graphics objects, like the ones you see in Figure 13-25, you may want some of them to line up with each other. Word includes a tool to make aligning objects quick and easy. Just follow these steps:

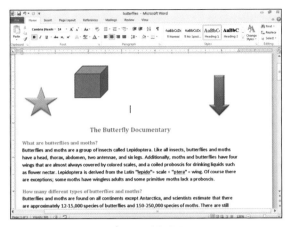

Figure 13-25
Multiple objects that need aligning.

1. Select the first object you want to align, then hold down the Ctrl key and select each additional object.

2. Choose Picture Tools > Format (or Drawing Tools > Format) > Arrange > Align. A menu of alignment options appears.

3. Choose one of the following alignment options:

   ▶ **Align Left:** Aligns the objects along their left edges

   ▶ **Align Center:** Centers the objects horizontally along their middles

   ▶ **Align Right:** Aligns the objects along their right edges

   ▶ **Align Top:** Aligns the objects along their top edges

   ▶ **Align Middle:** Centers the objects vertically along their middles

   ▶ **Align Bottom:** Aligns the objects along their bottom edges

Two additional options on the alignment choices apply when you have three or more objects selected. Distribute Horizontally calculates the total space from the left edge of the leftmost object to the right edge of the rightmost object and evenly divides the space between the selected objects. Distribute Vertically calculates the total space from the top edge of the top object to the bottom edge of the bottom object and evenly divides the space between the selected objects.

In Figure 13-26, I aligned the object tops and distributed the space horizontally.

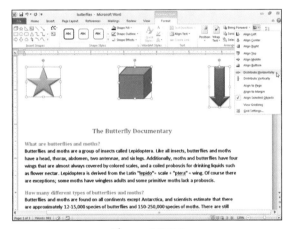

Figure 13-26
Selecting an alignment option.

Tip

Optionally, from the Align options, choose View Gridlines to display a grid that you can use to manually align the objects.

Stacking Objects

When you have multiple objects, sometimes you want them to overlap. Depending on the order in which the images were created, you may have one object covering up another object that you don't want covered. In Figure 13-27, you see a star, a box, and an arrow, with the arrow being the topmost object. In this sample, I want the box on the bottom and the star on the top, making the arrow the middle of the three objects.

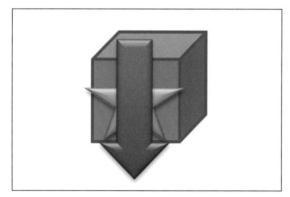

Figure 13-27
Incorrectly stacked objects.

When you restack objects, you can send an object back one object at a time or push it to the lowest object. Or you can bring an object forward one object at a time or bring it to the top of the stack. Follow these steps:

1. Select the object you want to reorder.

2. Choose Drawing Tools > Format > Arrange.

3. Choose one of the Order Objects options: Bring to Front, Send to Back, Bring Forward, or Send Backward.

Now take a look at the objects in Figure 13-28. I selected the arrow and chose Drawing Tools > Format > Arrange > Send Backward.

Figure 13-28
After changing the stacking order.

Grouping Objects

You can group multiple objects together to form a single object, which makes moving, resizing, and reshaping objects much easier. For example, instead of resizing each of four objects individually, you can group them together and resize only one. A really nice feature about the Group function is that if you need to, you can easily ungroup the objects, make any desired individual changes, and then quickly regroup them.

Select the objects you want grouped together and choose Drawing Tools > Format > Arrange > Group. In Figure 13-29, you see three independent objects on the right and one grouped object on the left. If you want to ungroup the object, select it and choose Drawing Tools > Format > Arrange > Ungroup. To regroup, select any one of the original objects and choose Drawing Tools > Format > Arrange > Regroup.

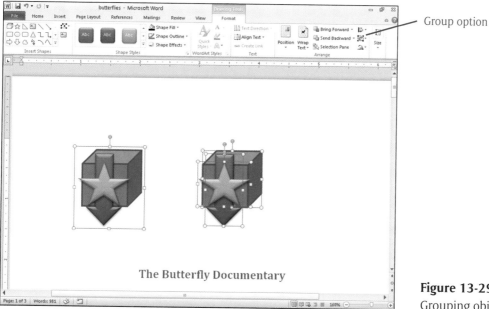

Group option

Figure 13-29
Grouping objects.

Symbolizing with SmartArt

ANOTHER ELEMENT YOU CAN PLACE in your document is called SmartArt. SmartArt objects are diagrams that show relationships, product cycles, workflow processes, and such. Using a diagram allows your viewers to better visualize a concept or idea.

First you must select the diagram type, and then you can customize it to meet your specific needs. There are seven basic diagram types, although each type contains quite a few variations. Here are the different diagram types:

> **Other Office Programs**
>
> Diagrams are also available in PowerPoint and Excel.

- ▶ **List:** Use this type for describing related items, usually sequential or showing a progression.

- ▶ **Process:** Use this type for describing how a concept or physical process changes over time. Figure 13-30 is an example of a process diagram.

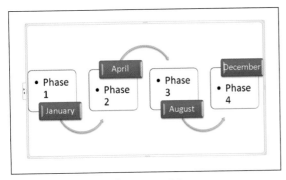

Figure 13-30
A process diagram.

▶ **Cycle:** Use this type to show progress from one stage to another when the process repeats itself.

▶ **Hierarchy:** Use this type to describe relationships between items or people, as shown in Figure 13-31. A company organization chart is an example of a hierarchy diagram.

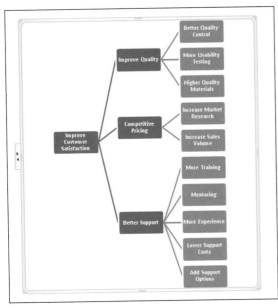

Figure 13-31
A hierarchy diagram.

▶ **Relationship:** Use this type to describe how two or more items are connected to each other.

▶ **Matrix:** Use this type for showing the relationship between the whole and its components.

▶ **Pyramid:** Use this for showing proportional or interconnected relationships.

Creating SmartArt

Begin by selecting Insert > Illustrations > SmartArt. The Choose a SmartArt Graphic dialog box shown in Figure 13-32 appears. Select the diagram type you want, and then from the List section in the middle, choose the diagram subtype and click OK. For the illustrations in this section, I am using a picture organization chart which is a hierarchy diagram.

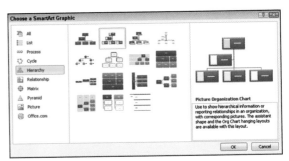

Figure 13-32
Choose the type of SmartArt you want to create.

Removing Diagram Shapes

Later in this chapter you will see how you can add additional shapes to your diagram. If, however, your diagram has shapes you do not want or need, you can easily delete them. In Figure 13-32, you see an organization diagram that automatically begins with a high level, an assistant level, and three sublevels. If you don't want the Assistant box, for example, you can remove it. Simply click the border edge of the shape you want to remove.

When the shape is selected, you see eight selection handles around the box. Press the Delete key to delete the unwanted shape.

Adding Text to a Diagram

Notice that each box in the diagram has a text placeholder. To add text to your diagram you *could* click each individual placeholder and type the desired text. A faster way, however, is to use the Text pane that appears on the left side of the diagram (see Figure 13-33). Selection handles surrounding the graphics shape are tied to your insertion point location on the Text pane. As you enter text, it automatically resizes to fit in the selected diagram shape.

Working with Hierarchy Levels

In the Text pane, when you press Enter, another blank line and a corresponding shape appear on the diagram. Since a hierarchy diagram (such as an organization chart), usually includes different levels, called *branches*, Word by default provides several higher headings and a few lower headings. You can promote or demote these headings as needed. In the Text pane, click anywhere in the line you want to promote or demote and do one of the following:

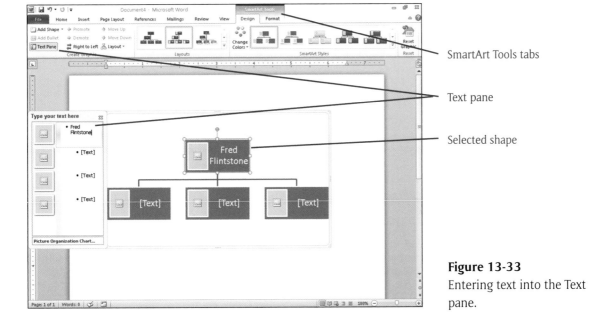

SmartArt Tools tabs

Text pane

Selected shape

Figure 13-33
Entering text into the Text pane.

To close the Text pane, choose SmartArt Tools > Design > Create Graphic > Text pane. Click it again to redisplay the Text pane.

▶ Press the Tab key to demote to a lower level. Optionally, choose SmartArt Tools > Design > Create Graphic > Demote.

▶ Press the Shift+Tab key to promote to a higher level. Optionally, choose SmartArt Tools > Design > Create Graphic > Promote.

As you promote or demote the text, the graphic immediately reflects the changes (see Figure 13-34).

Adding Diagram Shapes

The SmartArt Tools Design tab contains a button to add shapes; however, in most situations it is generally easiest to add shapes using the Text pane. Simply click at the end of the text in the shape located before where you want the new shape. Press Enter and the Text pane provides another line for typing and a shape to go with it. You can then add as many shapes as you want.

Unlike the hierarchy-type diagrams, the list, process, cycle, relationship, and matrix diagrams do not have branches, which makes them travel in a single direction. Look at the Text pane and diagram in Figure 13-35, where you see five shapes forming a circle. When working with these types of diagrams, all the Text pane lines are on the same level.

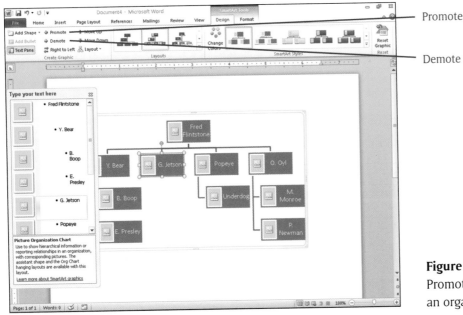

Promote

Demote

Figure 13-34
Promoting and demoting in an organization chart.

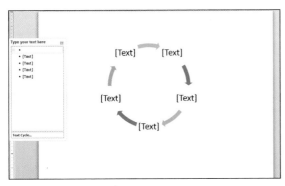

Figure 13-35
A single-level Text pane.

When adding shapes to a hierarchy diagram, you have additional decisions to make, such as at what level you want the new shape placed. If you are adding a peer-level shape, you use the Text pane. Click at the beginning of the line where you want the new shape and press the Enter key. On the resulting blank line, type the text for the new shape.

If, however, you want to add an assistant-level shape, follow these steps:

Add Assistant

The Add Assistant feature is available only if you are working with an organization chart.

1. In the Text pane, click the line for the shape to which you want to add an assistant.

2. Choose SmartArt Tools > Design > Create Graphic and click the Add Shape arrow. A list of choices appears.

3. Choose Add Assistant. The Assistant box appears. In the Text pane, instead of a bullet point like the other shapes, the Assistant appears at the bottom of the list with a right-angled arrow (see Figure 13-36).

Assistant

Figure 13-36
Adding an assistant.

In this sample diagram, there is a picture box for each box. You can click the picture box, and select a picture for each one. (See Figure 13-37.)

Click here to add a picture

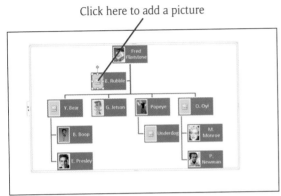

Figure 13-37
Adding pictures to the shape.

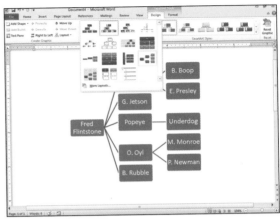

Figure 13-38
Select a different layout.

Changing the SmartArt Layout

If after working on your diagram you decide you should have chosen a different style, you do not have to start all over. Choose SmartArt Tools > Design > Layouts and select from the available layouts. As you pause your mouse over any layout, Live Preview shows you your chart as it would appear in the new layout. In Figure 13-38, you see the original organization chart changed to a horizontal hierarchy.

Remember that only an organization chart can have an assistant, so in this example, choosing a different layout forces the assistant to a peer level.

Changing Shapes

If you want to call special attention to a certain area of your diagram, you can change the shape. Optionally, you can change the shapes for all the diagram shape objects. For example, you want the assistant to be in the form of a circle instead of the square cornered box. Or perhaps you want a box to have rounded corners instead of the square corners.

Select the shape you want to change and choose SmartArt Tools > Format > Shapes > Change Shape. A gallery of shapes like the one you see in Figure 13-39 appears. Choose a new shape, and the diagram reflects the change.

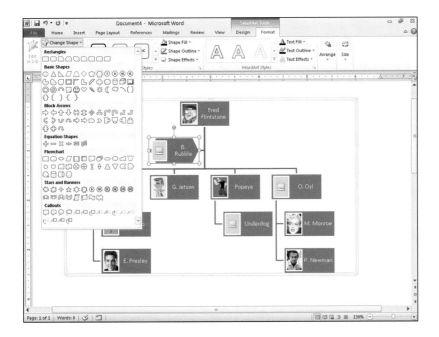

Figure 13-39
Selecting a new shape.

Tip

Changing shapes may force the text size on all the shapes to change. If your shape size needs modifying, choose SmartArt Tools > Format > Shapes and choose Larger or Smaller.

Changing a Diagram Style

If you want to add a little style to your diagram, you can select from a variety of predefined coordinated styles that would look good with your current diagram layout. You can also change the colors assigned to the diagram. The color choices available depend on the Word theme.

If you want to change the diagram colors, choose SmartArt Tools > Design > SmartArt Styles > Change Colors. A drop-down gallery similar to what you see in Figure 13-40 appears. Again, as you pause your mouse over any choice, Live Preview shows you how it looks on your diagram.

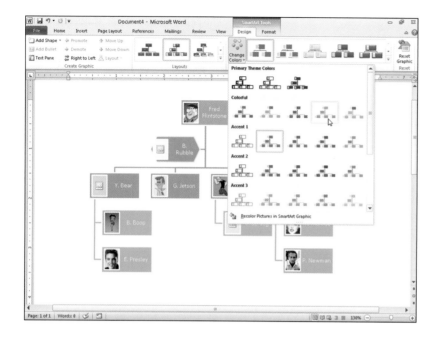

Figure 13-40
Adding a little color to your diagram.

If you want to change the box styles, such as adding shadows, embossing, or three-dimensional angles, choose SmartArt Tools > Design > SmartArt Styles and click the More button. Select from the choices you see. Figure 13-41 shows the diagram with an intense color depth and shadows.

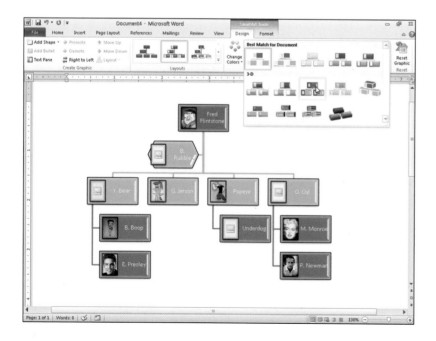

Figure 13-41
Adding diagram special effects.

You can also change an individual shape, color, or effects by selecting the shape and choosing SmartArt Tools > Format > Shape Styles and choosing from the number of different options provided, which include the shape fill color, outline attributes, and shape effects. See the Assistant shape in Figure 13-42.

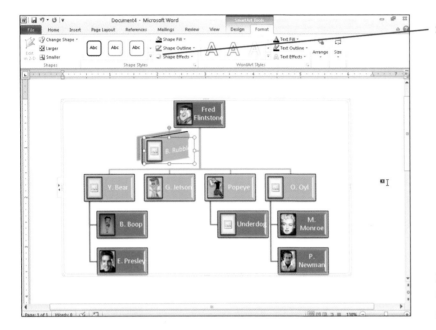

Shape Effects

Figure 13-42
Changing individual shape attributes.

Part 4
Word Tools

Picture Microsoft Word 2010 as the Swiss Army Knife of word processing. Your main tool, Microsoft Word 2010, is made up of many smaller tools. We all need the right tool for the job. In this part of the book, you'll discover Word tools to enhance the quality of your document and the speed in which you create them. You'll also discover ways to collaborate with others on a document and lots of ways to customize Word to better fit the way you work.

Employing Tools for
Quality

PICTURE YOURSELF AS A SKILLED CRAFTSPERSON—a carpenter, for example. Whether you're building a bird house or a beach house, you know you need to use the right tools to get the job done. So it is with Microsoft Word. Different tasks require different tools, and it's important to use the right tool for the job.

Up to this point, you've used quite a few of the basic Word features. This chapter is an assortment of some additional tools provided with Word that can make your word-processing tasks easier and help improve the quality of your writing.

As you work with Word, you may find you use some of the tools a lot and other tools very seldom, but as you proceed with your Word documents, I'm sure you'll find yourself looking at your screen and thinking, "Aha! I can use the [*xxxx*] feature to accomplish this."

Correcting Errors

WHETHER YOU ARE WRITING the great American novel, a standard business letter, or a résumé, spelling or grammatical errors can ruin the impression you're trying to create. Not only does Word have spelling and grammar checkers to correct document errors, it also has a thesaurus to help you find just the right word to convey your ideas.

Word has built-in dictionaries and grammatical rule sets that it uses to check your document. Word can identify possible problems as you type, and it also can run a special spelling and grammar check that provides you with more information about the problems and tools for fixing them. And although they have been greatly improved in Word 2010, these features aren't infallible; if you type "To *air* is human" instead of "To *err* is human," Word probably won't be able to tell you that you're wrong. However, combined with a good proofreading, these tools are very helpful.

Checking Spelling and Grammar as You Go

As you type your document, Word operates the spell checker tool in the background and identifies problems. Word tags potential spelling errors with a red wavy line under them. Right-click on an unrecognized word, and you see a shortcut menu appear with possible suggestions for correction (see the example in Figure 14-1). Click on the correct spelling, and the misspelled or unrecognized

word is replaced with your selection. Occasionally, Word cannot provide a suggestion. In those cases, you need to correct the error yourself.

Add to Dictionary

If Word interprets a word as a misspelling, but it is a word you use frequently, such as a name or business term, you can add it to your Dictionary so Word won't see it as a misspelling.

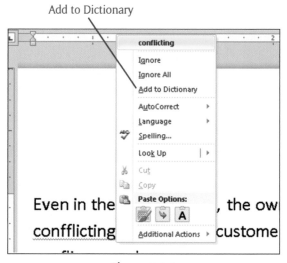

Figure 14-1
Fixing errors as you type.

As with spelling errors, Word identifies potential grammatical errors by placing a green wavy line under the questionable text. Right-click on the questionable word or phrase to display a shortcut menu with suggested grammatical corrections. Click the appropriate option, and Word replaces the incorrect word or phrase with your selection. Sometimes, however, Word cannot provide a suggestion; in those cases, you need to correct the error yourself.

Check for Yourself

Do *not* rely on Word's spell check and grammar features to catch all your errors. The tools are very helpful, but they are far from perfect and can miss many items. They can also flag items as errors that really are okay and can suggest wrong ways to fix both real problems and false errors. You alone are the one who knows what you want your document to say. Proofread it yourself!

Running a Spelling and Grammar Check

If you don't want to correct items as you type, Word can run a Spelling and Grammar check at the same time. Running the Spelling and Grammar check also provides additional options for dealing with incorrect items. Use the following steps:

1. Position the insertion point at the beginning of the document to check the entire document. If you only want to check a portion of the text, select the text first.

2. Choose Review > Proofing > Spelling and Grammar. If there are no errors in the document, a message box appears advising you

that the checks are complete; otherwise, Word displays the Spelling and Grammar dialog box shown in Figure 14-2, referencing the first error, whether spelling or grammar.

Tip

Optionally, press F7 to launch the Spelling and Grammar check.

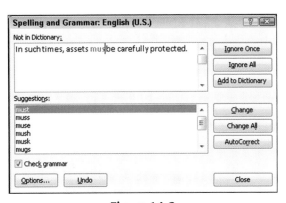

Figure 14-2
Using the Spelling and Grammar check to improve your document.

3. If the error is a spelling error, do one of the following:

   ▶ **Ignore Once:** Click this if you don't want to correct this instance of the spelling.

   ▶ **Ignore All:** Click this if you don't want to correct any instances of the spelling.

   ▶ **Add to Dictionary:** Choose this to add the word to the Dictionary so that in the future Word won't flag it as an error.

   ▶ **Change:** Choose a word from the Suggestions list and then click Change, which changes just this incident of the spelling mistake.

▶ **Change All:** After selecting a replacement from the Suggestions list, choose Change All if you think you could have made the same mistake more than once.

▶ **AutoCorrect:** After making a selection from the Suggestions list, click this option to add the unknown word and the correction as an AutoCorrect entry. If you make the same misspelling in a future document, Word automatically changes it to the correction.

4. If the error is a grammatical error, such as you see in Figure 14-3, take one of these actions:

Tip

If you don't want Word to check grammar, remove the checkmark from the Check Grammar option.

Check Grammar option

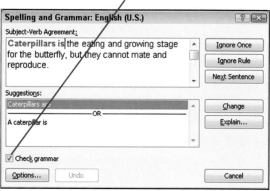

Figure 14-3
Catching grammatical mishaps.

▶ **Ignore Once:** Click this option if you don't want to change this instance of the grammatical problem.

▶ **Ignore Rule:** Click this option to ignore all instances of the same grammatical problem type.

▶ **Next Sentence:** Click this option to skip the error and continue the check. All instances of the same error are ignored.

▶ **Change:** Choose an option from the Suggestions list and then click Change, which changes just this incident of the grammatical mistake.

▶ **Explain:** Click this option to launch an article that explains the error and offers suggestions for avoiding the error.

5. When all potential mistakes are identified, Word notifies you that the Spelling and Grammar check is complete. Click the OK button.

Changing Spelling Options

Word provides quite a few options for both the spelling and grammar correction features. For example, if you don't want Word to check your spelling or your grammar as you type, you can turn off the feature. Click the File tab and choose Options. Click the Proofing category.

From the Proofing section, as shown in Figure 14-4, you can set or turn off any desired proofing options. Some of the options apply to all Office 2010 applications, and some apply only to Microsoft Word. There are even a few options that apply only to the current document.

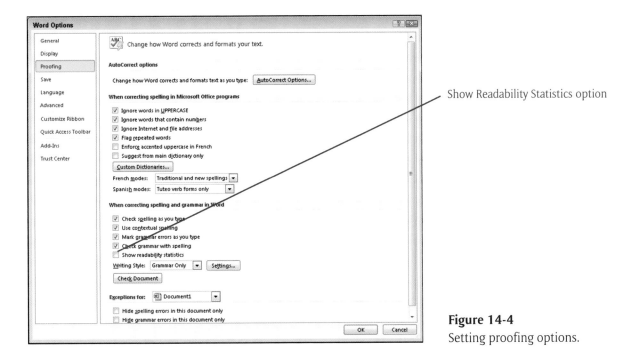

Show Readability Statistics option

Figure 14-4
Setting proofing options.

Readability Statistics

From the Word Options dialog box, click the Show Readability Statistics check box. After running a Spelling and Grammar check, Word displays statistics, such as the number of words, characters, paragraphs, and sentences, as well as average words per sentence or the readability grade level. See Figure 14-5 for an example.

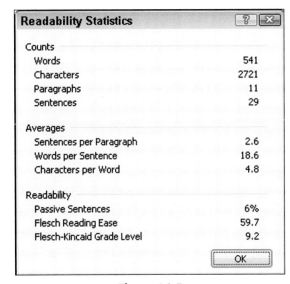

Figure 14-5
Viewing document statistics.

Finding Elusive Words with the Thesaurus

A KEY TO GOOD WRITING is using words that add interest and flair. However, remember that you need words appropriate for your audience. If you are addressing a group of grade school children, you'll use simpler words than if you are writing your college thesis. If you need a little help finding just the right word, try using Word's thesaurus.

Click anywhere in the word you want replaced and then choose Review > Proofing > Thesaurus. Optionally, press Shift+F7 to launch the thesaurus. A Research pane similar to the one shown in Figure 14-6 appears on the right side of the screen and displays various meanings of the current word and possible replacements. If you don't see the exact word you want, click a similar word, which displays its synonyms. Click the Back button to return to the previous word. When you locate the word that best fits your document, click the arrow next to it and choose Insert. Word replaces the current word with your selection.

Click the Research Close button (X) to close the Research pane.

Figure 14-6
Locating synonyms with the thesaurus.

Using Find and Replace

ORD'S FIND AND REPLACE features are real time savers. For example, you can quickly find out if you covered a particular topic in a lengthy report, or you can changes names, dates, and prices throughout documents with just a few keystrokes.

Using Find

Word's Find command is useful when you want to seek out text that you may have trouble visually locating in a document. The Find command doesn't change any text; it simply locates and highlights the specified text for you. Follow these steps:

1. Choose Home > Editing > Find, or press the Ctrl+F keys. The Navigation pane appears on the left side of the screen (see Figure 14-7).

2. In the text box, type the word or phrase that you want to search for. As you type, Word automatically highlights and displays each occurrence of the word or phrase you're looking for.

Starting Point

The Find command begins its search at the location of the insertion point.

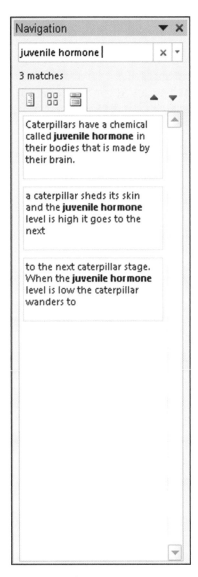

Figure 14-7
Finding document text.

3. The Navigation pane also lists the other occurrences of the searched text. Click any occurrence to instantly jump to the text. If you want to discontinue the search, simply close the Navigation pane.

Tip

Unless you specify whole words (see the next section), Word locates any instance containing the letters you specify. For example, if you enter *read* in the Find box, Word also locates words like *bread* or *reading*.

Extending Search Options

If you need to be a little more specific about what you're searching for, Word provides a number of extended options to assist you.

Open the Navigation pane by choosing Home > Editing > Find (or press the Ctrl+F keys), and in the search text box, type the word or phrase for which you want to search. Click the More Options arrow next to the text box, which displays a menu like the one you see in Figure 14-8. Choose Options, which displays the Find Options dialog box (also shown in Figure 14-8), and then select the options you want. Click OK when you are finished, and Word continues the search using the options you selected.

Take a brief look at the most commonly used options:

▶ **Match Case:** Check this to locate instances that match the upper- and lowercase letters as you entered them in the Find box. For example, if you typed *Go*, Word will not locate *go* or *GO*.

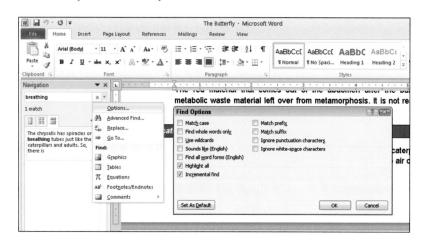

Figure 14-8
Specifying search options.

▶ **Find Whole Words Only:** Check this to locate instances of the entire word only. For example, if you enter *read* in the Find box, Word will ignore words like *bread* or *reading*.

▶ **Use Wildcards:** Check this to use the question mark (?) or asterisk (*) wildcards in your search. The ? character matches any single character, and the * character matches any number of characters. For example, if you enter *b?d* in the Find box, Word finds *bad*, *bed*, or *bidding*, but not bread. If you enter *b*d*, Word locates words like *bad*, *bed*, *abide*, *bidding*, *bread*, *bored*, and so forth.

Tip

Word also recognizes wildcard characters like the at sign (@) or angle bracket (<). See the Word Help system for a complete description.

▶ **Sounds Like:** Check this to locate instances that are phonetically the same as the text in the Find box. For example, if you entered *foul*, Word also locates *fowl*.

▶ **Find All Word Forms:** Check this to locate all grammatical forms of the search word. For example, if you enter *they*, Word also locates *their*, *theirs*, *them*, and *themselves*.

▶ **Highlight All:** Checked by default, this option tells Word to highlight all occurrences of the found text.

▶ **Incremental Find:** Also checked by default, the Incremental Find option allows Word to start searching as soon as you start typing in the Find box.

▶ **Match Prefix:** Check this to locate words that only begin, not contain or end, with the search word. For example, if you enter *mini*, Word also locates *minimum* or *miniature*, but not *administration*.

▶ **Match Suffix:** Check this to locate words that only end, not contain or begin, with the search word. For example, if you enter *ration*, Word also locates *demonstration* but not *rational*.

▶ **Ignore Punctuation Characters:** Check this to ignore punctuation marks, such as ' ? - " ! ; : , . and /. For example, if you entered *1478*, Word also locates *1,478* and *14.78*.

▶ **Ignore White-Space Characters:** Check this to ignore spaces and tabs. For example, if you enter *lonestar*, Word also locates *lone star*.

Finding Formatted Text

You can also locate text that contains a specified type of formatting. For example, you want to locate the word *apple*, but only if you underlined the word. Or perhaps you want to locate all text in the document in a 14-point Arial font. Follow these steps:

1. From the Navigation pane, click the down arrow next to the text box and choose Find Advanced. The Find and Replace dialog box opens.

2. Click the More button which expands the Find options, as shown in Figure 14-9. The More button turns into a Less button. Some of the options here are similar to those you viewed in the previous section.

Less button

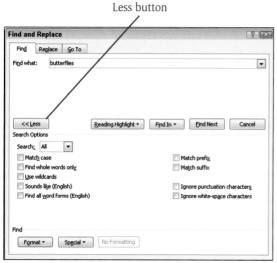

Figure 14-9
Expand the search options.

3. Click the Format button. You see a list of formatting options.

4. Click the formatting type you want to locate. Choices include Font, Paragraph, Tabs, Language, Frame, Style, and Highlight. A dialog box appropriate to your selection appears. In Figure 14-10 you see the Find Font dialog box.

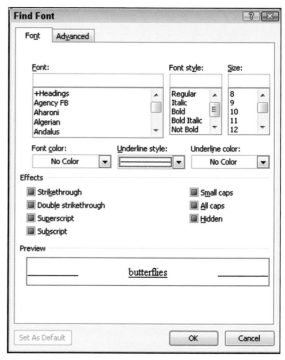

Figure 14-10
Searching for formatting.

5. Select the formatting you want to search for and then click OK, which returns you to the Find and Replace dialog box.

Tip

Instead of choosing font options from a dialog box, you can press a formatting shortcut key such as Ctrl+B for bold.

6. In the Find What text box, enter the text you want to search for. Or if you want to find the formatting only, regardless of the text, leave the Find What box empty.

7. Specify any other search options and click Find Next to begin your search. Click the Cancel button when you are finished.

Tip

Click the No Formatting button to remove any formatting specifications.

Figure 14-11
Searching for special characters.

Finding Special Characters

In Chapter 2, you discovered that Word hides many characters, such as the dots used for spaces, or an arrow for tabs, or even the paragraph mark ¶ at the end of a paragraph. You can have Word search for a number of special characters.

From the expanded Find and Replace dialog box, click the Special button. You see a list of formatting options, as shown in Figure 14-11. Choose the special character for which you want to search. Word places a code for the character in the Find What text box. Specify any other search options and click Find Next to begin your search.

Using Replace

If you want to locate some particular text and change it to something else, let Word do it for you with the Replace feature. The Replace feature is very similar to the Find function you just discovered. You can locate text and replace it with different text, or you can locate text and replace it with the same or different text, but perhaps with different formatting. Follow these simple steps:

1. Choose Home > Editing > Replace, or press the Ctrl+H keys. The Find and Replace dialog box appears with the Replace tab on top.

2. In the Find What text box, enter the text you want to search for.

3. Click in the Replace With text box and type a replacement word or phrase (see Figure 14-12).

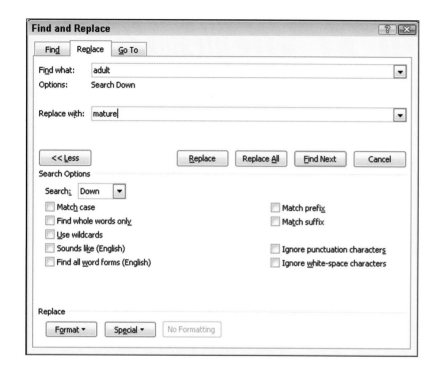

Figure 14-12
Entering Find and Replace text.

Replace with Nothing

To delete the "found" text, leave the Replace With text box empty. Word will replace the found text with nothing.

4. Specify any additional search or replace options, such as matching case or a particular format.

5. Click Find Next. Word locates the first match.

6. Choose one of the following:

   ▶ Click Replace if this is the text you want to change. Word replaces the text and locates the next occurrence.

   ▶ Click Replace All to replace all occurrences of the found text with the replacement text. Word displays a message box indicating how many occurrences it replaced. (See Figure 14-13.)

Tip

Use the Replace All button cautiously. Remember that Word takes you very literally. Make sure the Find and Replace options are exactly as you want them.

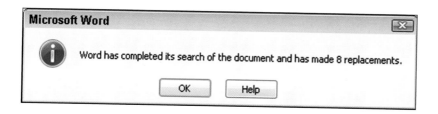

Figure 14-13
Using the Replace All command.

▶ Click Find Next to skip making changes on this occurrence and locate the next match.

7. Word notifies you when no more occurrences of the search text exist. Click OK to close the message box, and click Cancel to close the Find and Replace dialog box.

Applying Tools for
Speed

PICTURE YOURSELF RACING TO MEET the April 15th tax dead-line. You're feverishly filling out forms, performing calculations, and trying to remember all the details you know you're going to need. In order to make the process as quick and painless as possible, you have your tools ready: your calculator, your pencil, your receipts, and lots of caffeine.

Word includes a number of tools that help speed up the process of creating and editing documents, such as tools that can do your typing for you, and those that let you quickly make changes in your document. This chapter is about using Word tools so you can work as efficiently as you can.

Creating Bookmarks

JUST AS YOU USE A BOOKMARK to mark a certain place in a book, electronic bookmarks identify specified text locations for future reference. As an example, you might use a bookmark to help you quickly jump to certain topics in your document.

Tip

Bookmarks are useful for electronic reading only and do not affect a printed document.

Place the insertion point where you want to create a bookmark and choose Insert > Links > Bookmark. The Bookmark dialog box shown in Figure 15-1 appears.

Type a name for the bookmark and click Add. Word saves the bookmark and closes the Bookmark dialog box.

Tip

Bookmark names cannot include spaces or special characters except the underscore character (_).

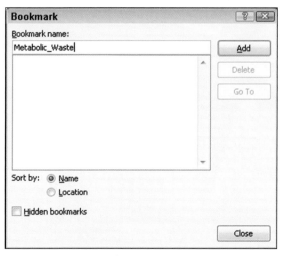

Figure 15-1
Creating a bookmark.

Now instead of scrolling through the document to locate the text, you can quickly jump to it. Click Insert > Links > Bookmark, which displays the Bookmark dialog box along with a list of all the bookmarks in your document. Select the bookmark you want and click Go To.

Optionally, you can get to a bookmark by using the Go To option, found in the Find and Replace dialog box. Choose Home > Editing, and then click the down arrow next to the Find option. Choose Go To. The Find and Replace dialog box appears with the Go To tab on top (see Figure 15-2).

Click Bookmark and then from the Enter Bookmark Name drop-down list, choose the bookmark you want. Click Go To and Word instantly jumps to the bookmark location.

Figure 15-2
Locating a bookmark.

Tip

Two alternative methods of displaying the
Go To option are pressing Ctrl+G or the
F5 key.

Specifying Hyperlinks

HYPERLINKS, SIMILAR TO bookmarks, take
you to a specific location. However, not only
can hyperlinks jump to a location in your
document, they can also jump to another file on
your computer, on your network, or to a Web page.
Like bookmarks, hyperlinks are useful for electronic
reading only and do not affect a printed document.

Word automatically creates some hyperlinks for
you. For example, if you type a Web address or
e-mail address, as soon as you press Enter or the
spacebar, Word underlines the area and creates the
link. The AutoFormat As You Type function is what
controls the automatic link creation behavior. You
will learn more about the AutoFormat As You Type
feature later in Chapter 17.

If you want to manually create a link, first select the
text or graphic you want the reader to click to launch
the hyperlink. Choose Insert > Links > Hyperlink,
which displays the Insert Hyperlink dialog box. The
Insert Hyperlink dialog box offers several different
options from which you can select:

▶ If you want to link to a different file or to a
Web site, choose Existing File or Web Page.
For a different file, locate and select the file
name so when the user clicks the link, the
referenced file will open. However, if you
want to link to a Web site, enter the Web
address in the Address text box. When the
user clicks the link, the Web browser will
open to the referenced Web page. Figure
15-3 illustrates a link to a Web site.

Figure 15-3
Creating a hyperlink to a Web site.

- If you want to link to a different location in the current document, click the Place in This Document button, then specify which heading or bookmark you want to reference. When users click on this link they will be redirected to the specified location.

- If you want to create a new document when the hyperlink is clicked, choose Create New Document and then enter a name and folder for the new document.

- If you want to send an e-mail when the link is selected, click the E-Mail Address button, then enter the recipients e-mail address and a subject. When the user clicks the link, the user's e-mail program starts. Figure 15-4 illustrates the e-mail link options.

Word displays hyperlinks in a different color text and with an underline. Press Ctrl and click any link to jump to the specified location. As you hover your mouse over the link, a tip appears with instructions for following the link and a notation to where the link will take you (see Figure 15-5).

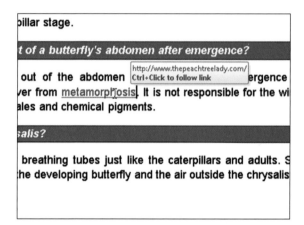

Figure 15-5
Hold down the Ctrl key and click the link.

Figure 15-4
Creating an e-mail hyperlink.

Generating Text with Building Blocks

ARE YOU TIRED OF TYPING your address over and over when composing letters? Or do you have a standard phrase that you need to frequently add to your documents? Word provides a couple of different methods you can use to quickly add the text into your document.

The first method is to use Word's AutoCorrect function, which you discovered in Chapter 2. Not only can you add words and symbols, but you can also generate a text paragraph or even a graphic with your signature. The only problem is that the AutoCorrect function limits each entry to 255 characters.

Office 2010 is designed to be modular, so it uses a function called *building blocks* that are divided into 14 different galleries. Think of building blocks as recycled material. You've already been introduced to some of the building blocks when you discovered some of the built-in options in Headers, Footers, Page Numbering, and Quick Tables. Take a brief look at some of the different building block galleries and what type of element each gallery holds:

▶ **AutoText:** Holds small text entries or graphics that you want to use again, such as a standard contract clause or a mission statement.

▶ **Bibliography:** Holds text in the form of a reference list of works by author, subject, or other relevant information.

▶ **Cover Pages:** Holds preformatted cover pages, such as those you might use for reports. Figure 15-6 illustrates one of the sample Cover Page building blocks.

▶ **Quick Parts:** Holds miscellaneous building blocks that don't fit any other gallery.

▶ **Equations:** Holds predefined equations objects.

▶ **Footers:** Holds a number of predefined footers that appear at the bottom of the page.

▶ **Headers:** Holds a number of predefined headers that appear at the top of the page.

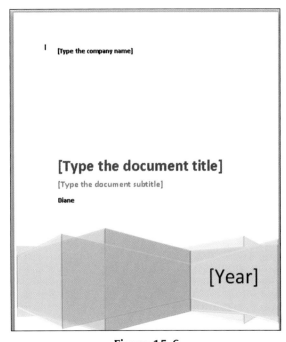

Figure 15-6
The Cubicles cover page.

▶ **Page Numbers:** There are four different page number galleries that hold predefined page numbers—some at the current location, some at the bottom or top of the page, and some in the margins.

▶ **Table of Contents:** Holds predefined tables of contents that are created based on heading styles in the document.

▶ **Tables:** Holds a series of predefined tables, such as those in the Quick Tables.

▶ **Text Box:** Holds predefined text box layouts and formatting.

▶ **Watermarks:** Holds several predefined watermarks, such as Draft, Do Not Copy, or Confidential. Watermarks are in light gray shading and appear in the background of a document, as shown in Figure 15-7.

Watermark

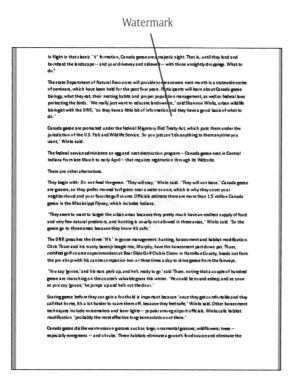

Figure 15-7
A Watermark building block.

Inserting Building Blocks

Now that you see all the different types of building blocks, take a look at how to insert any of the existing blocks into your document. Just follow these steps:

1. Make sure you are in Print Layout or Web Layout view. (You can insert a Building Block while in Draft view, but you will not be able to see it.)

2. Position the insertion point where you want to insert the building block.

3. Choose Insert > Text > Quick Parts > Building Blocks Organizer. The Building Blocks Organizer appears.

4. Click a building block to display a preview on the right side, as shown in Figure 15-8.

Figure 15-8
Click the Building Block Organizer to see a preview.

5. Click the Insert button. Word inserts the building block into your document.

Creating Custom Building Blocks

If none of the predefined building blocks suits your needs, you can create your own custom building block. Additionally, you can start with one of

278

the existing building blocks and customize it to a better fit and then save it for future use. Just follow these simple steps:

1. Create the text and formatting for the new building block.

2. Select the area you want to save as a building block

3. Choose Insert > Text > Quick Parts > Save Selection to Quick Part Gallery. The Create New Building Block dialog box appears.

4. Fill in the appropriate information, as shown in Figure 15-9.

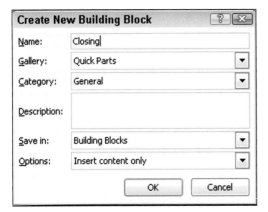

Figure 15-9
Naming a custom building block.

▶ **Name:** By default, Word picks up the first few characters of the text you selected; however, you can give the building block a short, more descriptive name.

▶ **Gallery:** Select which of the Gallery types you want. Most likely, you'll want to use the Quick Parts gallery.

▶ **Category:** You can further differentiate the items in the gallery by creating and assigning categories.

▶ **Description:** Enter a longer description to help you identify the building block and its purpose.

▶ **Save In:** Select whether to save the new item under the Building Blocks area, which makes it available no matter which template you use, or choose to save it only if you are using the Normal template.

▶ **Options:** Choices include whether to insert the building block at the current cursor position, start a new paragraph and then insert the building block, or to start a new page and then insert the building block.

5. Click OK. Now when you open the Building Blocks Organizer, you'll see your custom building block.

When you exit Word, you see the message box shown in Figure 15-10. Choose Save to save the changes.

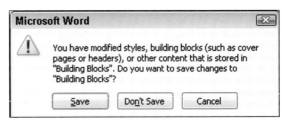

Figure 15-10
Saving building blocks for future use.

Tip

If you no longer want a custom building block, display the Building Blocks Organizer, select the building block you want to delete, and click the Delete button. Click Yes to the confirmation message that appears.

Adding Automatic Fields

WORD HAS A FEATURE called *fields* that you can use as placeholders in your document. You typically use fields with the kind of data that might change such as a date, numbering, or page numbers. In fact, in Chapter 4, when you created a header or footer, you probably used a field to insert the page number. Then in Chapter 7, you discovered fields when you created a Table of Contents and then you used fields again in Chapter 9, when you created form letters using Word's mail merge feature, such as when you specified a greeting or address block. Let's take a look at a few other fields.

Placing a Document Property

One group of Word fields is called Document Properties. And just like it sounds, document properties are miscellaneous pieces of information *about* your document. Pieces of information such as the document title, or the author are only a click away.

Before we place a document property into our document, let's take a brief look at where we can find and modify document properties. You'll find them on the Document Info screen. Click the File tab. From the Info screen, such as you see in Figure 15-11, on the right side of the screen, you see the document properties such as the Title, Comments, Author and lots of statistical information. If you click the mouse next to many of the choices, such as Title or Comments, you can type your own information into the text box. Word saves the document properties with a document, and anyone who opens the document can view the properties.

Figure 15-11
Viewing document properties.

But if you also want a property listed in the document body, position the cursor where you want the field and choose Insert > Text > Quick Parts > Document Property and choose the property you want from the list seen in Figure 15-12.

Figure 15-12
Document property list.

All properties appear as fields with a field code box surrounding it. As you pause your mouse over the property, a gray field surrounds it. If you click the field, you can edit or format the field as desired. If you want to delete the field, click the (non-printing) field tab that appears at the top left of the field and press the Delete key. Figure 15-13 illustrates a document with the Comment field displayed.

> Wastage is estimated at 15% across all food related product (validated trials). This will reduce once the 'Nudle-Rac' and associated IT systems
>
> Training, Quality Management Systems and Franchise Operations Manu completed effectively for $220,000 by the end of year 1.
>
> Plans for starting a Diane's Noodles franchise in Indiana

Figure 15-13
Displaying a document property.

Some of the document properties pull data from the properties under File > Info, and others remain blank so you can enter your own data. Then, if you want to use the property again, in another document location, Word remembers what you entered. For example, suppose you want your customer's company name in the document several times so you add the property field Company. You then type your customer company name in the first Company field box. If you then add the field

Company somewhere else in the document, it will automatically replicate what you entered in the first Company field. And, if you need to change the name, changing it in one field, changes it in all the Company fields.

Adding Field Codes

There are many other types of fields you can use in a Word document including statistical information and automatic numbering. Suppose you want the document creation date entered into a document. Using the Create Date field, you can insert the date and time that the document was first saved with its current name. Or suppose you have a document that you always want to display the current date.

When you create a document and you type in a date, the date is said to be *static*, meaning it doesn't change when the date changes. So if you type September 16, 2010, the document will always read September 16, 2010. If, however, you want the date or time to change with the calendar, you need to insert a *dynamic* date or time. Word handles these in the form of a field code. Just follow these steps:

1. Position the insertion point where you want the date.

2. Choose Insert > Text > Date and Time. The Date and Time dialog box appears (see Figure 15-14).

3. Click the date format you want to use.

4. Click the "Update automatically" check box and then click OK.

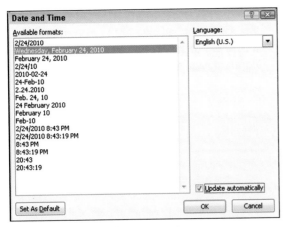

Figure 15-14
Adding an automatic date in the format you need.

Tip

If you only want the current static date and not a dynamic date, do not select the Update Automatically option.

Word inserts the current date field into the document. As you hover your mouse over the date, the field becomes shaded and if you click the field, the field placeholder appears (see Figure 15-15). Fields update automatically each time you open the document, but if you want to update a field manually, click the Update button at the top of the field placeholder.

Figure 15-15
The field placeholder.

Using Automatic Numbering

By design, the AutoNum field sequentially numbers paragraphs but there are many other practical uses for it. For example, suppose you have a lengthy document with a list of similar type elements; such as headings, tables, or figure references (such as this book), or graphics. You can use the AutoNum field to keep track of them for you.

In Figure 15-16 you see a document with headings. In front of each Heading, I inserted an AutoNum command. I also added the word Question in front of the AutoNum. So you see each Heading 1 with Question 1., Question 2., and so forth. The advantage to using the AutoNum field code is that if I move the third heading up to the top of the document, Word automatically renumbers the paragraphs for me.

Automatic Numbering field

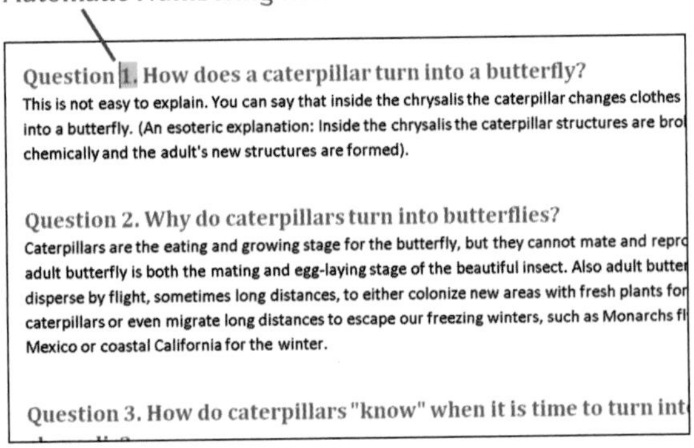

Question 1. How does a caterpillar turn into a butterfly?
This is not easy to explain. You can say that inside the chrysalis the caterpillar changes clothes into a butterfly. (An esoteric explanation: Inside the chrysalis the caterpillar structures are broken chemically and the adult's new structures are formed).

Question 2. Why do caterpillars turn into butterflies?
Caterpillars are the eating and growing stage for the butterfly, but they cannot mate and repro adult butterfly is both the mating and egg-laying stage of the beautiful insect. Also adult butter disperse by flight, sometimes long distances, to either colonize new areas with fresh plants for caterpillars or even migrate long distances to escape our freezing winters, such as Monarchs fl Mexico or coastal California for the winter.

Question 3. How do caterpillars "know" when it is time to turn int

Figure 15-16
Automatic numbering.

To add automatic numbering to your document, click the cursor where you want the first number and choose Insert > Text > Quick Parts > Field. The Field dialog box seen in Figure 15-17 appears. Choose AutoNum and click OK. Word inserts the AutoNum field into the document with the first number (1) and a period after it. Repeat adding the AutoNum field for each item you want numbered. You can use Word's copy and paste functions to copy the automatic numbering.

AutoNum

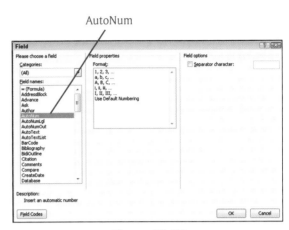

Figure 15-17
The Field dialog box.

Using Office Applications

MICROSOFT DESIGNED THE ENTIRE Office suite so that the applications can be used within each other. You've already discovered in Chapter 5, how you can e-mail a Word document using Outlook and in Chapter 12, you realized how to insert an Excel table into a Word document. But there's more you can do. This section is about integrating more of the Office elements.

Inserting a Word File

In your current document, if you need something you've already typed into another document, you could (A) retype the document; (B) open the document you want to insert, select the entire document, copy it, and then paste it into the new document; or (C) insert the other file into your existing file. I vote for C.

Position the insertion point where you want the file to begin and then choose Insert > Text. Click the Object arrow and choose Text from File. The Insert File dialog box seen in Figure 15-18 appears.

Locate and click the file you want and then choose Insert. The entire file appears in the current document. It's quick and easy!

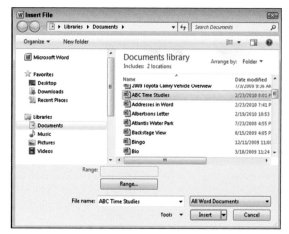

Figure 15-18
Inserting an existing file.

Using Charts from Excel

Suppose you're doing a report and you want to add a chart. You have two ways you can do that. One is to create the Excel chart in Word and the other is to insert an Excel chart in Word. That probably sounds a little strange to "create an Excel chart in Word", but because the Office applications are so tightly integrated, you can do just that. We'll take a look at creating a chart first.

Creating an Excel Chart

When you create a chart in Word, it's actually using the Excel program to do so. So to accomplish this, you need a very basic knowledge of using the Excel application. The following steps show you how to create an Excel chart in Word:

1. Position the cursor where you want the chart and choose Insert > Text > Object. The Object dialog box seen in Figure 15-19 appears.

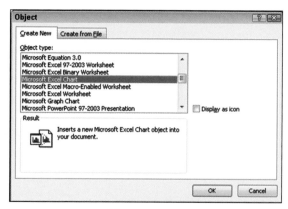

Figure 15-19
The Object dialog box.

2. From the Create New tab, select Microsoft Excel Chart and then click OK. A sample chart appears in your document and Excel worksheet and chart tabs appear on the Ribbon. See Figure 15-20.

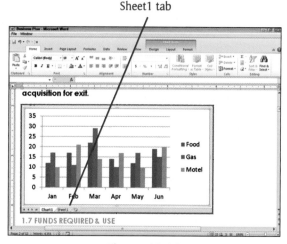

Figure 15-20
The sample Excel chart.

3. This chart is created from sample data so you need to replace the data with your own. Click the Sheet1 tab and replace the sample data with your own. See Figure 15-21.

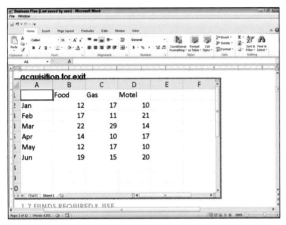

Figure 15-21
Modify the chart data.

4. Click the Chart1 tab to redisplay the chart.

5. If your data takes more or fewer cells than the sample, choose Chart Tools > Design > Data > Select Data. The Select Data Source dialog box appears and you see the worksheet data.

6. Highlight the cell data you want for your chart and click OK.

7. Optionally, use the other Chart Tools tabs to change the look of the chart or the chart type.

Tip

Word prints the chart with the rest of the document.

Inserting an Excel Chart

If you've already created and formatted the chart, you don't need to create it a second time in Word. You can simple insert the chart into your document. Inserting the chart using this method *embeds*

the chart into the document so that if the data on the chart changes, the Word document chart automatically updates when you reopen the Word document. Let's take a look at how this is accomplished.

Position the cursor where you want the chart and choose Insert > Text > Object. The Object dialog box appears. Click the Create from File tab and then click the Browse button. From the Browse dialog box that appears, navigate to and select the Excel workbook containing the chart you want then click OK. See Figure 15-22. Click OK to accept the choice.

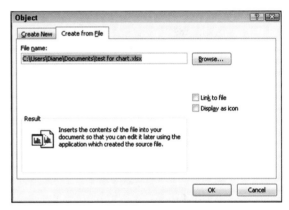

Figure 15-22
Selecting an Excel workbook.

Word displays the first worksheet in the Excel workbook. If the first worksheet is not the chart you want, click the worksheet tab that contains the chart. Also, like the chart you create in Word, the embedded chart will print with the rest of the document.

Inserting a PowerPoint Presentation

What about PowerPoint? Can you insert a PowerPoint presentation into your Word document? Yes you can, and similar to the Excel chart, the presentation is embedded into the document so if the original presentation changes, you'll see the changes as well in the Word document.

What is different is that you don't see the entire PowerPoint presentation in your document; you only see the first slide. You can view the PowerPoint slide show from within your document, but only the first slide prints.

Use the following steps to insert a PowerPoint presentation:

1. Position the cursor where you want the icon located and choose Insert > Text > Object. The Object dialog box appears.

2. From the Create from File tab, click the Browse button. The Browse dialog box appears.

3. Navigate to and select the PowerPoint you want to reference.

4. Click Insert. The Object dialog box reappears with the referenced file name.

5. Click OK. The first slide in the presentation appears in your Word document as you see in Figure 15-23.

Figure 15-23
The PowerPoint slide.

Tip

To view the entire presentation in a slide show format as shown in Figure 15-24, double-click the slide in the Word document.

Figure 15-24
The PowerPoint slide show.

Inserting an Access Link

While you cannot actually insert an Access database into a Word document, like you can an Excel or PowerPoint element, you can reference it so your document reader can quickly open and review the database. Of course, that's only going to work if your reader is viewing the document on the computer; not in paper form.

If you have an Access database that you want to reference, you have two ways you can do that. One is by creating a link to the Access database. To do that, see "Specifying Hyperlinks" earlier in this chapter.

The other method is to insert an Access icon in the document. When the reader double clicks the Access icon, the database will open and the reader can peruse through it. The following steps walk you through the process of inserting an Access database icon:

1. Position the cursor where you want the icon located and choose Insert > Text > Object. The Object dialog box appears.

2. From the Create from File tab, click the Browse button. The Browse dialog box appears.

3. Navigate to and select the Access database you want to reference.

4. Click Insert. The Object dialog box reappears with the referenced file name.

5. Click OK. An Access icon appears in your Word document as you see in Figure 15-25.

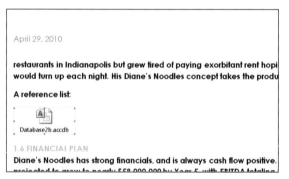

Figure 15-25
The Access database icon.

Double-click the Access icon to open the Access database. (See Figure 15-26.)

Figure 15-26
The opened Access database.

Collaborating with
Others

PICTURE YOURSELF AT A SATURDAY COOKOUT with friends. Your host and hostess supplied the basics for the meal—grilling items, beverages, condiments, and so on. Each of the guests contributed a dish to round out the meal—a special appetizer, a favorite side dish, or a stunning dessert. Together, everyone creates a fantastic meal.

Collaboration features enable everyone on the team to make a contribution to the finished document. Word's Track Changes features enable changes to be identified by user, and changes can be accepted or rejected as needed to finalize the document. If you prefer that changes not be made to the document, other users can add their comments so that you can incorporate their thoughts in your own words and then remove the comments. Word offers a third collaboration approach, the ability to compare documents edited by different users and decide which changes to keep. When you're working with a team, using Word's collaboration features ensures that the finished document reflects the best ideas contributed by each team member.

Tracking Changes

EVEN THE BEST OF WRITERS needs a little help, whether it's help with punctuation and grammar, help with word choice and phrasing, or help with ideas and the flow of information in a document. Circulating a document for review and correction by others provides the benefit of having input from a variety of team members with varying professional backgrounds, points of view, and skill sets. Whereas one person may miss an error or inaccuracy, it's less likely that four people will. And if two heads are better than one, well chances are that five or six heads will give you a range of ideas to draw on so that you can best communicate your message in any given document.

Circulating a document for review used to be a tricky process, even with early word processing programs. You typically could not tell what changes were made and who made them. This left you in the position of comparing the original file with the edited version (or versions) line by line, and choosing which changes to type into your final version of the file. This process could lead to omissions and miscommunications in the review process.

Some versions ago, a document review feature called revision marking was built into Word. Word 2007 and now 2010 included a renamed version of that feature called Track Changes. When enabled, the Track Changes feature does just what the name implies. As a particular user makes changes to the document, Word marks those changes so that you can see what has been changed. Even better, Word by default color-codes the changes according to the user who made them and uses different kinds of marks to indicate different types of changes.

Markup formatting for the changes includes the following:

- ▶ Strikethrough marks deletions.
- ▶ Underlining marks additions, also called insertions.
- ▶ Vertical lines at the left margin indicate changed lines.
- ▶ Double strikethrough marks in green show text that has been removed from a location.
- ▶ Double underscore marks in green show the new location for moved text.
- ▶ Formatting changes are shown with balloons in a markup area that appears to the right of the document in Print Layout view.
- ▶ Shading in a table shows inserted (light blue), deleted (pink), merged (light yellow), and split (light orange) cells.

Figure 16-1 illustrates how the Track Changes feature marks up a document.

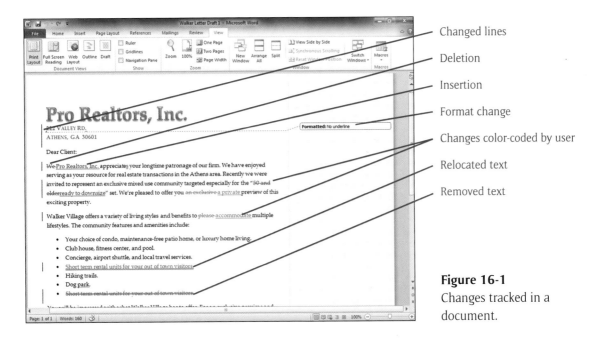

Changed lines

Deletion

Insertion

Format change

Changes color-coded by user

Relocated text

Removed text

Figure 16-1
Changes tracked in a document.

Once you've turned on Track Changes and have distributed the document for review, you can decide which changes to review and keep. You'll learn about the ins and outs of tracking and reviewing a document next.

Turning on Tracking

The Review tab on Word's Ribbon offers a wide variety of document review tools, including those for tracking changes. To turn on Track Changes, choose Review > Tracking > Track Changes (the top part of the button). When the Track Changes feature is active, its button is highlighted, as shown in Figure 16-2. Repeat the command sequence to turn the Track Changes feature off, such as when you want to make quick additions or deletions that you don't want marked as corrections.

After you enable Track Changes, save the document. Then, when you distribute the document to others and they open it, the Track Changes feature will already be enabled. Team members reviewing the document can read it and make the desired changes.

Figure 16-2
Track Changes feature activated.

Changing Tracking Options

As you learned earlier, Word uses particular
markup formatting to identify the user making
changes and the types of changes made. The
default settings do a great job of identifying
changes for you, but you may prefer to tweak how
those settings work. For example, you can change
the formatting used to mark insertions or deletions
or opt to use one color for insertions and deletions
rather than color-coding them by author (user).

To change the options for tracking, choose Review >
Tracking > Track Changes arrow > Change Tracking
Options. The Track Changes Options dialog box
shown in Figure 16-3 appears. Make the desired settings changes, and then click OK to apply them.

Tip

You can change tracking options before or
after distributing a document for tracking.

As you can see in Figure 16-3, the Track Changes
Options dialog box offers a wide variety of settings,
some of which apply to comments (a feature you'll
learn about later in this chapter) rather than
change tracking. Here's an overview of the features
for tracking changes that you may want to adjust:

Figure 16-3
Choosing Track Changes formatting.

▶ **Insertions and Color:** Choose what attribute to use to mark up inserted text, and
make a color choice other than By Author
to turn off color coding and use one color
for all changes instead.

▶ **Deletions and Color:** Choose what attribute to use to mark up inserted text, and
make a color choice other than By Author
to turn off color coding and use one color
for all changes instead.

▶ **Changed Lines and Color:** Specify a location
for the vertical lines that indicate changed
lines of text and a color for those markup
lines. The small preview area shows how your
choices for this pair of options will look.

▶ **Track Moves:** Use this check box to specify whether Track Changes will mark up moved text.

▶ **Moved From and Color:** Choose what attribute or character to use to mark up moved text in its original location, as well as choosing a color.

▶ **Moved To and Color:** Choose what attribute or character to use to mark up moved text in its new location, as well as choosing a color.

▶ **Inserted Cells, Deleted Cells, Merged Cells, and Split Cells:** Use these drop-down lists under Table Cell Highlighting to choose the highlighting colors for marking up the associated cell changes.

▶ **Track Formatting:** Use this check box to specify whether Track Changes will mark up formatting changes.

▶ **Formatting and Color:** Choose to use an attribute to mark up formatting changes—the default setting is (None)—and make a color choice other than By Author to turn off color coding and use one color for all changes instead.

Only Text?

I've used "text" in the preceding descriptions to simplify them. The Track Changes feature also marks up changes to objects, such as tables and graphics.

Changing the User Name

If you leave the default Track Changes settings in place, you will be able to see at a glance where each user has made changes in a file with Track Changes enabled, as you saw earlier in Figure 16-1. To identify who made a particular change, move the mouse pointer over the change, either in the text or in a balloon in the Markup Area at the right in Print Layout view. As shown in the example in Figure 16-4, a ScreenTip showing the author's user name, the date and the time of the change, and the change contents appears.

Pointer over change

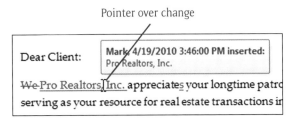

Figure 16-4
Viewing a change's author.

When you use Track Changes to mark up a document, Track Changes pulls your user name as specified in Word Options. If you need to update your user settings to make sure Word accurately identifies which changes you made, you can do so right from the Track Changes menu. Choose Review > Tracking > Track Changes arrow > Change User Name to open the General settings in the Word Options dialog box (see Figure 16-5). Update the User Name and Initials entries as desired, and then click OK.

Name and initials

Figure 16-5
Editing user information.

Viewing Tracked Changes

Just as you can change the overall view for a document, Word enables you to control which changes appear and how they look so that you can be as efficient as possible when completing your review of the changes.

By default, the Track Changes feature shows you the final version of the document, with the changes marked. If that is not how you wish to preview the document, you can click an alternate choice in the Display for Review drop-down list (see Figure 16-6) in the Tracking group of the Review tab. The Final choice shows the document with all changes in place and no markup. Original: Show Markup shows the original version of the text with changes marked. Original shows the document without any of the marked changes.

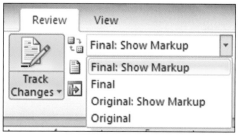

Figure 16-6
Choosing how to view changes.

The Show Markup drop-down list, also found in the Tracking group of the Review tab, enables you to turn off the display of particular tracked

changes. As shown in Figure 16-7, you can open the drop-down list by clicking Show Markup, and then click one of several choices to toggle display of the related markup on and off. A checkmark to the left of a choice means it is toggled on. So, for example, you could click the Formatting choice in the list to hide the markup display for formatting changes. This can be a handy thing to do if there are a lot of comments in the document and you're having trouble viewing all of the information in balloons in the Markup Area. You could choose Show Markup > Formatting again to turn the formatting markup display back on when you finish reviewing comments.

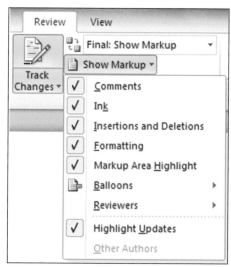

Figure 16-7
Choosing markup items to show.

The Show Markup drop-down list enables you to control display of other items using the Balloons and Reviewers submenus. On the Balloons submenu, you can choose to do any of the following:

▶ **Show Revisions in Balloons:** As shown in the example in Figure 16-8, choosing this option shows information removed from the document in balloons in the Markup Area. You must be working in Print Layout view or Web Layout view to see the balloons.

▶ **Show All Revisions Inline:** Choose this option to see revisions and comment markers right in the text and comments themselves in the Reviewing Pane.

▶ **Show Only Comments and Formatting in Balloons:** This default setting shows text changes inline and formatting changes and comments as balloons in the Markup Area.

Figure 16-8
Deletions shown in balloons.

The Reviewers submenu of the Show Markup drop-down list enables you to hide and redisplay comments by a particular reviewer. For example, if your boss reviewed a document and you want to focus on the changes that she made, you can hide the comments from all other reviewers except your boss. Choose Review > Tracking > Show Markup > Reviewers, and then click the name of the reviewer whose markup you want to hide, or redisplay if not checked. You can use the All Reviewers choice to remove the markup from all reviewers, and then revisit the submenu to check the names for individual reviewers to selectively turn their markup back on.

One final review viewing feature found in the Tracking group also applies to both Track Changes and comments. Choose Review > Tracking > Reviewing Pane to toggle the display of the Reviewing Pane on or off. The Reviewing Pane, shown in Figure 16-9, appears at the left side of the Word window by default. It lists each of the changes made and the reviewer who made it. A detailed summary of the number and nature of the changes made appears at the top of the pane. You can use the Show/Hide Detailed Summary button to toggle the detailed summary off or back on. To ensure that the Reviewing Pane calculates all the latest changes, click the Update Revision Count button.

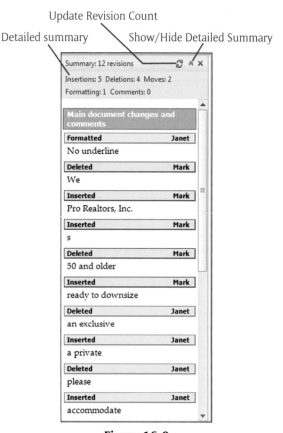

Figure 16-9
Changes and their authors listed
in the Reviewing Pane.

Reviewing Changes

The Track Changes feature considers all marked changes as *proposed* changes. The owner of the document—you—retains the ability to specify which changes should be incorporated into the document and which should be discarded. If one reviewer changed a statistic to a value that's incorrect and another reviewer made a change that you believe is grammatically incorrect, you can quickly undo those changes while going on to incorporate other changes that you believe improve and enhance the document.

The Changes group of the Review tab in the Ribbon offers tools to automate the process of reviewing changes. As shown in Figure 16-10, the Changes tools are as follows:

▶ **Accept:** Implements the change in the document, removing the markup formatting. Click the bottom portion of the button with the arrow on it to display additional options. Click Accept and Move to Next to implement the change and move to the next change. Choose Accept All Changes Shown to accept only those changes currently visible in the document (if you've hidden certain changes or changes by a particular reviewer, for example). To implement all the proposed changes, click Accept All Changes in Document.

▶ **Reject:** Click this button to remove the proposed change and remove its markup. Clicking the arrow for the button opens a list of choices like those for the Accept button. You can choose Reject and Move to Next, Reject All Changes Shown, and Reject All Changes in Document.

▶ **Previous and Next:** Use these buttons to move from change to change without accepting or rejecting the current change.

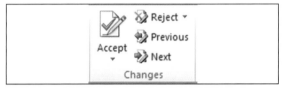

Figure 16-10
Tools for handling changes.

You can either work your way through the document and perform the review, or you can work with particular areas in the document as needed. For example, you can select a paragraph in the document, and then choose Review > Changes > Accept to accept only the changes proposed within the selection.

If the insertion point isn't in text with a change, clicking Accept or Reject will select the next change in the document. Alternately, you can use the Previous and Next buttons to move around and evaluate proposed changes.

When you finish working with the document changes, be sure to save the document to finalize it.

Printing the Markup

If a document contains tracked changes, they will print by default. Choose File > Print, click the top option under Settings, and click the Print Markup choice to toggle printing of tracked changes off or back on.

Working with Comments

MANY REVIEWERS of your documents may have input that requires explanation beyond short in-text tweaks or may have questions that need to be addressed outside of the content of what you've written. In such cases, you can encourage reviewers to use Word's Comments feature. Comments are notes or questions that reviewers can add to the document. The comments appear in balloons in the Markup Area by default in Print Layout and Web Layout views. In Draft view, you can see comments by displaying the Reviewing Pane (Review > Tracking > Reviewing Pane) or by moving the mouse over the comment marker to display the comment in a ScreenTip, as shown in Figure 16-11.

Pointer over comment marker

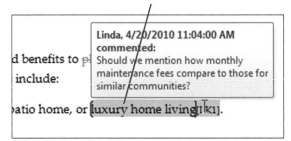

Figure 16-11
Viewing a comment.

Adding Comments

Unlike when you make changes using Track Changes, when you want to add a comment, you need to use a command to do so, as follows:

1. Select the text about which you want to make the comment. While you can select any amount of text, your comment will be more effective if you target it to a specific, limited portion of text, such as a sentence or phrase. Writers often find it easier to implement specific suggestions rather than generic ones.

2. Choose Review > Comments > New Comment. The insertion point is moved to a new comment balloon. If you are not displaying balloons, the Reviewing Pane opens, and the insertion point moves to a new comment there.

3. Type your comment text. You also can format text within the comment, insert line breaks and new paragraphs, and so on, as needed, to make the comment clear and complete.

4. Click in the document, outside the comment, to finish the comment. Close the Reviewing Pane, if desired.

Tip

New comments will appear even if Track Changes is not enabled. You can use the features together or separately.

Reviewing Comments

When you've received a commented document back from your readers and reviewers, the next step is to take a look at what they had to say and consider how to use that feedback in the finished document. Or if you're a reviewer, you can go back through the comments you've made and change or expand on them as needed to finish your commentary for the document's author. The Comments group on the Review tab includes Next and Previous buttons that you can use to navigate between the comments.

While you can jump around and work with comments using those buttons in any way you please, here's how to start the review from the top:

1. Choose View > Document Views > Print Layout. You also could change to Web Layout view if you're creating content for a Web page.

2. Press Ctrl+Home to move the insertion point to the beginning of the document.

3. Choose Review > Comments > Next. Word selects the first comment in the document in the Markup Area. As shown in Figure 16-12, the balloon outline for the selected comment changes to bold. The insertion point also moves within the comment.

4. Edit the comment if desired or click in the document and make edits according to the comment's recommendations.

Next button   Selected comment

Figure 16-12
Moving between comments.

5. Choose Review > Comments > Next and Review > Comments > Previous as needed to navigate to other comments in the document and work with them.

6. Click in the document, outside the current comment, to finish working with comments.

You also can work with comments in Draft view. When you use Review > Comments > Next to select the first comment, Word opens the Reviewing Pane, scrolls to the comment, and places the insertion point in it, as shown in Figure 16-13. You can click in the document to make changes and view other comments in the Reviewing Pane, jumping back and forth as needed. When you finish, you can click the Reviewing Pane's Close (X) button to close it.

Figure 16-13
Comment in the Reviewing Pane.

Tip

If you've previously used Review > Tracking > Show Markup to hide all comments or comments by one or more reviewers, make sure you redisplay those comments so that you can review or delete them as needed.

Deleting Comments

A finalized document need not include comments made by reviewers, unless you want those com-

ments to be available for reference or clarification in situations where references like footnotes and endnotes would be too formal. You can use one of three methods to delete comments:

► In any view, right-click the text that's been commented on and click Delete Comment, as shown in Figure 16-14.

► Choose Review > Comments > Next or Review > Comments > Previous to select the comment to delete, and then choose Review > Comments > Delete.

► Choose Review > Comments > Delete arrow > Delete All Comments in Document. This deletes all the comments in the document. Use Delete All Comments Shown, instead, if some of the comments are hidden.

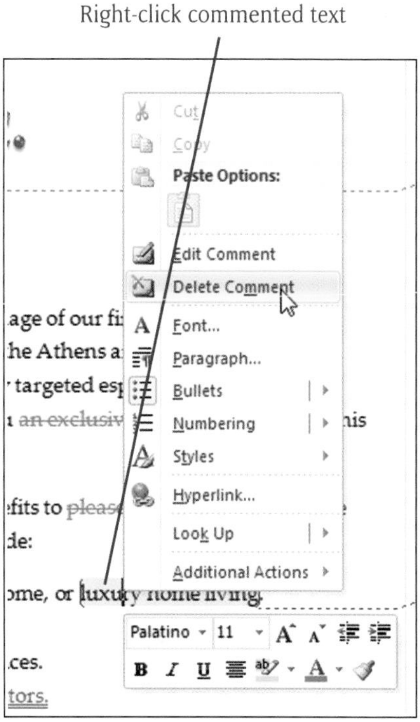

Right-click commented text

Figure 16-14
Deleting a comment.

Comparing Documents

MOST USERS BECOME comfortable with the Track Changes and Comments features within a work session or two. But that doesn't mean all reviewers will want to use those features or provide edited documents with their changes conveniently marked. Should you have flashbacks to your pre–Track Changes days if you receive a version of your document that has been edited but not marked up or marked up in separate copies of the file? Not at all. You can compare documents to sort through all the changes and combine them in a single finished product.

Word actually offers two methods for comparing documents. Using the first method, Compare, works best when you want to see the differences between an original document and a copy that's been edited by another person. This method is considered a *legal blackline* markup, but it effectively marks up a document just as the Track Changes feature does.

Follow these steps to compare an original document with an edited version:

1. Choose Review > Compare > Compare > Compare. The Compare Documents dialog box opens.

2. Use the Open buttons to browse and select an Original Document and Revised Document, as shown in Figure 16-15. If you've opened either document recently, it

may appear in the applicable drop-down list, in which case, you won't need to use the corresponding Open button.

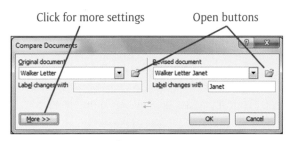

Click for more settings   Open buttons

Figure 16-15
Comparing documents.

3. (Optional) If you want to use an alternate name to identify the marked up changes, enter it in the Label Changes With text box under the Revised Document list. The name that appears initially is the user name of the person who edited and saved the file.

4. (Optional) To control which items Word marks up, click the More button and adjust the choices under Comparison Settings and Show Changes, accordingly.

5. Click OK. The Compare results appear onscreen, as shown in Figure 16-16. Note that by default, Word creates a new file named Compare Result X, and shows it with the marked up changes in the center pane. The Reviewing Pane appears at left with details about the changes. The panes at the right show the original and revised documents.

Figure 16-16
The completed comparison.

6. You can edit and save the Compare Result X file and manipulate panes as needed.

Managing the Source Document Display

After you've run the comparison, the Review > Compare > Compare > Show Source Documents choice becomes active. Use its submenu choices to determine whether either, both, or none of the source documents appears onscreen.

When you have numerous edited versions of a document, combining them ensures all the changes are reflected in a single document. Word's Combine process is nearly identical to the process for comparing documents. Follow the preceding steps, using the Review > Compare > Compare > Combine command instead. The Combine Documents dialog box looks and works identically

to the Compare Documents dialog box shown in Figure 16-15. The compiled results also look similar to those for a Compare process, as shown in Figure 16-17. The key differences are that the Reviewing Pane and combined document show the changes by both reviewers (identified by the user names that were active in their copy of Word when they edited and changed the file), and the initial name for the combined file appears as Combine Result *X*. Just as for the Compare process, you can work with the combined results, saving the file and managing the onscreen panes as needed.

Figure 16-17
The combined files.

Comparing More Reviewers

Combine and save the documents from the first two reviewers, and then combine that document with another document to add the changes by a third reviewer.

Customizing
Word

PICTURE YOURSELF AT THE CONTROLS of a Boeing 767 aircraft. The dashboard and console feature an overwhelming array of gauges, buttons, knobs, and levers, each with a very particular purpose in controlling how the plane operates. Used properly together, the controls enable you to achieve the feat of getting a monster plane off the ground and into the air.

Like a 767, Word offers dozens of settings and features that enable you to control its operation. Taking the time to set Word up to work the way you want it to can make you more efficient, so you can concentrate on your document's content rather than fumbling with commands. This chapter shows you the key ways in which you may want to customize Word.

Creating and Using Templates

EVEN WHEN YOU COOK a dish from scratch, you generally start with a recipe. The recipe ensures that you add the right ingredients in the right proportions at the correct point in the process, and that you cook the dish as needed. The recipe enables you to get a consistent result whenever you want to cook the dish again. Cooking without a recipe can lead to bad-tasting, overcooked, or undercooked food.

For a document that you need to create over and over—such as a newsletter or memo—a *template* can work like a recipe, prompting you to put the right information in the right place. A template file uses a special format (with a .dotx file name extension) so that it can become the basis for a new Word document. The template can supply not only formatting for the document, but also suggested contents and images. For example, Figure 17-1 shows a newsletter document with placeholder information that is set up to be saved as a template.

A template saves you time because it guides you in supplying the content for the document and has the formatting predefined. Using the template enhances your professionalism because it helps you create consistent-looking documents with reduced effort. For example, creating the example newsletter from scratch each month would be a time-consuming operation, and unless you could accurately remember all of the formatting you used, it wouldn't look the same from month to month.

Figure 17-1
Newsletter with placeholder content.

Tip

To save time, you can also modify an existing template that's installed with Word or that you download from Office.com.

Saving Your Template

To create a template, first create a document, add all the placeholder or suggested content that you want to include, and apply the formatting you want. (For example, Figure 17-1 shows that the newsletter is formatted with two columns.) Then follow these steps to save the file as a template:

1. Choose File > Save As. The Save As dialog box appears.

2. Type or edit the name you want to apply to the template in the File Name text box.

3. Choose Word Template from the Save As Type drop-down list.

4. Navigate to the C:\Users*User Name*\AppData\Roaming\Microsoft\Templates folder in the Save As dialog box. Saving to this location may make it easier to find and use the template, as you'll learn later. Figure 17-2 shows the Save As dialog box.

File type   Folder   Name

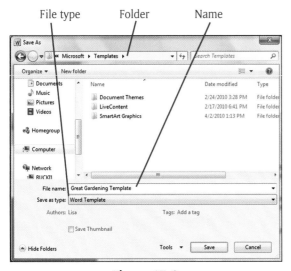

Figure 17-2
Saving a template.

5. Click Save. Word Saves the template file.

6. Choose File > Close to close the file.

Smarter Templates

If you get more advanced with your use of Word, you can display the Developer tab on the Ribbon and use it to set up automated controls that will help the user update place-holders with real content even more quickly.

Using Your Template to Make a New Document

Each time you use a template file, Word creates a new document based on the template. So unless you specifically open and edit the template, the original template file remains intact no matter how many documents you create from it.

Follow these steps to use a template you've saved to create a new document:

1. Choose File > New. The Available Templates list appears in the Backstage view.

2. Click My Templates, as shown in Figure 17-3. The New dialog box opens. It lists any templates that you've saved in the C:\Users*User Name*\AppData\Roaming\Microsoft\Templates folder.

My Templates   Select a template

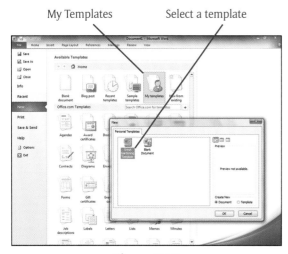

Figure 17-3
Creating a file from a template.

Determining Word Options

WORD OFFERS DOZENS of options for customizing how it operates. I'm not going to bore you by listing and describing every one. The use of Word options probably follows something like the 80-20 rule. Eighty percent or so of the time, you'll be working with the same 20 percent or fewer of the options. This section gives you an overview of where to find the various types of options and touches on the ones you'll use most frequently.

To work with Word Options, choose File > Options. In the Word Options dialog box that appears, click a category name in the list at the left to see that category's options.

3. Make sure that the Document option is selected under Create New.

4. Click the template that you want to use.

5. Click OK. Word creates the new document.

6. Edit the document as needed, and then save it.

Funny Tabs

Some writers call the categories at the left side of the Options dialog box "tabs." They don't look like tabs to me, but if you see that term used, know that it means the categories at the left.

General Options

The General category of options (shown in Figure 17-4) appears by default when you open the Word Options dialog box. You can change your User Name and Initials under Personalize Your Copy of

Microsoft Office. (You learned another way to make this change in Chapter 16.) The top section, User Interface Options, enables you to turn the Mini Toolbar and Live Preview off or back on, as well as change the Color Scheme and ScreenTip Style. You can choose Don't Show ScreenTips from the ScreenTip Style drop-down list to turn off ScreenTips altogether.

you to control which individual marks appear. Similarly, the Printing Options choices in the bottom section enable to you print items that wouldn't otherwise print, such as document properties or hidden text.

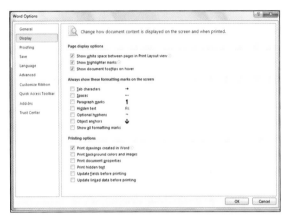

Figure 17-5
Word's Display options.

Proofing Options

The next category of options, Proofing, helps you to modify how the spelling, grammar, and AutoCorrect features work in Word. Figure 17-6 shows this category.

Figure 17-4
Word's General options.

Tip

You can resize the Word Options dialog box by dragging the side or bottom border, or lower-right corner.

Display Options

Click Display in the list at the left to open the options shown in Figure 17-5. In the Page Display Options section, enable or disable features like the white space between pages for Print Layout view. The middle section, Always Show These Formatting Marks on the Screen, is the one you will probably use most. You can select individual nonprinting characters here to display them onscreen. Unlike the Show/Hide button in the Paragraph group of the Home tab, which turns all nonprinting characters on or off, the Display options settings enable

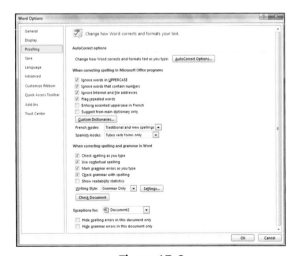

Figure 17-6
Word's Proofing options.

The options under the second section (When Correcting Spelling in Microsoft Office Programs) enable you to set up the spelling check feature to work faster and more effectively. For example, make sure Ignore Internet and File Addresses is checked to prevent the spelling check from stopping on every Web page URL in a document. On the other hand, if you want to start checking words in all uppercase or that have numbers, clear the Ignore Words in UPPERCASE and Ignore Words That Contain Numbers check boxes.

The When Correcting Spelling and Grammar in Word section enables you to control some automated aspects of checking spelling and grammar. For example, if the squiggly lines that appear under spelling and grammar errors as you type bother you, clear the Check Spelling as You Type and Mark Grammar Errors as You Type check boxes. Use the Exceptions For section settings at the bottom to hide those squiggly lines in the current document only.

Click the AutoCorrect Options button at the top of the Proofing category to open the AutoCorrect dialog box, shown in Figure 17-7. This dialog box has five tabs of options you can use for automated correction, typing, and formatting features, as follows:

▶ **AutoCorrect:** You learned in Chapter 2 how Word automatically fixes many typos that you make. The settings on this tab enable you to control correction for specific typos, such as having Word Capitalize First Letter of Sentences if you fail to do so. You also can add a new correction for your common typos by typing entries in the Replace and With text boxes, and then clicking Add.

▶ **Math AutoCorrect:** Use this tab to learn about and add shortcuts for inserting mathematical symbols. For example, you can type \Delta to enter the delta symbol (Δ), which may take less time than inserting the symbol manually.

▶ **AutoFormat As You Type:** Use the choices on this tab to control whether Word formats specific characters for you, such as formatting fractions (changing 1/4 to $\frac{1}{4}$) and ordinals. You can also control formatting list items, such as turning automatic numbered lists on and off.

▶ **AutoFormat:** This tab offers many of the same settings as the AutoFormat As You Type tab, but the choices here apply only when you run the AutoFormat feature. You need to add a button to the Quick Access Toolbar or Ribbon to make this command available. See the final two sections of this chapter to learn how to customize the Quick Access Toolbar or the Ribbon with additional commands.

▶ **Actions:** Formerly called SmartTags, the items checked here add settings to the shortcut menu when you type certain kinds of text in the document. For example, if Telephone Number (XML) is checked on this tab and you type a phone number into a document, you can right-click a phone number, point to the Additional Actions choice at the bottom of the shortcut menu, and choose or check for actions.

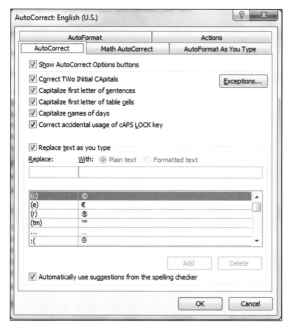

Figure 17-7
Finding AutoCorrect and other options.

Save Options

When you need to work with options for file management, click the Save category in the list at the left side of the Word Options dialog box to display the choices shown in Figure 17-8. The top section in the dialog box, Save Documents, holds the settings you're likely to use most:

Figure 17-8
Word's Save options.

▶ **Save Files in This Format:** Choose the default format in which files will be saved. It is handy to change the default format when you often share documents with users who don't have Word 2007. For example, you can save in Word 97-2003 Document (*.doc) format by default. Or for users who have another word processing program, you can choose a format such as Rich Text Format (*.rtf). (Some of the file types will not preserve all the document features you can apply in Word, such as certain types of formatting.)

▶ **Save AutoRecover Information Every X Minutes:** The AutoSave feature saves a version of all open files at the specified interval, so you can recover your files if for some reason Word shuts down or locks up when you haven't saved your work. Use the spin arrows or enter a value in the text box to specify how often Word should save versions of your files. Leaving Keep the Last Autosaved Version If I Close Without Saving option checked ensures that the most recent version will be made available for you to recover.

Tip

Choose File > Info and look under Versions to view the file versions AutoRecover has created. From there, you can click a version or choose Manage Versions > Recover Unsaved Documents to recover your work.

▶ **AutoRecover File Location:** Specify where you would like for the AutoRecover versions of your files to be stored. For example, changing to a network location can make sure you have other versions available in the event of a hard disk failure.

▶ **Default File Location:** If you'd like Word to suggest another save location by default the first time you save a file, choose the folder you want here.

The middle section of settings (Offline Editing Options for Document Management Server Files) only applies if you are working with SharePoint. At the bottom, the Embed Fonts in the File choice is important to check when you will be sharing files with other users who may need to heavily edit and reformat the document, or if you're sending the document to a commercial printer or print service within your organization. Embedding the fonts ensures the document will retain its formatting and print and look exactly as you'd expect. If the fonts aren't embedded and the computer where another user is editing or printing the file doesn't have all the document fonts, Word and Windows could substitute an alternate font and change the look of the document.

Parlez-Vous Français?

Use the Language category options to add and choose alternate languages for editing, display, and Help.

Advanced Options

The last category of options, Advanced, holds a mother lode of choices organized in 11 sections. As shown in Figure 17-9, you can scroll up and down to navigate to the option you need.

Scroll down to see more

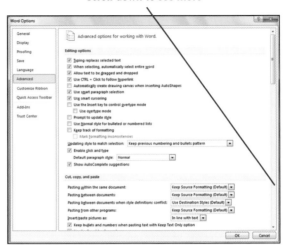

Figure 17-9
Advanced Word options.

Here's a look at the types of options available in this category:

▶ **Editing Options:** Here you can find options for turning a number of editing features on and off, such as Allow Text to Be Dragged and Dropped and Enable Click and Type.

▶ **Cut, Copy, and Paste:** Many of the settings here deal with how formatting behaves by default when you move or copy text. You also can control display of the Paste Options buttons here and use the Settings button to changes settings for the Smart Cut and Paste feature.

▶ **Image Size and Quality:** Here you can choose whether settings apply to the current document or All New Documents. From there, choose whether to Discard Editing Data or Compress Images, and to set a default resolution (target output) for images when printing.

▶ **Show Document Content:** These settings toggle the display of certain document features, such as picture placeholders (in place of the image itself), bookmark and field codes, crop marks, and the like. Turning these settings on and off can affect how quickly Word performs or can make it easier to identify document features that you need to edit. If you're working with a document you received from another user and there are font issues, you can use the Font Substitution button to choose substitute fonts.

▶ **Display:** If the options in the overall display category aren't sufficient for your needs, you can use the options in this section to further fine-tune how Word looks. You can control the number of recent documents that appears when you choose File > Recent, control scroll bar display, control measurement units (for example, use Inches or Points), and more.

▶ **Print:** This section offers several options for adjusting printing defaults. For example, you can choose to enable Use Draft Quality and Print Field Codes Instead of Their Values, as well as settings for duplex printing and document scaling.

▶ **When Printing This Document:** These settings also can apply to the current document or All New Documents. You can enable Print PostScript Over Text to have PostScript information from PostScript fields in a document converted from Word for the Mac format print above text or Print Only the Data From a Form to print on pre-printed form paper.

▶ **Save:** These settings supplement those in the Save category. Allow Background Saves is enabled by default. You also can enable Always Create Backup Copy for an additional means of protecting your data via creating .bak files, as well as saving settings pertaining to the Normal template and synchronizing remotely stored files.

▶ **Preserve Fidelity When Sharing This Document:** The settings here, when enabled, help form and linguistic data save more accurately when a file will be shared or reused.

▶ **General:** You can change settings for sounds and settings for opening files here, as well as entering a mailing address and using the File Locations and Web Options buttons to display even more detailed default settings for storing files and using Word with your Web browser.

▶ **Compatibility Options For:** Enables you to set up the displayed layout of the current document or All New Documents to emulate a prior Word version or another word processing program.

Adding to the Quick Access Toolbar

THE QUICK ACCESS TOOLBAR by default features three of the commands used most often by Word users: Save, Undo, and Repeat (redo). However, you're not just any Word user. You have your own needs, preferences, and quirks, and so you may work more effectively when *your* most used commands are a click away on the Quick Access Toolbar. You can add a button for any of the available commands in Word—including those not offered on the Ribbon—to the Quick Access Toolbar at any time.

Click the Customize Quick Access Toolbar button (the down arrow at the right end of the toolbar) to open the menu shown in Figure 17-10. Click any of the choices above the divider line to toggle its display on or off on the Quick Access Toolbar. The checked items are the ones that currently appear on the toolbar.

Click to open menu

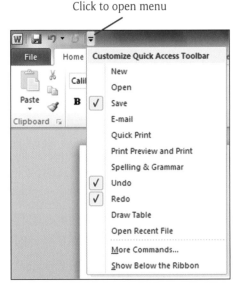

Figure 17-10
Customizing the Quick Access Toolbar.

Moving the QAT

The Show Below the Ribbon command on the Customize Quick Access Toolbar menu moves the toolbar so that you can reach it more easily by mouse.

If the command that you want to add doesn't appear directly on the menu, follow these steps to add it to the Quick Access Toolbar:

1. Click the Customize Quick Access Toolbar button, and then click More Commands near the bottom of the menu. The Word Options dialog box opens with the Quick Access Toolbar settings displayed.

2. Open the Choose Commands From drop-down list above the left-hand list of commands, and then click the location that likely has the command you want to add. For example, you can choose one of the Ribbon tabs, choose Commands Not in the Ribbon, or choose All Commands as shown in Figure 17-11.

Click command in this list   Added command

Select command location   Click to add

Figure 17-11
Finding and adding commands.

3. Scroll the left list of commands, and click the command you want to add to the Quick Access Toolbar.

4. Click the Add button between the two lists. The command moves over to the list at the right, which represents the list of commands currently on the Quick Access Toolbar, as illustrated in Figure 17-11.

5. Repeat Steps 2–4 as needed to add other commands to the right-hand list.

6. To change a command's position in the right-hand list, click the command and click either the Move Up or Move Down buttons (arrow buttons) at the right side of the list.

7. Click OK. Word displays the new command(s) on the Quick Access Toolbar.

More QAT Tricks

Use the Customize Quick Access Toolbar drop-down list above the right-hand list to control whether the QAT changes apply to the current document or all documents. You also can use the Reset button near the bottom to undo your customizations.

Customizing the Ribbon

WORD 2007 DID NOT OFFER the ability to customize the Ribbon, but Word 2010 does. Customizing the Ribbon rather than the Quick Access Toolbar offers greater flexibility because you can add more commands, and you can organize them by function on tabs. In fact, customizing the Ribbon requires first adding at least one new tab, and then designating the commands that you want to appear on that tab.

Some of the steps for creating a new Ribbon tab and adding commands resemble the steps for customizing the Quick Access Toolbar. Here are the specific steps for updating your Ribbon:

1. Right-click any Ribbon tab and click Customize the Ribbon. Alternately, you can choose File > Options and then click Customize Ribbon. Either way, the Word Options dialog box displays choices for customizing the Ribbon, which resemble those for customizing the Quick Access Toolbar.

2. Click the New Tab button below the Main Tabs list at the right. The new tab appears immediately with a generic name, New Tab (Custom) and a generically named group, New Group (Custom).

3. Click the new group, and click the Rename button below the list. Type a name in the Rename dialog box that appears (as shown in Figure 17-12), and then click OK.

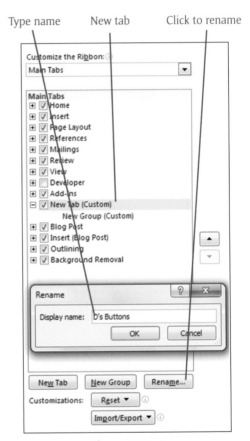

Figure 17-12
Naming the new tab.

4. Repeat the process in Step 3 to rename the group for the new tab.

5. Open the Choose Commands From drop-down list above the left-hand list of commands, and then click the location that likely has the command you want to add. For

example, you can choose one of the Ribbon tabs, choose Commands Not in the Ribbon, or choose All Commands.

6. Scroll the left list of commands, and click the command you want to add to the Quick Access Toolbar.

7. Make sure that the new group is selected in the right-hand list, and then click the Add button between the two lists. The command moves over to the list at the right, under the group name.

Tip

The first three commands that you add to a group will display the largest buttons.

8. Repeat Steps 5–7 as needed to add other commands to the group in the right-hand list. You also can drag and drop commands between the two lists.

9. To change a command's position in the group in the right-hand list, click the command and click either the Move Up or Move Down buttons (arrow buttons) at the right side of the list. Figure 17-13 shows some commands added to a new tab and group.

New group

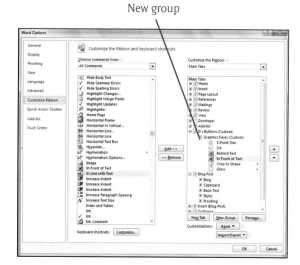

Figure 17-13
Commands in new group.

10. Click OK. Word creates the new tab and group. As shown in the example custom Ribbon tab in Figure 17-14, Word arranges and sizes the items within the group for you.

Tip

Click the Developer check box in the Main Tabs list at right to display and hide the Developer tab, a special-purpose tab for working with document controls and macros.

Tab name
Group name

Figure 17-14
Using a custom Ribbon tab.

Index